LEGISLATING
IMMORALITY

LEGISLATING IMMORALITY

THE HOMOSEXUAL MOVEMENT COMES OUT OF THE CLOSET

**George Grant and
Mark A. Horne**

Moody Press/Legacy Communications

Co-published by Moody Press, Chicago, Illinois and Legacy Communications,
Franklin, Tennessee.

ISBN: 0-8024-4919-0

To Our Wives
Karen and Jennifer
Whose Natural Affections
Sustain Us Tenderly
And
Whose Moral Legislations
Guide Us Mercifully

Y Gwyr Erbyn Byd

CONTENTS

A Note to the Reader / *ix*

Acknowledgments / *xi*

Introduction: Lance's Story / *1*

Part I: The War Zone

  1. A Walk on the Wilde Side / *11*

  2. De-Lighting America / *21*

Part II: Alien Affairs

  3. Indecent Exposure: Culture / *51*

  4. Fatal Distraction: Education / *71*

  5. Statutory Hate: Politics / *91*

  6. Dead Certainties: Medicine / *109*

  7. Troop Immorale: Military / *143*

  8. An Impuritan Ethic: Church / *163*

Part III: Altars and Arsenals

  9. Revealing Notions: Truth / *181*

  10. Unto Ages of Ages: Tradition / *199*

Part IV: A Call to Arms

  11. Just Say Yes: Hope / *225*

Conclusion: Lance's Reprise / *251*

Notes / *261*

Index / *287*

A NOTE TO THE READER

A ll the stories and vignettes in this book are true. In some, names have been changed; in others, editorial liberties have been taken to conflate time sequences and combine events for purposes of clarity or illustration. But in all instances, the substance of the situations, conversations, and circumstances are accurately portrayed and factually represented.

The greatest difficulty in researching and writing this book was not so much finding ways to accurately yet discreetly tell the stories of the individuals we interviewed as to faithfully yet sensitively convey the substance of the homosexual culture—its literature, social scene, art, music, and ideas. We struggled to find the appropriate balance between informing and defiling in much of the information in chapter 2 for instance. A tremendous amount of pertinent material was left out for this reason. But even with this offensive documentation deleted from the manuscript, the text remains quite disturbing. We know some readers will be outraged despite our best attempts to ameliorate the shock—but we felt that it was necessary to portray the forces arrayed against the family and the stability of our civilization as forthrightly as possible. It is our prayer that the benefits of such a portrayal will outweigh any offenses it might cause.

ACKNOWLEDGMENTS

And at last with my happier angel's own temerity
Did I clang their brazen knocker against the door,
To beg their dole look, in simple charity,
Or crumbs of history dropping from their great store.[1]

JOHN CROWE RANSOM

That this book exists at all is remarkable. We actually resisted the idea of writing it for quite some time. But then two dramatic events convinced us that despite our grave personal reservations and inhibitions the task simply had to be undertaken.

First, a special task force appointed by the Presbyterian Church, United States of America, released a controversial report on Christian sexuality entitled *Keeping Body and Soul Together: Sexuality, Spirituality, and Social Justice*. The report was shocking in its departure from historic biblical orthodoxy.

Then, a little more than a year later, President Bill Clinton appointed several prominent homosexual activists to strategic positions in his administration and announced that he would lift the historic ban on homosexuals serving in the military. That too was shocking—to both the citizenry and to military personnel.

These two events represented for us veritable cultural Rubicons. In crossing them, it became all too apparent to us that the homosexual movement had suddenly become a force to be reckoned with—and that the book was, in fact, long overdue. So we relented and went to work.

But even after we admitted the necessity of the task, the project remained supremely unpleasant for us. It involved research into unspeakable obcenities. It involved difficult and often dangerous interviews. It involved traumatic personal encounters with both the victims and the perpetrators of unimaginable perversions. And most telling of all, it involved the fiercest spiritual warfare that either of us has ever experienced.

Most books are the result of the thinking, encouragement, and diligence of many people. This one was obviously no exception. In fact, without the gracious help of others we would likely still be wrestling with cavalcades of indecision, doubt, and uncertainty.

Our publishers at Moody Press and Legacy Communications were a constant source of encouragement and support. Anne Scherich and David Dunham particularly afforded us their wisdom, their good humor, and their expertise—to say nothing of their patience, their constancy, and their long-suffering.

The stalwart men and women at the Presbyterian Lay Committee stayed the course and shared our concerns and our sense of urgency, all the while giving unselfishly of their time, energy, and expertise. Similarly, our coworkers Mary Jane Morris and Russ (St. Nick) Sorensen stood by us even when we were rather cranky due to sleep deprivation, writer's panic, and missed deadlines.

To all these friends, we offer our sincerest gratitude.

But it is to our wives, Karen and Jennifer, that we owe our deepest debt. No thanks could ever be enough for all that they do and all that they are (Philippians 1:3–11). *Deus Vult.*

INTRODUCTION: LANCE'S STORY

*The noise Time makes in passing by
Is very slight but even you can hear it
Having not necessarily to be near it,
Needing only the slightest will to try.*[1]

MERRILL MOORE

In ancient Greece and Rome, the festival of Bacchus was held each year to celebrate the spring harvest. It was always a chaotic and raucous affair. During the week-long festivities, the normally sedate city states of the Peloponnese succumbed to animal passions and compulsive caprices. They profligately indulged in every form of sensual gratification imaginable—from fornication and sodomy to intoxication and gluttony. It was an orgy of promiscuous pleasure.

Bacchus was the god of wine, women, and song. To the ancients, he was the epitome of pleasure. His mythic exploits were a dominant theme in the popular art, music, and ideas of the day. Chroniclers of the age tell us that the annual carnival—called the bacchanal—commemorating his legend was actually the bawdy highlight of the year. In fact, it dominated the Helleno-Latin calendar then even more than Christmastide does ours today.

But a wild picture of immorality that only poets and mobs can understand is always simultaneously a wild picture of melancholy that only parents and emissaries can understand. Thus, even as they reveled in the streets, the ancients were troubled by a sublime sadness. It felt like an ache in their throats or a knot in their stomachs, but it was actually an abscess in

1

their souls. Even as they celebrated their gay gaiety, they were forced to acknowledge their human unhappiness. Ultimately, the bacchanals' smothering culture of sexual excess proved to be the undoing of Greco-Roman dominance in the world. Historians from Thucydides and Herodotus to Himmelfarb and Schlossberg have documented that the social collapse of Greco-Romanism was rooted in the moral collapse of Greco-Romanism. The reason is as simple as it is universal.

Just as liberty and equality are opposite extremes often contrary to freedom, so sensuality and satisfaction are opposite extremes often contrary to happiness. There is, in fact, no real connection between the pursuit of happiness and the pursuit of pleasure. Happiness and pleasure could even be described as antithetical to one another, in that happiness is founded on the value of something eternal, whereas pleasure is founded on the value of something ephemeral.

Sadly, the lessons of history are all too often lost on those who most need to learn them.

Then and Now

The first time I witnessed a "Gay Pride Parade," I was astonished—and was reminded instantly of those ancient bacchanals. The raucous revelry, perverse promiscuity, orgiastic opulence, and appolyonic abandon I saw in the Montrose section of Houston was almost identical to the descriptions I had read of the Greeks on the precipice of their demise. The malevolent scene before me could have easily been transported three thousand miles and three thousand years to the bustling Plaka under the shadow of the Acropolis without missing a beat. The sights and sounds would have been no more alien there than here.

It was on that disorienting day in that discordant place that I first encountered the despondent distress of homosexuality—it was there and then that I first met Lance Ahlman.

We were as opposite as night and day. He was an exuberant participant in the day's festivities—cavorting in the aura of libertine excess. I was a member of an evangelistic team—inviting people to attend a Bible study I conducted for those who were interested in deliverance from the captivity of that same libertine excess. He was cocky, idealistic, and tragically self-sure. I was nervous, gloomy, and profoundly self-conscious. He was only just recently "out of the closet." I was only just recently married. He was appalled by my mission. I was no less alarmed by his.

Ironically, we became quick friends.

Paradox is at the root of all true friendships. The tensions of likes and dislikes, similarities and differences, comparisons and contrasts must be delicately balanced for mere comradery to mature into genuine openness. And so our odd relationship grew in fits and starts.

He periodically attended the Bible study I led, but always left infuriated. Marshaling tattered second-hand arguments from wishful-thinking liberals and salon-chair expositors, he railed against the plain teaching of Scripture on sexuality in general and homosexuality in particular. He first tried the tired tack of assailing Biblical authority. Failing at that, he tried some creative exegetical gymnastics. In desperation he attacked particularly onerous episodes in church history or obviously noxious inconsistencies in church practice. His torturous logical contortions became convincing evidence that all too often a man's theology is shaped by his morality—not the other way around. He simply would not give up a fancy under the shock of a fact.

Even so, Lance seriously sought for a substantive justification for his sexual orientation and practice. He had first yielded to his homosexual urges while serving a hitch in the army. In the beginning he thought he had come to the end of a lifelong search for meaning and significance. It turned out to be just another false start.

Because of the then strictly enforced ban on homosexual activity in the armed forces, he and his lovers felt more than a little inhibited. So, he opted out of the military at the first opportunity and joined Houston's ribald homosexual community.

But even that failed to satisfy him. His unhappiness continued to gnaw at him—mind, body, and spirit. He yearned for something more than what the saturnalias of the gay bars offered. He yearned for something more than what the bacchanalias of the gay parades offered. Laboring night and day like a factory, he poured through every scrap of literature he could find on the subject, both what I gave him and what he could dredge up on his own.

"I had become desperate," he told me sometime later. "I knew that I was so lost I didn't know which way was up. I was so lonely—and the anonymous sex I had at the bars and bathhouses only intensified that loneliness. The only place that I found any kind of authenticity was at the Bible study. But that grated on me terribly. I can remember sitting outside your apartment in my car debating whether or not I should go in. I felt damned if I did and damned if I didn't. Now I know that I was simply under conviction, but at the time I just knew that I was miserable."

For a few months, he tried to assuage his anguish by going to the services of a local prohomosexual congregation. "I thought that might relieve the pressure I was feeling," he explained. "But it only made things worse. The inconsistency of that kind of pick-and-choose Christianity was obvious to me right away. I determined that I had only two choices: accept Christianity as a whole or reject it as a whole. The option of winnowing out the parts I liked and trashing the rest—cafeteria-style—just seemed like the height of hypocrisy."

Indeed, hypocrisy is the tribute error pays to truth, and inconsistency is the tribute iniquity renders to integrity.

For several years Lance struggled with the enigmas of grace and truth. He watched as several of his former friends and lovers were alternately rescued by the Gospel or consumed by AIDS. Meanwhile, the downward spiral of his promiscuity accelerated alarmingly.

There were times when he would cut off all contact with me for months on end. Then he would show up at my door for desperation counseling. Finally, late one Friday night, he yielded and trusted Christ for the very first time.

"There was no instant flash of revelation," he said. "No fireworks. No bells and whistles. I had just come to the end of myself."

For the longest time, he had resisted the inexorable tug of grace in his life. But all the while he knew that he did not have an opposing theory so much as an opining thirst. Ultimately that thirst drove him to drink at the sure and eternal Fountain.

Lance has been a different person ever since. "I had become convinced that I was born a homosexual. Now I know that I was just born a sinner. I never could find a cure for the former. Thankfully, the cure for the latter found me."

As a result, his life has become an emblem of hope to any and all trapped in the vicious downward spiral of licentiousness. He is happily married and the proud father of four beautiful children. "People can change. Sexual orientation is not cruelly predestined by some freak genetic code. There really is hope. I'm living proof."

Why This Book?

We have been privileged to see God similarly at work in the lives of innumerable homosexual men and women through the years. That is why we have never shared the fear many Christians have of the "gay liberation movement." We have personally witnessed *real* liberation too many times. Spiritual longing is the soft underbelly of the modern homosexual bacchanalia. Even militant groups such as ACT-UP, Queer Nation, Wham, and NAMBLA don't seem to us to be a significant challenge to the Gospel.

But there is one threat we are very concerned about—if successful, it could stymie any efforts to reach people like Lance with the message of hope and truth. That threat is an uninformed and compromised church.

And thus this book.

Growing out of tense and terse apprehension that a tidal wave of misinformation and accommodation in the church might actually engulf church life and mission—this investigation was undertaken so that congregations might have the background necessary to make wise decisions; so that believers might be equipped to effectively minister to the hurting; so that we all might have the courage to stand against the tide.

This book is offered under the assumption that whatever is right is actually good, that whatever is good is actually just, and that whatever is just is actually merciful. The kindest and most compassionate message Christians can convey to homosexuals and their defenders is an unwaveringly Biblical message. The wisest and most decorous standard we can raise before a watching world is an unashamedly truthful standard.

Much of the material you will read in these pages will shock you. It is shocking to us as well, despite the years we have spent dealing with and ministering to the homosexual community. We present this material because it is not possible to declare that the gay and lesbian movement is dangerous or perverse without detailing in some way or another its dangers or perversions. Even so, mere sensationalism not only fails to convince; it is a breach of Christian ethics. We have tried to walk that fine line between informing and defiling.

Thus we have taken as our guideline the prescription of the apostle Paul:

Have no fellowship with the unfruitful works of darkness, but rather expose them. For it is shameful even to speak of those things which are done by them in secret. But all things that are exposed are made manifest by the light. (Ephesians 5:11–13)

We have attempted to expose unfruitful works without dabbling in shameful talk. But be forewarned: by throwing the searchlight of truth on filthy deeds, we will necessarily be forced to describe filth. Our prayer is that such a shocking revelation will alert us even as it did the believers in the apostles' day:

> Awake, you who sleep. Arise from the dead. And most assuredly Christ will give you light. (Ephesians 5:14)

Structure

This book grew out of several projects, both individual and collaborative. During the flaps in the media over the appointment of several homosexual activists to key posts in the Clinton administration and the intended lifting of the ban on homosexuals in the military, Mr. Horne wrote several timely articles, editorials, and reviews. We have incorporated portions of those into the text in various places. During several research and writing trips over the past several years, Dr. Grant has compiled a journal of vignettes, interviews, and personal observations. After much discussion we decided to include many of those in the book essentially unaltered—even to the point of leaving the first-person narrative style intact. In addition, the two of us have collaborated on three related projects: a short book on the crisis over homosexuality in mainstream Protestantism titled *Unnatural Affections: The Impuritan Ethic of Homosexuality in the Church*[2]; a long article on the homosexual counterculture in the armed forces for *Caveat,* a journal of conservative thought;[3] and another article in a mass-market compilation volume entitled *Gays in the Military: The Moral and Strategic Crisis.*[4] We have included much of that material in this work.

Structurally, the format of the book is straightforward:

Throughout the first section, the parameters of the homosexual movement are defined and measured. In chapter 1 a series of vignettes profiles the current crisis in one prominent homosexual community through the lens of individual lives and conversations. Chapter 2 examines the broader world of homosexuality—including its disturbing lifestyle practices.

The second section probes the impact of the homosexual movement on the institutions of our culture. Chapter 3 looks at the inroads gays have made in the world of popular entertainment. In chapter 4 the interaction between the radical homosexual movement and the educational system is examined. Chapter 5 looks at the ever-shifting, ever-changing world of politics and how activists have co-opted it for their own sordid ends. Chapter 6 is an exposé of the collaboration between those same activists and the medical research and management industry. Chapter 7 surveys the current controversy over gays in the military. Chapter 8 focuses on the emergence of a powerful homosexual influence in the institutional church.

The next section of the book probes the historical and theological roots of the issue. Chapter 9 summarizes the principles and precepts of the Scriptures on the question of homosexuality. Chapter 10 sums up twenty centuries of church tradition and teaching on homosexual practices.

And finally, chapter 11 reviews the whole of the issue—with a list of suggested practical applications to help us restore our culture to sanity and justice.

Each chapter begins with quotations from the "Fugitive Poets," a group of literary traditionalists living and working in the South during the first half of this century. The passages were carefully selected to reflect the moral themes contained in the chapters that follow.

In the end, our arguments are conspicuously presuppositional. There is a simple reason for this: the modern homosexual movement is not problematic because it is politically obnoxious, or culturally offensive, or socially subversive, or organizationally anarchic, or emotionally destructive, or personally selfish, or medically pathogenic. Rather, it is problematic because the "faith once and for all delivered to the saints" says that it is problematic. Period. All other concerns, though real, are but incidentally symptomatic.

So you will not find in these pages sensational hysteria about the destructiveness of the gay lifestyle—as awful as it is; or long diatribes about the maledictory effect of the gay agenda—as frightening as it is. Instead, you will find the facts stated as dispassionately as possible, often in the words of homosexual advocates and spokesmen themselves—though innumerable expletives were deleted. And perhaps even more important, you will find a plea for the church to simply do what it is supposed to do and to be what it is supposed to be.

Deo soli gloria. Jesu juva.

PART I

THE WAR ZONE

The browning honey-horns droop and faint,
Exhale in rainbow drops a timorous essence,
And spend their whiff of fragrance all unheeded
On lustful winds who whirl far to the South
Heated with expectation of lying that night
On the voluptuous breast of weeping willow,
Flowing its hair beside some moon-lit river.[1]

ANDREW NELSON LYTLE

1

A WALK
ON THE WILDE SIDE

All our debate is voiceless here,
As all our rage, the rage of stone;
If hope is hopeless, then fearless fear,
And history is thus undone.[2]

ROBERT PENN WARREN

J ust beyond famed Cooper Union, between Astor Place and Tompkins Square, is a little neighborhood affectionately dubbed the East
Village by its residents. Like so much of the rest of New York, it is a
community of violent contrasts: historic Stuyvesant Street is lined with
stately landmark homes, whereas shabby boutiques, disreputable tene-
ments, and "shooters galleries" dominate the surrounding blocks; homeless men and women sleep in the doorways of chic art galleries and
along the sidewalk in front of fashionable lofts and condominiums; impeccably tailored Wall Street moguls and would-be moguls hurry to
work amidst peddlers hawking their dilapidated wares; petition-gatherers
for every imaginable cause desperately distribute their leaflets to world-
weary commuters and gawk-eyed tourists; fly-by-night hucksters vie for
sales outside vintage establishments such as the Strand, the Yiddish
Theater, and Pageant Book and Print.

This was once a comfortable literary neighborhood where James
Fenimore Cooper, W. H. Auden, Allen Ginsberg, and Jacob Adler lived
and worked. In the sixties it became a haven for the hippie drug culture.

Rock and roll came alive at the Electric Circus on St. Mark's Place and at Fillmore East on Second Avenue. When Greenwich Village rents began to soar in the seventies, gentrification began in earnest and the substantial Jewish, Polish, and Ukrainian populations were gradually displaced by uptown yuppies.

The St. Mark's Church-in-the-Bowery on Tenth Street was built in 1660 as a Dutch Reformed chapel on Governor Peter Stuyvesant's farm—"bowery" or "bouerie" literally means "farm." Late in the seventeenth century it became an Episcopal parish church for the emerging community of small freeholders and yeomen and has been in continuous use ever since. In the late seventies the church helped to launch the famed Poetry Project, and by the early eighties it had become the neighborhood's center of *avant garde* radicalism, activism, and dissent. But the continuing evolution of the East Village has made even its most adventuresome forays into the uncharted realms of multicultural political correctness seem terribly tame in comparison.

By the late eighties the neighborhood had become the fulcrum of New York's massive homosexual movement. Just around the corner from the old church on St. Mark's Place—at the site of Cooper's last knickerbocker home—are the notorious St. Mark's Baths. Closed for a time in the wake of the worst of the AIDS epidemic, this grimy establishment nevertheless continues to symbolically dominate the social, cultural, and political life of the community.

That is where I met John Langford.

He was standing in line outside the Baths, anxious to get in. It was a dismal, gray New York afternoon. A wintry witchery hung in the air. The shivering file was as quiet, as servile, and as sullen as a welfare queue. It was a paradox as strange as any I'd ever witnessed: a straggle of men on the precipice of their intended gaiety looking for all the world like lambs being led to the slaughter.

John was nervously fingering the butt of a cigarette he had just snuffed out. I tried to strike up a conversation: "Hey, what're all you guys waiting in line for? What kind of place is this?"

With averted eyes he mumbled: "It's a . . . uh, its a . . . well, it's a bathhouse. You know."

I feigned innocent confusion. "A what?"

He looked up momentarily. "A bathhouse. You know. A sex parlor. A gay sex parlor."

"Oh my."

"Well, you know, it's not really the kind of place for tourists . . . or uh, straights. It's kind of wild, you know. Steam rooms. Hot tubs. Private booths. Anonymous sex. Group gigs. Orgies. You know, whatever turns you on. Each to his own."

"I guess. But isn't it . . . well, dangerous? I mean with AIDS and everything?"

He smiled a wry smile. "Yeah. Yeah, it is."

"So, uh . . . so why . . . "

"Why am I here? Why do I do this kind of thing? Good question. I, uh . . . I wish there was a good answer. I'm gay. This is what homosexuals do. That's it, I guess. This is what we do. And whatever the risks . . . well, those are the risks we have to take."

"Have to?"

"Yeah. Have to."

He appeared to be about twenty-five or so. His haircut was close-cropped around the sides but with a tumble of coiffed dark curls on top. Dressed in the outré hip-hop fashion of the day—loose jeans, layered shirts, a bulky stadium jacket, and expensive Nikes—the hesitation in his voice belied the cocky pose he struck.

The line didn't seem to be moving, so I probed a bit further.

"Do you really believe that? Do you really believe that you have absolutely no choice in the matter?"

"Humm, well . . . I don't know. Yeah, I guess. I really haven't ever thought much about it before."

"Really?"

"Yeah, I guess that sounds kind of crazy, doesn't it—not ever really giving the way I am, the way I act, a second thought. But that's how it is with *most* people, isn't it? We really don't examine why we do what we do. We just kind of fall into these patterns of behavior . . . I, uh . . . see, I was a psychology major. Anyway. I think that is just the way it is. We're all compulsive to one degree or another. If danger is involved in our peculiar compulsion—or even morality or religion or whatever—we just overlook it. We conveniently forget about it."

"And so you never think about it at all?"

"Well . . . only late in the night. When all torments come in uninvited to haunt."

"Torments or conscience?"

"Whatever."

⚜   ⚜   ⚜

A couple of doors down is the St. Mark's Bookshop. It is a thriving store that specializes in small-press books, philosophy, and women's studies. It is just about all that remains of an hypnotically fascinating row of second-hand bookstores that once made the East Village a bargain hunter's paradise.

It was there that I met Lisa Beveridge.

She was a strikingly beautiful woman who seemed to have gone to extraordinary extremes to hide that fact from the world. She wore baggy parachute pants, an oversized lumberjack flannel shirt, and hiking boots. Her hair was bobbed short, and she wore no makeup or jewelry. She was, however, adorned with a bevy of buttons bearing the slogans of various lesbian activist groups: "Refuse and Resist," "I'm a Lesbian . . . Get Used to It," "Abortion On Demand and Without Apology," "Queens, Queers, and Quays," and "Dykes on Bykes." They were pinned willy-nilly on her khaki photojournalist's vest.

She was browsing among the sundry literary offerings in the "Gay Sexuality" section. It struck me as more than a little strange that virtually all of the titles that were not brazenly pornographic seemed to focus on some kind of spiritual quest: *A Zen Soul-Guide to the Sexual Zeitgeist, Buddhist Lesbian Love, Psychic Cross-Dressing, The Sensual Satisfaction of the Soul-Spirit, Beautiful Butch Bodhisattvah,* and *Shamanistic Sex.*

Lisa was not looking at the porn. So, I thought I might try to strike up a conversation: "Are you interested in spiritual things?"

She turned and smiled cordially but her eyes betrayed an immistakable look—that canny, shrewd, disabused, *très gauche* coast look—conveying an experienced suspicion of any and all trendy self-help fads and religious fascinations. She chuckled. "What are you? Some kind of shrink or preacher or something?"

"Yeah. Something."

She chuckled again. "Well, I have to tell you, I don't believe in that stuff. In fact, I actually despise all these odd psychoanalyzing cults." She pointed toward the shelf of books: "And this co-dependency business and all its New Age corollaries *really* leaves me cold. Pop-psychology is so banal."

Her friendly manner and her easy articulateness seemed to contrast oddly with her chosen predilections. She continued with a wry winsomeness. "You name it: Muktananda, Sri Rajneesh, Divine Light Mission, Branch Davidian, EST, Transcendental Meditation, Dianetics, Synanon, Baptists, Eckankar, B'hai, Baba Ram Dass, Presbyterians—they're all just hoaxes. You know what I mean?

"Well, uh. . . ."

"Just nonsense. Junk. Fads. All of them are the same."

Then, she threw me a curveball: "All, that is, except one." She leaned toward me and confided: "It's my Thursday evening Prosperity Visualization Seminar. It's like a combination of all of the best in Arica, Zen, Jung, Freud, Rand, and—get this—Christianity."

"Oh. . . ." At first, I couldn't tell if she was kidding.

She wasn't.

She set the book she had been looking at down on the shelf and began gesturing: "I used to have a big problem with affluence, you know, really visualizing it. So, I was stuck at a kind of preternatural bourgeois level. I just couldn't get a handle on who I was supposed to be. Or even *what* I was supposed to be. I simply couldn't appreciate myself. I couldn't find a way to affirm my longings or passions. But now, thanks to Prosperity Visualization, I'm in touch with my feelings. And I can actually *own* them—for perhaps the first time. I'm up for prosperity now. I'm up for it, and it's happening."

"So, this group helps you get rich? Or just accept those who are already rich?"

"Both. Definitely both. See, that was my problem. My anima. Really bad karma."

"So what does all this have to do with your, uh . . . with your, uh . . ."

"My queerness?"

"Well . . . "

"Everything really. I had to get past the barriers of the present and probe the conflicts of the past in order to see clear to the future. Prosperity Visualization helped me to do that deep down in my Spirit Woman."

My face must have betrayed my doubt.

"It's really beautiful," she said. "Not at all like all that other ridiculous hocus-pocus or psycho-babble. It is totally spiritual. My queerness—like my financial situation—is not just coded into biology. It is spiritual."

ࢶ　　ࢶ　　ࢶ

Tompkins Square, three blocks east, was the site of a bloody confrontation between police and drug users just a few years ago. It is hard to imagine. Like so many of New York's parks, it is a surprisingly serene oasis set amid the hustle and bustle of the city. And like Central Park, Union Square, Bryant Park, and Washington Square, it is a favored site for protests and demonstrations.

On the day I visited, Queer Nation—a radical breakaway faction of the equally radical ACT-UP homosexual activist organization—had scheduled a "Stonewall Love-In" there. Recently relandscaped and renovated, the park is normally crowded with brown-baggers, strollers, and even a few joggers. But by the time I arrived, it had been abandoned into the hands of the rally organizers. A small platform had been erected, and a makeshift sound system and podium had been installed.

At first there were only a couple of dozen activists there. They were milling around, tending to a few last minute details, rechecking the schedule of events, and generally making merry. Representatives from several renowned fellow traveler organizations began to unfurl their banners and to set up long folding tables loaded with pamphlets and paraphanalia around the perimeter of the park. Three or four burly members of the local Women's Action Coalition were raising a giant black and blue display that announced "High-Octane Anger." Meanwhile, two volunteers from Planned Parenthood were laying out the necessary supplies for a "Condom-Fest," scheduled for later in the afternoon. As the crowd began to swell, a full complement of the vaunted minions of the American Left made appearances: there were representatives from the ACLU, People for the American Way, NOW, Fund for the Feminist Majority, NARAL, Greenpeace, NAMBLA, Sierra Club, CISPES, the Children's Defense Fund, the NEA, and the Audubon Society. Even the slightly less reputable partisans of the Left's many obsolete "Lost Causes" circulated among the protestors: the New Symbionese Liberationists, the American Maoists, the Trotskyites, the Weathermen, the Neo-Jacobins, and the Black Panthers.

Before long, the park was a carnival of inflated rhetoric, exaggerated emotions, and excited hormones. Though they tended to be a rather colorful lot, I was surprised to observe that the protestors were virtually indistinguishable from the typical hippyish rent-a-crowds that populate such things as Earth Day celebrations, Amnesty International benefit concerts, or Pro-Abortion photo-ops. Absolute conformity is never so sure as among absolute nonconformists.

In recent years, the haunting and emaciated figures of men on the very threshold of death have become regular fixtures at local Gay Pride parades and protests. This one was to be no exception. From across the square, a couple of orderlies were helping several wheelchair-bound AIDS patients make their way toward the rally. They were residents of a neighborhood hospice for the dying. The anguish of uncertain eternity was etched on their faces.

A man standing near me at the East Seventh Street entrance noticed my interest. "Sad, isn't it?"

"Yes," I said. "Yes it is. Tragic, really."

He nodded agreement. We chatted for a few moments—but all the while, his eyes never left the hospice residents. His name, he said, was Larry Slovenic, and he worked as an investment banker for a prestigious midtown firm. His dark wool suit was a conservative Brooks Brothers cut; his crisp white shirt was an expensive pinpoint pima; his designer tie was an Italian silk larrose; and his shoes were rich Spanish thread-needles. He was a perfect image of success—a paradigm of *sartor resartus*. "It really scares me," he said after a long pause. "There but for the grace of God. . . ."

At that, his voice trembled and his eyes brimmed with tears. "The doctor says it's just a matter of time. I, uh . . . I don't know what I'm going to do."

I shuddered with realization. "You've tested positive?"

"Yeah. I just found out two weeks ago. I haven't told . . . well, hardly anyone yet. I mean, what do you say? How do you say it?" He turned toward me now, his face collapsed into a map of suffering, criss-crossed with deep lines gouged out by inner travail. "I'm afraid. I don't want . . . I don't want to die."

I listened. I sympathized. I tried to console him. But at the very *mention* of the Gospel, he turned suddenly, violently belligerent. He set his jaw and blustered. "I'm not sorry I'm gay. I won't apologize for what I am. I *refuse* to feel guilty for this. Anyone who suggests that I should be . . . well, that just makes me furious. Absolutely *furious*."

There is a pious truism that admonishes us to "separate the sin from the sinner." But like so many other truisms, it is easier said than done. It is easier said than done simply because nine times out of ten, sinners won't allow it.

The rally was just getting underway. One of the organizers was at the podium leading an angry chant: "We're here and we're queer." The crowd was working itself into a cathartic frenzy. Fists were raised. Curses were hurled. Tempers flared.

Larry turned toward me with a fierce glare. Over and over again he repeated the chant—his face red, his veins bulging. "I'm your worst nightmare," he shouted. "I'm America's worst nightmare. I'm a mad fag with nothing left to lose."

†   †   †

After I left the unpleasant scene of the rally, I walked up Broadway toward Madison. Though it was already getting dark, the streets were crowded and the shops abuzz with activity. Young women clad in the latest fashions—but wearing the city's obligatory tennis shoes instead of pumps or heels—stopped at the bakery, the green-grocer, and the corner market. Hot dog, pretzel, and falafel vendors enjoyed a brisk trade. Harried executives unwound by stopping in at a local pub or browsing in the sidewalk bookstalls. Street musicians took their places amid the throng. Buskers and panhandlers rattled their cups and pled their cases. The happy cacophony bore testimony to the fact that despite all the ills of this poor fallen world, the ordinary affairs of life go on.

Mark Callihan is a beat cop. He walks these streets and witnesses these scenes every day. In fact, he was born just a few blocks north of the East Village and has spent his entire life here. "I've seen a lot of changes over the years," he told me. "Some of them good . . . most of them, well . . . not so good. But it's still home to me."

He had just emerged from an eclectic store across Broadway from the Strand that specialized in comics, cybernetics, and other assorted science fiction bric-a-brac. A woman with a shaved head and a plethora of ominous tattoos was carrying on an animated conversation with him—he later told me that they had gone to high school together. A light drizzle had begun to fall. A bag lady stood nearby singing loudly—show tunes, I believe, from *Porgy and Bess*. Meanwhile, shoppers continued to whirl past, as if in a dizzying, dervish dance.

"I love this city," Mark told me. "I love this neighborhood. I love its amazing diversity. We've got a little bit of everything here. It's wonderful. That's why I get so upset when I see it threatened by criminal mischief, by selfishness, and by sheer irresponsibility—by the drugs, the gangs, the porn, the low-life hustlers, the bookies, the pimps, the welfare cheats, and the gay agitators."

"Gay agitators?"

"Yeah. You know, the ones that are always making a nuisance of themselves—throwing themselves in front of traffic, dumping blood onto the sidewalks, disrupting public meetings, vandalizing churches, flaunting public lewdness, and generally riling the entire city up. It's awful."

"They do that? I mean, often?"

"Hey, they're angry. They're desperate. Ever since this AIDS thing started, they've been . . . oh, I don't know. It's difficult. Still, there's just no excuse. . . ." He shook his head in frustration.

After a long thoughtful pause, he went on. "You know, this is a very difficult subject to discuss. Rationally, I mean. Objectively. Almost anything I might say inevitably sounds like an overreaction, or prejudiced, or homophobic, or something. The problem is that most people just have no idea . . . they can't even begin to imagine . . . what goes on. What it's like."

He looked across the street where a huddle of shoppers continued to rifle through the paperback bins at the Strand despite the fact that the rain was starting to come down harder now. A homeless man dodged traffic in the center of Broadway, tracing imaginary designs above his head with a ragged umbrella. A young Hasidic couple hurried along, strange archaisms draped across their frail frames. A small group of teens, oblivious to everything else around them, bopped along to the syncopated beat that blared from their gargantuan boom-box. Two elderly women compared the respective virtues of cucumbers at a vegetable market with all the fervor of bond traders. A tall distinguished-looking man, dapper and dashing, walked behind a pair of perky Pekinese that were clearly relishing their regular evening jaunt. Mark took all this in with obvious satisfaction. He smiled.

"As crazy as this world obviously is, I just have to wonder if there is any way to communicate to ordinary people who live ordinary lives the truth about homosexuals and the lives they lead. Is there any way to even *describe* what they do, how they act, what they believe? How do you do it without sounding either hysterical or just plain . . . well, *filthy?* Just plain *disgusting?* I just have to wonder. I really do."

"Yeah. I know what you mean," I sighed. "I do too. I just have to wonder."

2

DE-LIGHTING AMERICA

Thin lips can make a music; hateful eyes can see;
Crooked limbs go dancing to a strange melody
The surly heart of clowns can crack with ecstasy;
Rootbound oaks toss limbs if winds come fervently.[1]

DONALD DAVIDSON

S ince the advent of modernity, the cultural centers of revolutionary thought and rhetoric have been as diverse as the social cataclysms they have spawned. During the great English Civil War they were the manor houses of Sussex and Ely. During the American War of Independence they were the taverns of Boston and Philadelphia. During the French Revolution they were the cafes and salons of Paris. During the Enlightenment they were the galleries of Vienna and Berlin. And during the Russian Revolution they were the lodges of St. Petersburg's secret societies.

But since the First World War, the centers for revolutionary thought and rhetoric have invariably been small literary bookstores. The influential Bloomsbury group—including Virginia Wolfe, John Maynard Keynes, Lytton Strachey, E.M. Forster, Duncan Grant, William Butler Yeats, Aldous Huxley, D.H. Lawrence, and Bertrand Russell—often gathered at the Gordon Square Bookshop near the British Museum in London. The eclectic *Gauche* fine arts cabal—including Gertrude Stein, Ernest Hemingway, James Joyce, Andre Gide, F. Scott Fitzgerald, Ezra Pound, Joan Miro, and Pablo Picasso—made the Shakespeare and Company bookshop on the Left Bank in Paris the social hub and intellectual clearinghouse of their movement. The Gotham Book Mart was the up-town center of gravity for many of New York's chic Greenwich radi-cals—including Mabel Dodge, Rockwell Kent, Margaret Sanger, John Reed, Upton Sinclair, Julius Hammer, and Clarence Darrow. During the heyday of California's bohemian and beatnik movements, the City Lights Bookstore in the Bay area's North Beach neighborhood became the fountainhead of creative protest—drawing such luminaries as Jack Kerouac, Henri Lenoir, Shig, Grace Slick, and Jerry Garcia.

Arguably the cultural and intellectual locus of the homosexual movement today is also a bookstore.

A Different Light Bookstore in San Francisco is located just across the street and down the block from the Harvey Milk Plaza and a few doors over from the magnificent mission-style Castro Street Theater. The bookstore is a veritable cornucopia of gay literature, paraphanalia, art, and artifacts and has naturally served as a central gathering place, a social catalyst, and a political prod for upscale gays in this, the most influential homosexual community in the nation.

At first glance it appears to be nothing more than a rather pedestrian neighborhood bookstore. The split-level floor plan is dominated by at-tractive modular wood shelving, bright fixture displays, and well-spaced aisles. But upon a closer inspection the store reveals its startlingly unique character.

The racks lining a niche just beyond the checkout counter are domi-nated by what one might be tempted to call pornographic magazines—except that they do not actually portray what most people associate with explicit sensual temptation or sexual satiation. In fact, they defy catego-rization altogether. Their brutality and degradation is utterly shocking. It is not so much that they appear crude that makes them so appalling, as that they appear cruel. They more resemble torture than sex.

Similarly, the shelves along the walls are overstuffed with a vast array of books—but of a sort that simply cannot be imagined by the average mind. They comprise an horrific and hellish Dewey Decimal inventory: books on bestiality; books on pedophilia; books on sado-masochism; books on physiogeny; books on necrophilia; books on de-mentiogeny; books on incestualism; and books on biliaphilia.

Vulgar posters, uncouth bumper stickers, perverse buttons, crude banners, crass newsletters, obscene trinkets, profane souvenirs, sacri-legious T-shirts, ribald pamphlets, and indecent brochures round out the stock.

"This store actually represents the very best of the homosexual community," Michael McWilliams, a regular customer, said to me. "It is the intellectual and literary center of San Francisco's gay universe. And as a result, it is the intellectual and literary center of the *world's* gay universe."

My consternation and incredulity must have been all too evident.

"Hey, *this* is traditional morality . . . or rather, traditional immorality. Prudish and uptight Christian ideals about sex are the real novelties—not this stuff. The history of the world looks a whole lot more like this than it does like a Sunday school lesson."

As much as I wanted to disagree with him, I knew that he was probably right.

Traditional Immorality

History is indeed replete with the sad saga of mankind's perverse folly.

In ancient societies for instance, there was nothing resembling the Christian sexual ideal of covenantal, heterosexual, and monogamous love. Fertility cults involving temple prostitution and orgies, both heterosexual and homosexual, were commonplace. Brutality, perversity, and promiscuity were a natural part of the well-worn human landscape in times gone by.

Through the ages, the story of fallen man has been tragically predictable. Apart from the ameliorating grace of God, human societies were invariably inclined to progressive defilement:

> Professing to be wise, they became fools, and changed the glory of the incorruptible God into an image made like corruptible man—and birds and four-footed animals and creeping things. Therefore God also gave them up to uncleanness, in the lust of their hearts, to dishonor their bodies among themselves. (Romans 1:22–24)

They became trapped on a sadly debauched downgrade:

> For this reason God gave them up to vile passions. For even their women exchanged the natural use for what is against nature. Likewise also the men, leaving the natural use of the woman, burned in their lust for one another, men with men committing what is shameful, and receiving in themselves the penalty of their error which was due. (Romans 1: 26–27)

Thus, according to author Peter Leithart, ancient paganism naturally gave rise to perverse sexual practices. He says that this was because:

> It was essentially a worship of nature, and the practice of ritual sex was rooted in this naturalistic worldview. In ancient mythology, in which we can see distortions of the Genesis account, order emerged from chaos. . . . In the chaos and fertility cults man participates in divine life and recovers fertility by a ritual reenactment of the original act of a myth, often of the creation from chaos. Ritual chaos, in short, recreates, reorders, and reanimates the world. Sexual orgies are one part of the ritual reenactment of that chaos.[2]

Furthermore, in many of those postdeluvian societies, homosexual relationships were encouraged as a positive good. This is most notably true in the case of the ancient Greeks. Sodomy was not only practiced, but held up as a philosophical ideal. According to Leithart, "Plato's most poetic hymns on love grew out of reflections on pederasty."[3] Indeed, in a prototypical statement the philosopher opined:

> Through the nightly loving of young boys, a man, on arising, begins to see the authentic nature of true beauty.[4]

Plato's teacher, Socrates, argued that promiscuous homosexuality was a "superior form of love" because it united "the love of a beautiful body" with "the love of a beautiful soul." And this was something that he believed could only rarely be accomplished through chaste heterosexuality.[5]

Sadly, idealization of perversion was not unique to the Hellenic culture. A myriad of sociological and anthropological studies reveal that other ancient civilizations, almost without exception, reveled in promiscuity, homosexuality, and sensual abuse.[6] Rome was perpetual satyricon.[7] Egypt, Persia, Carthage, Babylon, and Assyria were all steeped in pederastic tradition.[8] And the ancient empires of the Mongols, Tartars, Huns, Teutons, Celts, Incas, Aztecs, Mayans, Nubians, Mings, Canaanites, and Zulus likewise celebrated depravity, degradation, and debauchery.[9]

Dennis Prager, a contemporary Jewish scholar contrasts Old Testament Israel with these surrounding pagan societies:

> Except for the introduction of a universal, moral, supernatural God, nothing was as radically different, as unnatural, and as anti-social as its prohibition of homosexuality. . . . Man-boy love has been an accepted, even

lauded feature of most civilizations. It dominated Greece, and has been an accepted norm in the Arab and Muslim world until the present century. Sir Richard Burton reported that the Chinese love of homosexuality was only equaled by their love of bestiality.[10]

Camille Paglia, Professor of Humanities at the University of the Arts in Philadelphia, concurs:

Worldwide, in Greece and Rome as in the Near East, China, and Japan, pretty boys have usually been considered by men to be as sexually desirable as women. Christianity is unusual in finding the practice of boy-love abhorrent.[11]

The lesson of history is indisputable: apart from cultures guided and directed by the Bible, human society has never maintained what most of us might regard as "traditional family values." In point of fact, only the gradual missionary expansion—and ultimately the cultural dominance—of Christianity can explain the existence of the sexual ethic we today consider natural and normative.

And that came only at great cost.

To the Uttermost

The last mandate of Christ to His disciples—commonly known as the Great Commission—was to comprehensively evangelize all the world. He said:

All authority in heaven and on earth has been given to Me. Therefore go and make disciples of all nations, baptizing them in the Name of the Father and of the Son and of the Holy Spirit, and teaching them to obey everything I have commanded you. And surely I am with you always, to the very end of the age. (Matthew 28:18–20)

The immediate implications of this mandate were quite revolutionary and have literally altered the course of world history.

In this charge Jesus asserts that all authority in heaven is His (Psalm 103:19). The heights, the depths, the angels, and the principalities are all under His sovereign rule (Psalm 135:5–7). Moreover, all authority on earth is His as well (Psalm 147:15–18). Man and creature, as well as every invention and institution, are under His providential superintendence (Psalm 24:1). There are no neutral areas in all the cosmos that can escape His authoritative regency (Colossians 1:17).

On that basis, Christ says, believers all across the wide gulf of time are to manifest His Lordship continually—making disciples in all nations by going, baptizing, and teaching.

It was this mandate that originally emboldened the earliest disciples to preach the Gospel—first in Jerusalem and Judea, then in Samaria, and finally in the uttermost parts of the earth (Acts 1:8). It was this mandate that sustained a faithful church through generations of hardship, persecution, calamity, and privation—provoking it to offer light and life to those ensnared in the miry clay of darkness, defilement, and death. It was this mandate that eventually sent explorers and adventurers such as Columbus, Vespucci, Balboa, da Gama, Magellan, and Cabot out across the perilous uncharted seas.[12] And ultimately, it was this same mandate that became the catalyst for a remarkable resurgence of missionary efforts—both in word and in deed—that followed on the heels of that great European expansion and colonization.[13]

Just as no corner of the globe was ultimately left untouched by the explorers, soldiers, merchants, and colonists bearing up under notions of the "White Man's Burden" and "Manifest Destiny," the selfless and sacrificial efforts of the missionaries that invariably accompanied them left virtually no stone unturned either. Peoples everywhere tasted the abundant benefits of the Gospel they preached.[14] And, chief among those benefits of course, was a new standard for sexual morality—a standard that was almost entirely unknown anywhere in the world until the advent of the Gospel.

As these sundry emissaries moved out from Christendom to the "uttermost parts of the earth" they were shocked to discover the horrors of untamed heathenism. They were confronted by the specters of endemic poverty, recurring famine, unfettered disease, and widespread chattel servility. Cannibalism, ritual abuse, patricide, human sacrifice, abortion, petty tyranny, paternalistic exploitation, live burials, infanticide, exterminative clan warfare, and genocidal tribal vendettas all predominated. In addition, they found sexual perversity all too prevalent and homosexuality all too commonplace.

Again and again, they had to affirm in the clearest possible way—in both word and deed—that Jesus Christ is the only perfect sacrifice for the sins of the world and that through Him had come the death of death and the end of debauchery (Romans 5:6–18).

Most of the Westerners knew that this liberating message would likely be met with strident opposition. And it was.

Nevertheless, as they circled the globe, penetrated the jungles, and crossed the seas, they preached a singular message: light out of darkness, liberty out of tyranny, and life out of death. To cultures epidemic with poverty, brutality, lawlessness, and disease, those faithful Christian witnesses interjected the novel Christian concepts of grace, charity, law, medicine, and sexual morality. They overturned despots, liberated the captives, and rescued the perishing. They established hospitals. They founded orphanages. They started rescue missions. They built almshouses. They opened soup kitchens. They incorporated charitable societies. They changed laws. They demonstrated love. They lived as if people really mattered.[15]

As a result, the tradition of "traditional morality" gradually supplanted the older "traditional immorality" inherent in this poor fallen world and its "state of nature."[16]

The Empire Strikes Back

Just as the hands of a clock can be turned back, so the progress of historical events can be annulled. We need look no further than our own ever-shifting social mores for evidence of that: traditional immorality has arisen phoenix-like from the dust heap of the past.

Thus, in the midst of the present dramatic and cataclysmic moral reversals, author and theologian Peter Jones is compelled to ask:

Why is homosexuality on the rise? Why is it endorsed by *Time* magazine, promoted on publicly funded radio, and featured in children's comic strips—with great moral fervor in the name of democracy? Why is feminism such a powerful force today? Why is the movement developing its own goddess spirituality? Why is witchcraft taught in certain California school districts? Why is feminist spirituality making enormous inroads into Christianity? Why is abortion a vitally important part of the feminist manifesto? Is ecology just a neutral concern about the survival of the planet, or does it too have a religious agenda? Why is American Indian nature religion being actively promoted? Why is the work ethic no longer working? Why is multiculturalism and political correctness so important on many college campuses?[17]

Jones concludes this querying litany of woes asking: "Are all these seemingly disconnected issues *related* in any way?"[18]

His answer is an unequivocal yes.[19]

He says that despite the great attainments of Christendom's missionary march around the globe, ancient paganism is now resurgent. Morality's ascent was hardly a permanent attainment of historical uniformitarianism. The old "gnostic empire," he says, has "returned with a vengeance."[20]

In fact, from the sixteenth century onward, the Christian ethic of chaste fidelity began to be undermined first by the neo-pagan Renaissance—due to an exaltation of the pagan Greek classics—and then further by the neo-gnostic Enlightenment. The French *philosophe,* Voltaire, recognized this when he bluntly stated, "Once, a philosopher; twice, a sodomite!"[21]

For more than a millennium the church had maintained that any and all sexual activity outside the sacred bond of marriage was sinful—thus, for instance, it thought homosexuals were responsible for their behavior and that their behavior was immoral—but the new secular movements kept looking back to the old pagan promiscuity.

Again according to Leithart:

> In the final analysis, as one would expect, the Enlightenment rejection of Christian sexual morality led to a justification of all sexual perversions. In an important sense, Western Enlightenment sexual ethics were far more perverse than their pre-Christian models, for they were self-consciously rejecting Christianity, and like the dog that returns to his vomit, were in the last condition worse than the first (2 Peter 2:22). We are still living with the consequences of the Enlightenment's triumph over Christianity.[22]

This triumph involved the acceptance of three central tenets that were and are directly contrary to the confession of the church:

First, the Enlightenment encouraged a virtual worship of nature. The natural environment was the standard against which moral behavior was to be measured. This of course necessitated a rejection of the Bible as the ethical foundation of culture. Nature became, according to historian Carl Becker, "the new revelation."[23]

Second, because nature was considered normative, and humanity was viewed as a mere product of nature, anything people did "naturally" in thought, word, or deed was considered normal or even good. In other words, these modern secular movements denied the existence of original sin. By Renaissance and Enlightenment standards, only that which suppressed what men did naturally could be considered evil.[24]

Third, this environmental humanism ultimately led to a kind of insipid primitivism—an obsession with "the virtues of either distant primitive civilizations, or of the distant, and more virtuous past of European civilization itself."[25] After all, if nature is good, then the closer people are to nature the better they will be. Since the primitive peoples invariably had perverse sexual customs, the new humanistic thinkers used them as evidence that Christian morality must be an "artificial aberration." Typical in this regard was the influential work of Jean-Jacques Rousseau, who asserted that monogamy was an "artificial contrivance" exploited by women to "establish their empire."[26]

As these ideas took a higher and higher cultural profile, leaders in government and academia—and gradually even in the church—began increasingly to believe that the vast material differences between Christian societies and pagan societies were actually not rooted in religion but in the situational vagaries of education, technology, sociology, and race. They thus advocated an amalgamation of "the best of both worlds," wedding the technological achievement of the West with the moral license of the East—a combination that the dumb certainty of experience has since demonstrated to be "the worst of both worlds."

Bearing Fruit

Not surprisingly, Enlightenment thought had a profound effect on the daily lives of those who whole heartedly embraced it.[27] Rousseau, Voltaire, Danton, Robespierre, Babeuf, Darwin, Buonarroti, Marx, Nechayev, Tolstoy, Nietzsche, Tkachev, Freud, Wells, Shaw, Kinsey, Sanger, Baldwin, Ingersol, and Russell, though undoubtedly successful, accomplished, and influential, were simultaneously self-consciously immoral—each at least dabbling with homosexuality.[28]

The life and work of Thomas Paine is instructive in this regard. Paine remains well known as a passionate American patriot because he authored *Common Sense,* a best-selling booklet that helped spark the War for Independence.[29] A stalwart defender of the right of secession and nullification, he is celebrated in the narrative history of this land as a genuine hero.

But there was a dark side to Paine that most students of history know little or nothing about.

Although Paine championed the idea of liberty, he also propagated a "secular, millenarian insistence" that "we have it in our power to begin the world over again" by the "establishing of a new constitutional union."[30] As a result, he did not remain in America long after the war, but emigrated first to Regency London and then eventually to Jacobin France in 1791—in search of an Enlightenment utopian "new world order."[31]

In France, Paine lived as the guest of the revolutionary journalist Nicholas Bonneville.[32] There he became increasingly devoted to neo-pagan ideas and perverse sexual relationships.

Historian James Billington explains:

> Paine, who lived in a *ménage à trois* with Bonneville and his wife from 1797 to 1802, believed that the Druids and Pythagoreans had combined to provide an occult ideological alternative to Christianity. *An Essay on the Origin of Free Masonry,* written after his return to America (with Bonneville's wife) and immediately translated into French by Bonneville, insisted that the natural sun worship of the Druids had not been destroyed but merely diverted into Masonry.[33]

The rambunctious neo-pagan revivals of nature worship and pederastic sexual license that Paine and his cohorts reveled in were actually not terribly uncommon during the French Revolution. According to Billington:

> Paine's closest American friend in Paris, Joel Barlow, imagined that there were "natural" sexual origins for festive revolutionary symbols. He traced the trees of liberty to the phallic symbol of the Egyptian cult of Isis—carried thence to Greece and Rome, where Bacchus was know by the epithet Liber, so that the Phallus became the emblem of Libertas. Barlow derived the Phrygian red cap of liberty from a Roman symbol for the head of the phallus, and he decried with solemnity the substitution of the maypole and the celebration of May first for the older and richer phallic festival of the Liber Deus on the Vernal Equinox: men have forgotten the original object of the institution, the phallus has lost its testicles, and has been for many centuries reduced to a simple pole.[34]

Following in the Enlightenment footsteps of Paine were a whole host of modern intellectuals. As an English university student, John Maynard Keynes, perhaps the most popular and influential economist of the twentieth century, joined an elite, intellectual, secret society known as the "Cambridge Apostles." Originally formed as a debating society to defend the Gospel at Cambridge, by the time Keynes became a member in 1903 the Apostles had changed remarkably.[35]

As Richard Deacon states in his history of the society:

> From about 1830 onwards there had been distinct undercurrents of homosexual orientation in the Society, though . . . these were for the most part sublimated and platonic rather than physical. But from the turn of the century the sublimated turned into the consummated and homosexuality became almost a creed.[36]

This academic homosexual cult was self-consciously viewed by them as an emulation of the Greek pagan philosophers the Enlightenment had so ceremoniously elevated. One member who, years later, regretted his sexual promiscuity as a student wrote of "how mistaken was my early view, finding expression in Plato and appealing to me there, that the love for men is of a higher kind than that for women. It may be, but it seldom seems so."[37]

Deacon notes:

> The theory that the love of man for man was greater than that of man for woman became an Apostolic tradition. It was summed up in one of the later Apostolic secret phrases of this period—the "Higher Sodomy." Note the capital letters. This was said to reflect the view that women were inferior to men both in mind and body, and that this put a homosexual relationship on a much higher plane.[38]

Once he became a member, Keynes, along with one other Apostle, was instrumental in increasing the level of perversity in the secret society. "The homosexual phase in Apostolic life bloomed in the latter part of the last century," Deacon writes, "reached hot-house proportions in the early part of this century, becoming blatantly and even ostentatiously aggressive under those two predacious pederasts, Giles Lytton Strachey and John Maynard Keynes."[39]

Indeed, Keynes later boasted about the society's immorality, saying, "The Apostles repudiated entirely the customary conventions and traditional wisdom. We were in the strict sense Immoralists."[40] Unlike his partner, Strachey, Keynes practiced his perverse sexual ethic not only because of an admiration for pagan morality, but also because of an abiding hatred of Christianity:

> The two men were devoted to the same sexual cult and had the same contempt for conventional thought. But there was a difference between the two men. In Strachey's case this was more a question of perversity for its own sake than any carefully thought out philosophy. Keynes was reacting positively against the Puritan ethic: he hated Puritanism in any form and not least in the form it had long taken at Cambridge. Both men, however, regarded homosexuality as the supreme state of existence, "surpassing Christian understanding," and being superior to heterosexual relationships.[41]

Interestingly, the antipathy to Christianity undergirding Keynes' sexual ethic also influenced his social theory:

> Keynes' hatred of Puritanism is important in the light of his economic theories. He was to become the man who has gone down in history as the most outstanding economist and the architect of social progress of the past seventy years, though some would dispute such an assessment. But it was his hostility to the Puritan ethic which stimulated and lay behind his economic theories—spend to create work, spend one's way out of a depression, and spend to stimulate growth. It was also his hatred of Puritanism which caused him in early life to devote rather more time to pursuing homosexual conquests than to economics. . . . Keynes' much-admired theories on how best life can be improved by pouring out so-called Government money—i.e. the money taken from the people in taxes—were marked by an abysmal ignorance of what life for the masses was like and how much they survive in the long run solely by their own efforts and not by the benevolence of any government. Cambridge may have acquired over the ages too great a respect for the Puritan ethic, but it must be remembered that a degree of Puritanism has usually been beneficial to Britain, whereas an over-reaction against it has often been disastrous.[42]

Despite their best efforts at propounding their fiercely anti-Christian notions, however, for at least two centuries the Paines and Keyneses of this world were profoundly unsuccessful in debunking the solid Christian consensus in the West. But their relentless assault on morality continued unabated. Many humanists believed it was simply a matter of time before their intellectual shenanigans would eventually prevail.

Apparently, they were right.

Of course, what makes homosexuality distinctive is its sexual proclivities, not its intellectual progenitors. This is evident even to the most
casual observer.

When *The Advocate,* a "mainstream" national newsmagazine for homosexuals, decided to stop running sexually explicit classified ads, they
received an irate letter:

> I am surprised by *The Advocate's* pandering to those who want to de-sex
> the gay and lesbian culture and life-style. We suffer discrimination because
> we have same-sex partners, not because we like movies, theater, art, etc.
> Removing the sex ads only gives support to those who claim that sex is
> something dirty and nasty that should be neither noticed nor discussed.[43]

Indeed, the essential point of discussion about homosexuality is not
that Enlightenment thought has produced a peculiar promiscuity, it is
what this peculiar promiscuity actually is. "Ye shall know them by their
fruit" (Matthew 12:33).

Of course, this poses a complex problem: discussing what homosexual practice actually is and what it actually entails is generally considered either a serious breach of social ethics or a sensational lapse of
polite propriety. And for good reason: the description is nothing short of
appalling. Such unpleasantness is not to be thoughtlessly embraced. But
then, neither should it be shirked.

Author David Chilton has noted:

> There are some . . . who would object to . . . a frank treatment, going so
> far as to call it homophobic. This strikes me as odd: apparently we should
> not be squeamish about what homosexuals actually *do*—dear me, that
> would be homophobic—but we should be squeamish about someone giving
> an accurate *explanation* of what they do. Such an attitude is, in fact, a
> standard perversion of our age, which stresses refinement over decency,
> aesthetics over ethics.[44]

Ironically, this kind of cautious hesitation and inverted prudery is
perfectly suited to advance the homosexual agenda. Marshall Kirk and
Hunter Madsen, authors of a gay political strategy manual, endorse this
"squeamishness" as a tactic for effective propagandizing:

> In the early stages of the campaign, the public should not be shocked and
> repelled by premature exposure to homo*sexual* behavior itself. Instead, the

imagery of sex per se should be down-played, and the issue of gay rights reduced as far as possible, to an abstract social question.[45]

Homosexuals want us to believe that same-sex couples are just like heterosexual couples except for the small difference that they happen to be, well, the same sex. This is patently untrue.

Promiscuity

That homosexual practice is something utterly and completely alien from heterosexual practice can be demonstrated first and foremost by the profligate prolificacy of gay sex. Heterosexual activity, even at its most promiscuous, hardly comes close to homosexuality.

As renowned clinical psychologist Frank M. du Mas has stated:

Promiscuity among homosexuals is well known. . . . Promiscuity is much more prevalent among male homosexuals than female homosexuals, but even female homosexuals tend to be promiscuous by heterosexual standards.[46]

The evidence for this assertion is more than merely anecdotal.

In 1983, for example, a group of homosexuals kept diaries of their sexual encounters. When the results were collated, it was discovered that the average homosexual male had fellated 106 different men. Furthermore, on average the homosexuals were sodomized seventy-two times.[47] Indeed, an average homosexual can easily have thousands of sexual partners in his lifetime.[48]

Worse, many—if not most—of all homosexual encounters are anonymous. As the brilliant and vociferous proponent of sexual license Camille Paglia has noted:

One of the problems that most vexed me in my meditation on sex is the promiscuity of gay men. Again and again, I was astonished to learn from gay friends of hot spots in notorious toilets at the diner, the bus terminal, or, Minerva help us, the Yale library. What gives? Women, straight or gay, do not make a life-style of offering themselves without cost to random strangers in sleazy public settings.[49]

In fact, while promiscuity among lesbians appears to be slightly less prolific than that of gay men, it is still a far cry from that of average heterosexual women.

According to the family advocate Tony Marco:

> Evidence exists of high levels of lesbian promiscuity, which correlate with high disease-incidence statistics among lesbians. Jay and Young's *Gay Report* revealed thirty-eight percent of lesbians surveyed had between eleven and more than three hundred lifetime sexual partners—far beyond the norm for heterosexual women. In *Homosexualities*, Bell and Weinberg reported that forty-one percent of white lesbians admitted to having between ten and five hundred sexual partners.[50]

Even those homosexuals who maintain long-term "committed" relationships display a shocking level of wantonness. David Chilton writes:

> Anonymous, promiscuous sex is a hallmark of homosexuality, and this can be true even in what are called "monogamous" relationships. *New York* magazine lamented the case of one AIDS sufferer who had had, ironically, a rather stable sex life, staying with the same lover for more than ten years—*except for one night a week.* That makes, at the very least, over fifty partners a year, and possibly five hundred! A heterosexual who acted that way might be called promiscuous.[51]

And it is a kind of promiscuity altogether unknown in even the most depraved heterosexual circles. The sheer number of sexual encounters might militate against any possibility of tenderness, romance, and sensuality. But the impersonal and mechanical anonymity utterly negates it.[52]

Homosexual bathhouses—or as they are sometimes called, without a hint of irony, health clubs—cater specifically to this perverse hankering for anonymity. Researchers Enrique Rueda and Michael Schwartz have noted that "the degree of promiscuity in the baths defies the imagination of those not familiar with homosexuality."[53]

Author Randy Alcorn concurs:

> In gay baths men meet and copulate with total strangers and often have sex with multiple partners. Government official Dan Bradley described his first visit to a gay bath: "I must have had sex with ten different guys that first night. I was like a kid in a candy store." The baths allow sexual relations in front of others or in private cubicles, often without even the exchange of

names. Some bath houses or "gay health clubs" have rooms for group sex and pornographic movies.[54]

The lesbian scene is hardly better. *The Advocate* recently ran an article on lesbian sex clubs. It reported:

1992 did usher in a new wave of women-only sex clubs in cities like San Francisco, Los Angeles, and New York, generating newfound interest in promiscuous public sex among lesbians. While the idea of female sex clubs is nothing new, the sheer number of women these clubs have drawn over the year is.[55]

According to the article, this development is the result of much diligent labor. It quotes the owner of a lesbian bar in New York saying that she'd "spent months agonizing over how to get girls" to engage in illicit acts "in a more anonymous way."[56]

For some, the gentrified atmosphere of such clubs is too tame for their animal appetites. Indiscriminate sex with strangers is not enough. They have a need to "exhibit" their promiscuity. Thus, homosexuals are notorious for "taking over" public parks.

Frank Browning, an articulate homosexual advocate, admits:

The sexual revolution upon which the gay social movement built itself has indeed probed the limits of wildness. For all the talented dancers of "A Chorus Line," "Cats," and myriad other Broadway shows, for all the courageous and eloquent AIDS activists, for all the dedicated civil rights lawyers and public officials, for all the doctors, designers, and urban planners, there remain the people who frequent the Windmill and Land's End in San Francisco, Griffith's Park in Los Angeles, the Black Forest in Washington, the Ramble in Manhattan's Central Park, the Fens in Boston, and the Woods, with their hanging plastic shopping bags of condoms, on Fire Island. Indeed, respectable community leaders and park *habitués* are very often the same people. Everywhere, within a few steps of the civil rights agenda of social acceptance, there still murmurs the wild man of jungle lust.[57]

Another daring rendezvous for homosexual men is the public rest room.

As gay activists Jay and Young report:

The use of public toilets for cruising and sex is so well-known that a technical book by Cornell University entitled *The Bath Room* includes a whole section discussing the homosexual issue in the design of modern public restrooms. . . . Psychiatrists have on occasion suggested that men choose public places because they find the danger attractive. Most contemporary gay writers, however, indicate that sex in public places is chosen for its convenience or its anonymity or both, and a few have suggested that there is something revolutionary about both promiscuous and public sex.[58]

Conservative columnist and individual-rights advocate Thomas Sowell also observes:

Complaints have come from men who find that using the toilets means being either solicited or being witnesses to homosexual activity. Homosexual men have been attracted to the toilets at the University of Florida from as far as forty miles away. This university, as well as Dartmouth, Georgetown, and the University of California at San Diego, have been forced to install stainless steel panels between toilet stalls to prevent the drilling of holes in the walls for homosexual activity.[59]

Indeed, Kirk and Madsen, in their book promoting the homosexual ethic, express concern that the popularity of sexual sport in public may be hurting their image. "Perhaps the most malignant form of gay misbehavior is public sex," they write.[60] Nevertheless, they concede, it is part and parcel of the movement.

They describe their shock in encountering a proliferation of brazen sexual advances in and around the public rest rooms at Harvard University during their tender undergraduate days.[61] In order to squelch this unwelcome activity, school authorities were ultimately forced to remove the doors to the toilet stalls—thus destroying everyone's privacy—and have the campus police regularly patrol the area. Amazingly, the local *Harvard Gay and Lesbian Newsletter* printed a ribald protest, "mocking the straight staff, students, and police."[62]

Kirk and Madsen go on to explain that homosexuals simply do not hesitate to flaunt their perversion with everything from public nudity to open solicitation and from brash exhibitionism to foul hygiene.[63]

Filthy Deeds

There is more to habitually engaging in such practices than mere promiscuity. The fact is, homosexual behavior is, to be blunt, more suited for the bathroom than the bedroom. The reason is obvious: it makes contact with human waste unavoidable.

Indeed, common homosexual practice actually revels in indescribably profane excretory, urinary, and ingestatory acts. Besides the obvious unsanitary nature of such activities, physical damages—from intestinal confluence to fecal incontinence—are all but inevitable as well.[64]

But the relationship between homosexuality and human waste goes beyond unintended consequences. The homosexual community not only romanticizes excretory intimacy, it makes such activity an integral aspect of its culture.[65] Study after study has shown that what homosexuals euphemistically call "water sports," "golden showers," or "scat games" are central to their sexual milieu.[66]

In *Sapphistry*, a best-selling handbook to lesbian sexuality, Pat Califia argues that such activities ought not be the exclusive domain of gay men. She writes that excretory intimacy is "a perfectly natural form of sex" for gay men and women alike.[67] To think otherwise, she says is "mere phobia."[68]

Is this what Plato, Voltaire, and Rousseau have led us to? Is this really the end result of liberty, equality, and fraternity? Is this the enlightening the Enlightenment had in view?

Whatever its cause, one thing is certain: it isn't the intellectual fruition of the Renaissance or even modern "good, clean sex" that homosexuals want us to accept. Rather it is a barely disguised "filthy wallowing" dredged up from the annals of a far distant barbarian past.

From Bad to Worse

Even if homosexual practice is—to resort to supreme understatement—so unsanitary, what business is it of the rest of us? Does the filthiness and promiscuity of homosexual practice justify the "repressive" measures that our society has historically placed on nonheterosexual activities? Public health and public indecency, after all, can be dealt with as separate issues, at least theoretically. Homosexual relations, we are told, is an activity that occurs between consenting adults.

But that's the problem. It's not. It's not an activity that occurs "between consenting adults." Not by a long shot.

Concerned parents of a fourteen-year-old girl contacted the police in Highland Village, Texas, to lodge a complaint. They had discovered that their young daughter had become sexually involved with a young adult male. The police investigated and began to search for a young man named Tyler Bradd Lawson, who had recently joined the local teenage dating scene. The case became complicated when they began to think they were after *two* young men, Tyler and his twin brother, Brett. But they finally found their suspect and resolved the mystery of the two brothers.

They were a woman.

According to police, Niki Faye Eichman, a twenty-year-old lesbian, posed as two men. They charged her with sexual assault of a minor.

Eichman, a former child-care worker who was working as a convenience store clerk, had allegedly created a fake identity in order to seduce girls. Her victim did not learn of her true identity until police told her. "She learned when we learned," a policemen said.

And her reaction? "There are no words to describe that," he asserted. "It wasn't good. She is getting therapy—psychiatric help."[69]

Although the extent to which Eichman was willing to go may be extreme, her obsession with youth is not unique among homosexuals. The homosexual movement has openly advocated legalizing pedophilia. As one "revolutionary" bluntly stated:

> We shall sodomize your sons, emblems of your feeble masculinity, of your shallow dreams and vulgar lies. We shall seduce them in your schools, in your dormitories, in your gymnasiums, in your locker rooms, in your sports arenas, in your seminaries, in your youth groups, in your movie theater bathrooms, in your army bunkhouses, in your truck stops, in your all-male clubs, in your house of Congress, wherever men are with men together. Your sons shall become our minions to do our bidding. They will be recast in our image; they will come to crave and adore us.[70]

And that's not all:

> We shall sculpt statues of beautiful young men. . . . The museums of the world will be filled only with paintings of graceful, naked lads. . . . Perfect boys . . . will be bonded together in communal setting, under the control and instruction of homosexual savants.[71]

The homosexual movement does not simply want antisodomy laws repealed. It is not content to end discrimination. It is not merely looking for tougher, more inclusive civil rights statutes. It wants age-of-consent laws abolished as well.

The homosexual tabloid *Bay Area Reporter* recently ran an editorial which said in part:

> What is a pedophile? A pedophile is not a rapist, or a murderer, or a devil, but a person who loves. . . . As a gay child, I would have welcomed sexual relations with males of adult age as well as my own. . . . Gay liberation is stuck in backwaters as long as gay children are denied their sexuality and as long as parents are allowed to push gay children into the roles of hetero adults. . . . Most of the heteros just don't know how to give gay-affirming support to their children (the gay ones as well as the non-gay ones). Let's give them a hand.[72]

Tony Marco notes:

> It should come as no surprise, then, that gay extremist manifestos, such as "The 1972 Gay Rights Platform," have consistently called upon governments to: (1) repeal all state laws prohibiting private sexual acts involving consenting persons—not just consenting *adults,* and (2) repeal of all laws governing the age of sexual consent.[73]

These are not isolated instances, but rather a recurring theme in the homosexual subculture. Dr. Judith Reisman states:

> 10–20 percent of *The Advocate* ads sexually solicited boys/teens within a larger pool of 58 percent prostitution ads. Up to 23 percent of sex customers wanted "hairless" or smooth bodies while 38 percent used youth cues ("boys," "youth," or "son") to recruit boy lovers.[74]

But perhaps the strongest evidence of the homosexual movement's link to pedophilia is its open acceptance of the North American Man/Boy Love Association (NAMBLA). Congressman William Dannemeyer explains:

> NAMBLA is a highly visible national organization, though a small one. They put out a newspaper filled with pictures of male children, they hold conventions, and they appear on network talk shows. Their announced political goal is the elimination or severe alteration of the age-of-consent laws, and they argue their case using the rhetoric of the civil rights movement. Little boys, they say, have as much right as adults to engage in consensual sex, and only a repressive society would prevent them from enjoy-

ing such exquisite pleasures at the earliest possible age. One international pedophile has popularized the slogan "Sex before eight, or it's too late."[75]

Interestingly, leaders and activists within the movement consider NAMBLA a perfectly legitimate organization and apparently do not mind being associated with it in the least. As Dannemeyer notes, NAMBLA members are permitted to appear in the annual New York Gay and Lesbian Pride March alongside such groups as the Gay Men's Health Crisis, the National Gay and Lesbian Task Force, ANGLE, ACT-UP, Queer Nation, the Human Rights Campaign, NOW, Dykes on Bykes, and Dykes with Tykes.[76] The same people who consider parents homophobic for not wanting homosexuals to be public school teachers march side by side with those who cherish child molestation as a virtue.

Movement leaders forthrightly admit the predominance of pedophilia. Roger Magnuson writes:

A survey done by two homosexual authors reveals that three-fourths of homosexuals had at some time had sex with boys sixteen to nineteen or younger. One reported, "My lover and I are into young boys thirteen to eighteen years old. . . . I am actively involved with many of them insofar as the social services, family courts, schools, probation departments, etc., are concerned." Another said, "How long will we boy lovers have to wait? How long before we can walk honestly and proudly hand in hand with our young friends and not have to palm them off as our nephews or our stepsons?"[77]

In *Sapphistry,* Pat Califia provides a blanket defense of pedophilia, statutory rape, and child pornography:

Is a boy of seventeen who seeks out older men for sex a child? Is a girl in high school who knows she is a lesbian a child? When children of two or three years of age are prevented from exploring their own genitals and told not to ask questions about their own bodies, who is being protected and what threatens them? Legally, young people are not entitled to any kind of sexual expression. The juvenile justice system often deals harshly with young people whose only "crime" is their homosexuality. Will the anti-pornography movement create a climate in which children can explore their own sexuality with whomever and however they choose? Will it guarantee them the information and security they need to make those choices? Or will it create a more repressive climate in which even less information about sexuality is available and even less sexual variation is tolerated?[78]

She even goes so far as to extend her sanction to sex with preadolescents:

> Some lesbians feel that any sex between a child and an adult is coercive because adults are physically bigger than children and have much more social power. Other lesbians feel that it is not uncommon for an affectionate relationship between an adult and a child to contain an erotic component. They believe it may be possible to express this eroticism in ways that are enjoyable and pleasant for the child. They also believe that children are capable of initiating sexual relationships (with adults as well as other children), since sexual desire can exist in children as well as adults. This is a difficult and controversial issue, perhaps best judged on a case-by-case basis. The horrors of child abuse are a major concern to feminists. However, while protecting children, we should not overlook their right to freedom of sexual expression.[79]

According to a poll taken by the National Gay Task Force, the two major priorities of the homosexual movement at present are the right of admitted homosexuals to be public school teachers and the right of homosexuals to adopt children.[80]

And despite their ominous appetite for molestation, they appear to be on the verge of achieving those goals in community after community all across America.[81]

That certainly does not bode well for the health and welfare of children. Tony Marco has put it bluntly:

> Child molestation is regarded in every state as a criminal offense. Yet it's common knowledge that homosexuals are notorious practitioners of sex with minors.[82]

He cites a survey done by two homosexual researchers which revealed that 73 percent of the homosexuals surveyed had had sex with boys sixteen to nineteen years of age or younger.[83] The fact is, though making up only 2 percent of the population, homosexuals are responsible for more than one-third of all reported child molestations.[84] According to Dr. Reisman's research:

> The rate of one in four abused girls and boys suggests a worst-case scenario of 1,225 boys victimized by gays to every twenty-five girls victimized by heterosexuals. These data are supported by the scholarly literature which finds abuse

of boys "five times greater than the molestation of young girls" with a mean number of one pederast offender molesting 150.2 boy victims compared to a pedophile offender molesting 19.8 girl victims.[85]

At least 30 percent of convicted male child molesters have committed homosexual acts and at least 91 percent of those who molested non-familial boys admitted to no sexual contact ever in their lives except with homosexuals.[86]

In their book on promoting the acceptance of homosexuality in America, Marshall Kirk and Hunter Madsen confess:

> Although it seems incredible that gay men could be so reckless, many . . . take their cue from William Burroughs, who, speaking through one of his characters in *Queer,* declared of a straight boy with which he wished to have sex, "So he's not queer. People can be obliging. What is the obstacle?" And we emphasize, such behavior isn't at all uncommon. We were once informed, by a cheery gay acquaintance, that, trapped in the crush of a recent rock concert audience, right behind a thirteen-year-old boy, he had taken advantage of the horrified youth's inability to move away.[87]

Beyond Reason

A few years ago, a public ruckus erupted in the media when a display of the photography of Robert Mapplethorpe was sponsored and funded by the federal government. One of the controversial photographs involved a graphic picture of a man with his hand and forearm shoved up into another man's rectum.

The picture not only disgusted and outraged taxpayers, it also shocked them. Most had never considered that such an act was remotely possible or that it could ever be done by anyone other than a cruel torturer—much less that it was an appropriate subject for publicly-funded art. But Robert Mapplethorpe was a homosexual, and what he photographed was nothing more than a common homosexual act. He was simply, as he said, "documenting a little slice of American life."[88]

One recent study showed that over a third of homosexual men engage in the activity Mapplethorpe portrayed—commonly known as "fisting."[89] Another study found that nearly half "accepted fisting as a nor-

mal part of sexual play."[90] Essentially, fisting "involves the penetration
of the rectum by the hand or by sundry hand-held objects.[91]"

Florence King, a prominent bisexual essayist and humorist, notes
that such brutality is not limited to gay men.[92] And Pat Califia confesses
that both anal and vaginal fisting are now "becoming more popular
among lesbians."[93]

Apparently, this kind of barbaric brutality is a normal and accepted
part of the homosexual lifestyle. Randy Alcorn notes that "gay leather
shops sell spiked collars, whips," and other paraphernalia for inflicting
pain, which, when used, often results in injuries requiring medical attention.[94]

In a recent article on "safer sex," the lesbian magazine *Deneuve*
went so far as to offer unprintable instructions for the use of various
torture devices: needles, razors, and tongs.[95]

Dr. Judith Reisman, president of the Institute for Media Education,
has recently completed a preliminary content analysis of *The Advocate*
magazine, the preeminent publication of the nation's homosexuals. She
has found that homosexuals "publicly solicit violence roughly five hundred times per gay magazine per month."[96]

But the barbarism of homosexuality is not merely sadomasochistic.
Many homosexuals also indulge in bestiality—that is to say, sex with
animals.[97] In fact, Pat Califia includes animals in her list of sexual fantasies for lesbians.[98] After affording her readers a ribald mechanical tuto-
rial she attempts to alleviate concerns about the psychological problems
that might result from such behavior by saying:

> If you are not compelling the animal to accept your attentions and you are
> gentle, you will not harm it emotionally or physically.[99]

It gets worse still.

Karen Greenlee is a prominent lesbian activist with even more peculiar tastes. In a recent interview she discussed her triumph over society's
repressive attitudes:

> For awhile I found myself thinking, "Yeah, this isn't normal. Why can't I
> be like other people? Why doesn't the same pair of shoes fit me just
> right?" I went through all that personal hell and finally I accepted myself
> and realized that's just me. That's my nature and I might as well enjoy it.
> I'm miserable when I try to be something I'm not. . . . The reason I was

having a problem with it was because I couldn't accept myself. I was still trying to live my life by other people's standards. To accept it was to accept peace.[100]

Greenlee's particular fetish is odd, even for the wild anything-goes world of lesbianism. For one thing, she says she prefers "young men in their twenties."[101] But that is by no means all there is to it. In fact, when she told a homosexual friend about her particular sexual preference, he told her she was "in danger of going to Hell."[102]

What proclivity could possibly cause such a reaction? Necrophilia. Not long ago she was fined over two hundred dollars and held eleven days in jail after she stole a hearse carrying a corpse. She confessed to sexual encounters with between twenty and forty cadavers during four months of employment at a suburban California mortuary.[103]

Interestingly, perversity goes around full circle in the homosexual movement. Frank Browning writes of the parties in the late eighties that were called "Jack and Jills." These were orgies that were attended by both male and female homosexuals. According to Browning, "as chance would have it, queer Jacks occasionally found themselves playing with dyke Jills." In this topsy-turvy environment a young homosexual man once asked him, "If I'm having vaginal intercourse, is it gay sex or straight sex? And is it sick?"[104]

The disturbing fact is that "homosexual" behavior could much more accurately be described as "pansexual" or "omnisexual." It is the full-scale return of ancient paganism—with all its brutality and barbarism.

The fact is, if homosexuality is normal, so is everything else. Whatever decisions we do or do not make about the homosexual movement, at the very least we ought to realize what is at stake.

Conclusion

In 1893, a Parliament of Religions was held in Chicago. At hand were delegates from dozens of pagan cults and religious sects from around the world to meet and dialogue with Western church leaders in what organizers called the "universal and trans-religious spirit of cooperation, toleration, and empathy that unites all mankind regardless of its sundry religious impulses."[105]

A group of Presbyterian missionaries—representative of thousands of faithful men and women who had seen firsthand the horrors of heathen lands and had sacrificed dearly to bring them help and hope—quenched that spirit of indiscriminant and promiscuous toleration with a report that stated succinctly the unique and distinctive appeal of the Gospel:

> Just as Buddha, Mohammed, Confucius, Krishna, and Zoroaster remain to this day decayed by irrevocable death, so the religions that bear their names carry with them the stench of the grave. Poverty, barbarity, death, and lasciviousness must be the lot of those men and nations that follow after them. The horrors of children left to die, women sacrificed to dumb idols, families destroyed by fleshly perversion, and the sick given over to their own devices are the fruit of the flesh that no heathen ravings can be rid. Only the Gospel of our Savior Jesus Christ, the Way, the Truth, and the Life, can lend the bequest of life. Only Christ has Himself escaped the shackles of death, and only the faith in Him that comes through grace can free men from the oppressions of the spirit of Sodom, which we must sadly affirm, is the same as your precious spirit of cooperation, toleration, and empathy.[106]

Another dissenting voice came from a veteran missionary from China who asserted:

> If ever the time comes when we willingly place pagan ideas on a par with Christian ideas, we must realize that regardless of our sophistication, education, or refinement, the brutality that is inherent in paganism will surely overtake us. It is the height of conceit to ignore the great lessons of cultural history by attempting in the name of toleration that which can only kill, steal, and destroy. God have mercy on us.[107]

Still another delegate, a converted Polynesian islander, argued:

> I have witnessed first hand, in my own community and in my own life the liberty that comes with the Gospel. It is no hate, it is no intolerance, it is no bigotry that tells men and women how to be free from the horrors of death, defilement, and destruction. It is no love, it is no tolerance, it is no freedom that tells men to do as they wish to the detriment of all that is sacred, sure, and secure.[108]

The organizers of the Parliament were none too pleased—but the message was inescapably clear. Again and again, the faithful concurred, the age old commitment of the distinctive Gospel of Christ must not, can not, and will not be compromised.

When it is, not only does heresy sweep through the church, but perversion sweeps across the land.

PART II

ALIEN AFFAIRS

Alone to the weight of impassivity,
Incest of spirit, theorem of desire,
Without will as chalky cliffs by the sea,
Empty as the bodiless flesh of fire:
All space, that heaven is a dayless night,
A nightless day driven by perfect lust
For vacancy, in which her bored eyesight
Stares at the drowsy cubes of human dust.[1]

ALLEN TATE

3

INDECENT EXPOSURE: CULTURE

Not yet is there that heat and sober
Vivisection of more clamant air
That hands joined in the dark will answer
After the daily circuits of its glare.
It is the time of sundering.[2]

HART CRANE

On April 25, 1993, they converged on the Washington mall in large numbers. But "large numbers" is not what they had expected. In fact, they had anticipated nothing less than "enormous" numbers.

Organizers for the march on Washington had planned for "some one million gays, lesbians, and bisexuals"[3] to "demand equal rights and increased AIDS funding."[4] Instead, Park Service estimates placed the number of protesters "somewhere in the 300,000 range."[5]

Just prior to the march David Mixner—chief strategist for the march organizers and personal counsel to Bill Clinton on sexuality issues—admitted that a small turnout would be "embarrassing," even "disastrous."[6]

It seems that his worst fears had been realized.

"The homosexual community showed all its muscle today," commented Washington resident James Holliday:

And it is a whole lot weaker than almost anyone thought. It seems that the vitality and momentum that Hollywood and the national news media tried to throw their way simply fizzled out altogether.[7]

But all was not for naught. The protesters who did make it to the nation's capital tried to make the best of a disappointing situation.

Organizers scheduled hundreds of workshops, seminars, and gala balls to coincide with the march. Covering the gamut of interests—from an antiracism workshop to a "meat and greet" showcase, from a congressional briefing on homosexuality in the black community to a NOW sponsored "lesbutante ball," from a business fair to an ACT-UP "civil disobedience action seminar," from an ACLU banquet to a gay and lesbian "harmonic convergence" choral festival, from a national "transgender" caucus meeting to a "dandy midnight cruisy cruise," from an "inter-faith mass wedding" to a "leather fetish" conference, and from a park beautification project to a "clean needles" demonstration—the events were supposed to "represent the full diversity of the gay, lesbian, and bisexual community."[8]

But apparently those scheduled events were not quite adventurous enough for many of the attendees. And so they found the time to patronize the clubs and bars in the notorious Dupont Circle gay community as well as indulge in public sodomy and fellatio beneath the Washington Monument.

According to John Tollarud, a veteran Park Service employee, the public decorum of the protestors was shocking—even by Washington standards:

> I thought I had seen it all. But I was entirely unprepared for this. Public nudity is one thing, but open, brazen sex acts, along the Washington mall, on the sidewalks, in the parks . . . well, I've just never seen anything like it. And I hope I never do again. I used to think that we should all be open-minded and just let people do what ever they want to do. But if this is what they have in mind: to turn our cities into a pornographic spectacle, well, they can just forget it.[9]

Similarly, Jane Ellerston, a Justice Department employee who witnessed much of the goings on from a vantage at her office building, commented:

> It was almost as if they completely lost all self-control. They just went berserk. Even on the stage between celebrity speeches or musical interludes, they would parade around in the nude, they would simulate sex acts, and they would unleash a constant barrage of profanity. If the media had not carefully censored and sanitized their coverage of the events, the

American people would have turned on the whole movement in a flash. In fact, if the movement did not have the full sanction and complicity of popular culture—the Hollywood establishment, the television producers, the celebrities, and the major media—I'm convinced that the entire movement would simply self-destruct.[10]

But of course, the movement does have the sanction and complicity of popular culture, and as a result it thrives. Even in the face of disappointment and distress, it thrives.

ABC *World News Sunday* anchor Carole Simpson, for instance, called the march "one of the biggest civil rights demonstrations ever staged in the nation's capital."[11] On the *MacNeil-Lehrer Report,* Judy Woodruff said they gathered "to demand freedom from discrimination."[12] NBC's Linda Vester echoed the official party line on *Nightly News*: "Organizers had a long list of demands. The top three: civil rights protection, an end to the ban on gays in the military, and more funding for AIDS research."[13]

Somehow though, the media failed to report the other "demands" of march officials:

The redefinition of sexual re-assignment surgeries as medical, not cosmetic, treatment . . . and in schools, a culturally inclusive lesbian, gay, bisexual, and transgender studies program at all levels of education.[14]

In addition the media failed to report on:

- Hundreds of lesbians who marched topless down Pennsylvania Avenue;

- Police orders not to arrest participants who violated public decency statutes;

- Topless women and nude men who cavorted, kissed, and embraced in the Navy Memorial fountain;

- Lebian marchers who filed past the White House chanting "Chelsea, Chelsea, Chelsea!"

- Platform speakers who simulated sex acts on stage and roared out obcenities via giant amplifiers;

- Remarks by the platform program's host openly lusting after Mrs. Clinton, saying: "We finally have a First Lady you can #%*@."[15]

Camille Paglia writes:

Happy are those periods when marriage and religion are strong. . . . Unfortunately, we live in a time when the chaos of sex has broken out into the open. . . . Historiography's most glaring error has been its assertion that Judeo-Christianity defeated paganism. Paganism has survived in the thousand forms of sex, art, and now the modern media. . . . A critical point has been reached. With the rebirth of the gods in the massive idolatries of popular culture, with the eruption of sex and violence into every corner of the ubiquitous mass media, Judeo-Christianity is facing its most serious challenge since Europe's confrontation with Islam in the Middle Ages. The latent paganism of western culture has burst forth again in all its daemonic vitality.[16]

Hollywood vs. Christendom

In his fascinating book *Hollywood vs. America: Popular Culture and the War on Traditional Values,* popular movie reviewer Michael Medved provides prodigious evidence that Hollywood has become—to use Paglia's phrase—a "pagan institution."[17] And no little part of that paganization process has come at the behest of the industry's very powerful homosexual movement. He writes:

No one could deny that the formidable gay presence in the entertainment business encourages industry leaders to take a far more sympathetic view of homosexuality than does the public at large. In a 1990 study of "Hollywood opinion leaders" by University of Texas government professor David F. Prindle, sixty-eight percent said they supported "gay rights," compared to only twelve percent who endorsed that position in a 1987 national *Times Mirror* poll. More recently, an impressive array of Hollywood establishment's most influential figures have provided support for leading gay rights organizations. In August 1991, top executives from all four television networks and from the eight largest movie studios served together on the host committee for a gala dinner to benefit the National Gay and Lesbian Task Force.[18]

The importance of homosexuals to the motion picture industry is an acknowledged fact among celebrities themselves. Toward the end of 1992, the cover of *Vanity Fair* sported a glitzy photo of Elizabeth Taylor—who has made a recent career move into AIDS activism—elegantly flaunting a condom. In the magazine, she told an interviewer, "Without homosexuals there would be no Hollywood."[19]

Not surprisingly then, more and more movies are being produced with homosexual themes. These include *Sunday, Bloody Sunday,* a film in which a man and a woman compete for the same man; *Lianna,* in which a women "discovers" she is a lesbian; *My Beautiful Laundrette,* which centers on a male homosexual couple opening a Laundromat; *Parting Glances,* on the subject of AIDS; *Desert Hearts,* which positively portrays a divorced woman falling for a casino waitress in the 1950s; *Torch Song Trilogy,* which presents homosexuals as "regular people" who want home and family just like heterosexuals; and *Longtime Companion* and *Peter's Friends,* both movies about AIDS that portray homosexuals "sensitively" and "positively."[20]

In addition, according to Medved, viewers are treated to the visual or audible presence of urination in *The Cook, the Thief, His Wife, and Her Lover, Twenty-One, The Power of One, Deep Cover, Shakes the Clown, Doc Hollywood,* and *Closet Land.* And these desensitizing "subtle allusions" and "gracious nods" to homosexual fantasies and practices are just the tip of the iceberg. Medved reports that MGM studios recently bought a script for a half-million dollars and the chairman has committed to pay an additional quarter-million dollars to the acclaimed screenwriter—Joe Eszterhas, who wrote *Jagged Edge* and *Basic Instinct*—once production begins. The plot of the film—tentatively titled *Sacred Cows*—revolves around bestial perversions too brazen to mention.[21] But not only does MGM claim it is about to make this movie, but it is reported that they are considering Paul Newman or Lloyd Bridges to take the starring role.[22]

Despite the abundance of such condescension, homosexual activists are not yet entirely satisfied. Go figure.

A case in point is the way the homosexual community reacted to *The Crying Game,* a film released to rave reviews at the beginning of 1993. This thriller portrays a British soldier who falls in love—and becomes somewhat sexually involved with—a homosexual transvestite. But all the while, both the soldier and the audience think that *he* is a *she.* Once the soldier realizes that his lover is a man, not a woman,

he—perhaps quite understandably, given the magnitude of the deception—becomes physically ill.

The movie was lauded with extravagant praise by reviewers and nomi-
nated for several prestigious awards. But apparently moviegoers considered
it to be little more than a cheap cinematic trick. They stayed away in
droves from what they justifiably considered a "homosexual movie."[23]

The movie reviewer in *The Advocate,* however, characterized *The
Crying Game* as a "dishonest thriller."[24] Why?

> Because if the producer were making a really daring film about gender
> bending, then he'd own up to what should be his real theme—a man's
> discovery of his attraction to transvestites and his inner struggle to under-
> stand what this means.[25]

Apparently, from a homosexual point of view it is unrealistic that as
soon as the soldier sees the naked body of the transvestite:

> Our hero is off to the john for a quick vomit, keeping careful distance from
> the former object of his affection.[26]

For homosexuals, in the "real world," men who fall in love with
men who disguise themselves as women are not deceived but latently
homosexual. To portray life otherwise, is "maintaining silence on gay
sexuality."[27]

Give them an inch and they'll take a mile. Give them a mile and
they'll take it all.

PCTV

Television is a powerful tool for propagandizing a people, and the leaders in the homosexual movement are only too well aware of this fact.
Marshall Kirk and Hunter Madsen, in their classic book on homosexual
strategies, *After the Ball,* state:

> The visual media—television, films, magazines—are the most powerful
> image makers in Western civilization. For example, in the average Ameri-
> can household, the TV screen radiates its embracing bluish glow for more
> than fifty hours every week, bringing films, sitcoms, talk shows, and news
> reports right into the living room. These hours are a gateway into the pri-
> vate world of straights, through which a Trojan horse might be passed.[28]

Not ones to miss a chance to penetrate "the private world of straights," the homosexual movement has exerted a profound impact on television. Syndicated columnist Joseph Farah writes:

> Kathryn Montgomery, author of *Target: Prime Time,* a book about the role of advocacy groups in shaping television programming, has said that homosexuals are the most effective and well-organized of the special-interest organizations lobbying the TV industry. Ever since the mid-1970s, network officials have permitted and encouraged their producers and writers to submit their scripts dealing with homosexuality for review by the Gay Media Task Force, a Hollywood-based lobbying office.[29]

As a result of this activism—combined with the compliant sympathy of most industry insiders—homosexuality is becoming more and more blatant on the TV screen. A decade ago, ABC's sitcom *Soap* centered on a gay character as did CBS's more recent *Doctor, Doctor* and Fox's *Brothers.*

NBC's *L.A. Law* featured a subplot on a show about an athlete who lost an advertising contract because he announced he was homosexual.[30] The show also presented the first lesbian kiss on television. Executive producer David Kelley claimed that getting the scene on the air "was easy. The network was supportive."[31]

ABC's *Thirty-something* went even farther—showing two men in bed together after having sex. Notably, the short scene caused the network to lose over a million dollars in revenue due to viewer and sponsor outrage. Nevertheless, ABC officials assured the producers that they would support future episodes. Sure enough, they lost another half million or more by showing the "couple" exchange a kiss.[32]

ABC's *Roseanne* was the first show where an established character "came out of the closet." The articulate, talented, and bisexual Sandra Bernhard plays a divorced woman who "discovers" she is a homosexual when she falls for another woman—played by Morgan Fairchild.[33]

That's Not the Way It Is

Network news coverage is often just as biased as the "entertainment" programming—sometimes even more so.

One California pastor was enlightened by his treatment on a TV call-in show, which featured a panel of "experts" on AIDS. All of the panel members claimed that AIDS was caused by HIV but that the virus could not be spread through any form of "casual contact."

The pastor was rather skeptical of this bold and confident assertion so he called the program to inquire further. When a young woman—named Barbara—answered the phone, he asked his question:

> I'd like to ask your panel members if they really believe their own rhetoric. Would any of them actually be willing to share a drinking glass with an AIDS victim?

Actually, he admitted later:

> My question had a stinger on its tail: one member of the panel actually had AIDS, so I suggested that the experts' willingness to perform the experiment could be tested on the spot. After a few moments of awkward silence, the woman . . . told me to hang on, and she put me on hold. Ten minutes or so later, the phone clicked. I suddenly found myself listening to a dial tone.[34]

Undeterred, the pastor hit his redial button and called back. Barbara answered again and asked him for his question:

> "Hi. We must have been cut off accidentally. I was waiting to ask my question."
>
> "What was your question?"
>
> "I wanted to know whether anyone on your panel would share a glass of water with an AIDS victim."

A few moments of awkward silence followed once again. And finally she answered:

> "Well, we've decided not to use your question."
>
> "Why not?"
>
> "Because this is a program to inform people about AIDS."
>
> "Uh, right. That's why I asked the question. I want to be informed."
>
> "But we want to give people information. We don't want to scare them."[35]

Scaring people, after all, might have made people "less accepting of homosexuals." Concern for people's health—indeed, their very lives—took second place.

Sadly, such perfidy is not limited to local television news departments. Even the major networks engage in such censorship, manipulating their audiences in absurd ways.

When controversy broke out over Robert Mapplethorpe's federally funded photographs of explicit sadomasochistic acts, for instance, the media portrayed the opponents of using tax dollars to subsidize pornography as "censors." But, in fact, it was the network news media that censored its news footage so that no one could actually know what it was that the opponents were objecting to.

The way that the media manipulates their coverage in favor of the homosexual agenda sometimes goes far beyond mere censorship or suppression. Sometimes it actively promotes misinformation. Paglia points out one such case:

> The intrusion of strident liberal politics into the assessment of Mapplethorpe has done a great disservice to this remarkable artist. I was outraged, for example, at an early *Nightline* program on the controversy in which the ABC correspondent ostentatiously posed in a room lined with propped-up examples of Mapplethorpe's photos of black men. It was a blatantly biased attempt to suggest that Jesse Helm's opposition to Mapplethorpe was simply racially motivated.[36]

Television is especially damaging because viewers assume that what they see must be true. Often they don't realize in how many ways the camera can lie. In this case, the old saying "Seeing is believing" is a formula for deceiving the audience.

All That's Unfit to Print

Just as in television and movies, newspapers and magazines are almost invariably prohomosexual in their editorial slant.

Homosexual author Frank Browning confirms this bias by comparing a 1963 article in the *New York Times* to a 1990 article in *Newsweek*. Of the *Times* piece, he writes:

The story's thirty-five hundred words detailed the haunts, behaviors, and characteristics of New York's "invert" population. Reporter Robert C. Doty left not a doubt about the ominous threat that the inverts presented. . . . With enormous dismay, the *Times* announced to the world that homosexuals had transformed themselves from mere individual unfortunates into an organized and threatening community. Between 1960 and 1965, there appeared a flurry of such reports in general-circulation "family" journals— *Life, Look, Time,* and *Newsweek,* among others. Often, the tone was less hostile than Doty's ominous description of a shadow world in the *Times,* but the new "gay" denizens appeared, at best, as sad unfortunates.[37]

The 1990 *Newsweek* on the other hand, presented a much different picture of homosexuals:

Most gay activists I know were pleased and reassured by the content of the article and by a publication of *Newsweek*'s stature having chosen to devote so much attention to gay concerns. The contrast with the *Times* report of only a generation earlier could not have been more stark. Gay people had come of age as a respectable, if troubled, American minority.[38]

Indeed, virtually all news magazines and newspapers today present homosexuals as a "respectable minority." But is this portrayal accurate? Does it reflect what really is at stake in the legitimizing of homosexuality? Browning has second thoughts about the perspective of today's media:

I found something distressing about the clean, well-scrubbed presentation of all these fiercely proud, wholesome, socially successful homosexuals. Of the two accounts, *Newsweek*'s ebulliently supportive, the *Times* nasty and hateful, there seemed to me a deeper truth in the latter. Through all his ominous imagery and forthright disgust, Robert Doty found and reported to his readers a disturbing territory of desire that . . . presented a genuine threat to the polite, orderly daylight world of homogeneous civility. Unlike *Newsweek*'s earnest gloss, Doty drew his eye down sharply, clearly, on a critical issue in American life: what sort of desire is acceptable and where it should be expressed.[39]

The problem, of course, is that if major magazines and newspapers permitted their readers to see what the homosexual lifestyle is really like, the gay rights movement would suffer a severe and immediate setback. Frank Browning may be able to get away with an occasional honest statement in a book with a cover displaying two bare-chested young men in affectionate embrace that is tucked safely away in the "gay studies" section of a bookstore. In the mass media, however, as Browning's comments on *Newsweek* demonstrate, the truth is distorted to present homosexuals as "just like heterosexuals."

Sometimes biased reporting is demonstrated in smaller ways. When a group of parents rallied in front of the school board building in Brooklyn they were amazed at the coverage they received. The fifteen-hundred citizens were concerned about the inclusion of sexually explicit materials in the grade school curriculum. Shortly after they arrived they were confronted by about thirty members of a group called the "Lesbian Avengers." This small cadre of radicals magically became a much larger group of five hundred when the media later reported on the event.[40] As pro-lifers can only too readily attest, journalists constantly understate the size or significance of a movement they don't like and overstate the power of those they agree with.

Even local community newspapers have gotten into the act. In Everett, Washington, for instance, Sally Huston and Jennifer Quall were "married" on August 5, 1990. They submitted an announcement of their nuptials to their local newspaper, *The Herald*. The newspaper formed a committee to decide how to treat the ad. They concluded the homosexual marriage should be recognized.

There was only one problem: the women weren't married. Washington state does not recognize homosexual marriages—yet.

So, in order to accommodate their peculiar situation, *The Herald* scrapped their "Wedding Book" page and replaced it with a generic "Celebrations" page where homosexual "unions" and heterosexual marriages could be treated on an equal basis. Needless to say the announcement was widely and sympathetically reported in the national press.[41]

Over a year later, the *Austin American-Statesman* announced the "marriage" of Sara Strandtman and Karen Umminger. The newspaper's publisher stated, "We did it because we thought, and still do think, we're honoring a part of the diversity of the community."[42] Interestingly, like Washington, the state of Texas does not legally recognize same-sex marriages.

Bibliophile

Mainstream book publishing has also become quite amenable to the homosexual agenda in recent years. One obvious reason for this is that,

relatively speaking, there are a great number of homosexuals in the
book publishing industry.

Copy editor Steven Boldt wrote in the homosexual newspaper the
New York Native:

> Either gay people are over-represented in commercial publishing, or the
> estimate of ten percent for the general population is way too low. When I
> was at Dell Publishing—or, as it was known in some circles, Boy's
> Town—in the early 1980s, at least half the fifteen men in the editorial and
> cover art departments were gay, including several in top management.
> When I was managing editor at Pocket Books in the mid 1980s, I had a
> photograph of my lover on my bulletin board. . . . Obviously not all com-
> mercial houses are as gay as were Dell and Pocket, but after a decade in
> publishing and having been on staffs or having extensively freelanced for
> Dell, Pocket, Bantam, Crown, Zebra, St. Martin's, Time Warner, and Simon
> and Schuster, I don't doubt that most books published by them with gay
> content were read before publication by a lesbian or a gay man in a posi-
> tion to suggest changes to their editor.[43]

The predominance of homosexual ideas in the industry is naturally
reflected in the kinds of books that are ultimately published—and conversely in the kinds of books that are rejected out of hand. Homosexual
books are a "growth market."

The success of gay books has motivated the mainstream publishers
to dramatically increase the number of homosexual titles—and perhaps
more important, to lend them greater marketing support. Random House
recently released a novel about a major league shortstop in love with the
team's second baseman. Plume Books is selling more openly homosexual titles. Book-of-the-Month-Club and Quality Paperback book club
both now commonly carry homosexual titles.[44]

Several of the mainstream publishers have even begun to develop
special labels aimed at homosexuals. St. Martin's Press, for instance,
has put out "Stonewall Inn Editions" that are named after a "famous"
riot that occurred in 1969 when police raided a homosexual bar in
Greenwich Village. The Stonewall riot is described in homosexual literature as "the shot heard around the homosexual world."[45]

In addition to the influence that homosexuals exert on mainstream
book publishing, homosexuals have also created their own publishing
houses. Alyson Publishing is a venture that has made dramatic inroads

into the public education system. Naiad Press is a "feminist and lesbian" publisher, the oldest in the country.[46]

Selling Sex

The real boons in homosexual publishing are not books by or about homosexuality per se. Rather they are in the proliferating sex education trade.

Simon and Schuster, for example, published *The Teenage Body Book: Guide to Sexuality,* which tells youths on the cover that it contains "straightforward, no-nonsense answers to the questions you have about sex during these vital years of your life." It was written by Kathy McCoy—who won the American Library Association's Best Book for Young Adults award for a previous book.[47] Not only does the book tell children that it is just fine for them to have sex in their early teens and presents abortion as a perfectly legitimate option, it also happily endorses homosexual behavior. Besides the usual fatalistic propaganda about sexual identity that makes up the central tenet of homosexual ideology, McCoy goes on to actively encourage homosexual encounters among teens—specifically group masturbation or masturbation with a same-sex friend.[48]

This is only one of many books aimed at young readers that endorses, if not encourages, homosexuality. Kinsey-associate and professional sexologist Wardell Pomeroy, for instance, has written two popular paperbacks that are recommended by sex education groups such as Planned Parenthood as ideal for youngsters and can be found in almost any well-stocked bookstore. Both *Girls and Sex*[49] and *Boys and Sex*[50] assure teens that homosexual practice is perfectly normal and healthy as long as one doesn't allow oneself to feel guilty. Thus, while openly and exclusively homosexual books are relatively new, mainstream publishers have been cranking out this sort of homosexual propaganda aimed at children for over a decade.

Even fictional comic books are now promoting homosexuality among young people. When the character Northstar announced his homosexuality in a recent issue of the Marvel Comics title *Alpha Flight,* the story was covered by most national daily newspapers and popular national weeklies. Marvel received thousands of letters both for and against the character's open homosexuality. The issue quickly sold out—the price rising almost immediately from just over a dollar to more than thirty dollars.[51]

But Marvel's endorsement of homosexuality was nothing new to the comics trade. The other major comic book company, DC Comics, had already introduced several homosexual characters—as well as an "arborsexual woman."[52] Homosexual activists couldn't be happier.

As one homosexual free-lance writer, said:

> The largest audience for comic books is, of course, teens and pre-teens. And in the real world, where gay and lesbian teens are often susceptible to depression and low self-esteem, positive gay role models, even fictional ones like . . . Northstar will have a welcome audience.[53]

Industrial Pollution

The decision to publish homosexuals is not entirely based on ideological alignment. As Arnold Dolin stated of his company's venture into homosexual products, "It's a commercial decision. We see a hungry audience."[54]

The fact is, despite their small numbers, homosexuals have a great deal of buying power. The average male homosexual household has an average income of $51,325 per year, and the lesbian household has an average of $45,927. The national average annual household income, on the other hand, is $36,520. Furthermore, homosexuals have much more "discretionary income," than heterosexuals.[55] The reason for this is that, unlike those who they contemptuously refer to as "breeders," homosexuals generally do not have children to support and can afford go out to eat or go on cruises more often than heterosexual couples.

The affluence of homosexuals is especially important for newspaper, magazine, and book publishers, since almost 60 percent of homosexuals have graduated from college, as opposed to the US average of 18 percent.[56] As a result, homosexuals are more likely to read than heterosexuals.

The vast buying power of the gay community is evidenced in the *Damron Address Book,* which boasts, "Over six thousand listings: USA, Canada, Mexico."[57] Though admittedly a major emphasis of the guide is on pornographic outlets—"adult" bookstores, subscriptions to pornographic magazines, order forms for pornographic videos, phone sex numbers, "hustler" rendezvous sites, pick-up bars, "gyms" and "spas," and outright sex clubs—it also provides general tourist information and helpful hints for the busy traveler.

Not only does *Damron* advertise for private establishments, it also provides guidance to public "cruisy areas," where homosexuals can go for sex with loitering strangers. Next to the listings of these various parks, highway rest stops, and bus terminals many times the letters "AYOR" appear—standing for, of course, "at your own risk." Some even say "extreme risk" and warn of the presence of "police decoys."

A. L. Burruss Park in Marietta, Georgia, near Atlanta is one such park. In March of 1991, police began cracking down on homosexual cruisers, logging dozens of arrests for sodomy, sexual solicitation, and exhibitionism. The park had been literally "taken over" by the cruisers, especially during lunchtime hours and on weekends. Marietta police Lieutenant Tim Fant told reporters, "They overran the park, and we intend to take it back."[58]

Because of the homosexual activity going on, families had not been able to use park facilities for four years. Cleaning the park, however, cost the local police a great deal—and not just in dollars and cents. Staff writer David Noel for the *Marietta Daily Journal* writes:

> The raids have taken their toll on the undercover officers, who are often groped by the men before the arrests, Lieutenant Fant said. One officer started wearing a protective cup, similar to those used by baseball players, during his assignments in the park, he said. "It is very stressful on my people," Lieutenant Fant said. "It's more mental. The biggest thing you have to do is keep your sense of humor about it. It can make you feel literally sick to your stomach."[59]

No kidding.

Fant also mentioned that nearby Wildwood Park and also Gold Branch Park had the same problem. All three were advertised as cruising areas in *Blue-Boy,* a magazine based in San Francisco. As Fant put it: "This is a whole different culture."

Indeed it is. And even two years later Wildwood Park is still a hotbed of public homosexuality. *Damron* lists it as an Atlanta "cruisy area," to be utilized "at your own risk."[60]

In the section on Mexico, *Damron* is even worse. Readers are warned, "Gay life in Mexico is not nearly as free and open as it is in the United States or Canada," but notes also that "if you play it cool and go by the rules, Mexico can be rewarding." How so? Because "much of Mexico is very poor. Consequently, many *boys will be available for the price of a cocktail*."[61] Nothing like pedophile prostitution to reward homosexuals who "play it cool" south of the border.

Homosexual rights advocates Marshall Kirk and Hunter Madsen properly assert:

> The fact is that gay bars and other businesses have a perfectly wretched record of failure to serve the community. Indeed, where not to do so would lose money, they've shown themselves willing to *harm* the community. It's hard to forget that when AIDS-related Kaposi's Sarcoma was first rumored to be linked to the use of nitrite inhalants, the manufacturers of Hardware, Quicksilver, and Ram responded by taking out expensive magazine ads for their "Blueprint for Health"—in essence, exercise, eat right, keep a good thought, and "learn to ignore the prophets of doom"—when the moral thing would have been to take the loss and go into another line of business. It's hard to forget that, by and large, the gay bathhouses of New York and San Francisco shut down not as they should—voluntarily, as soon as it became evident to a reasonable person that what they were selling was death, and in abundance—but under legal duress, kicking and screaming in protest, and spewing out a sewer system of cheap rationales for their continued operation. Yes, it's hard to forget, and impossible to forgive.[62]

Not wanting the sex industry to get all the profits, mainstream industries are realizing that homosexuals are a potential market for many other products besides sexual items. Companies such as CBS, Benetton, Philip Morris, Seagram, and Time Warner, among others, are marketing their products to homosexuals.[63] On Wall Street, Shearson Lehman Brothers, Inc., has authorized an acknowledged homosexual broker to both advertise and write a column on financial advice in a homosexual publication.[64] In the September 1992 *Vanity Fair,* Banana Republic ran an ad of two men closely embracing.[65]

Ever mindful of political and social opportunities, homosexuals are well aware of how to use their consumer clout to their cultural advantage. In January of 1991, the Dallas Gay Alliance credit union helped increase the visibility of homosexual consumers by issuing a Visa credit card that was emblazoned with the homosexual symbol of a pink triangle.[66] As a group, homosexuals are using their influence to pressure companies to "offer benefits and health insurance for partners of gay and lesbian employees."[67]

A handful of companies are already offering benefits to homosexuals and their "partners" as if they were married couples. In June of 1992, Levi Strauss began offering health coverage for "unmarried partners" of its homosexual employees. Other companies with such policies include Ben and Jerry's Homemade, the Vermont-based ice cream company; MCA/Universal and Disney, the entertainment giants; and Borland International and Lotus Development, both computer software companies.[68]

Besides legitimizing homosexual relationships and sponsoring prohomosexual programs and movies, industries can also promote perversity by their philanthropy. Levi Strauss, for example, decided to stop supporting the Boy Scouts of America financially about the same time they began their coverage of "partners." They objected to the fact that the Boy Scouts do not admit homosexuals into their organization.[69] Though company representatives insisted their decision was motivated solely by principle, the San Francisco-based company happily admits that "three out of four gay men prefer Levi's jeans . . . over other brands."[70]

Though homosexuals are attempting to get other companies to offer benefits to the partners of homosexual employees, it is doubtful that they will achieve widespread success. Despite their financial clout, insuring what is such an unhealthy lifestyle would end up costing the company and the other employees severely. Of course, if homosexuals can get the government to *require* companies to treat homosexual couples the same as families, then they might—indeed, they will—succeed.

Conclusion

There is only one thing a person can say in this day of brash intemperance that requires real courage—and that is a truism. A truism is often so biting and precise that it is discomfiting. It is anathema and thus scorned.

Making the accusation of media bias is a perfect case in point. Like a truism, it is universally acknowledged. And like anathema, it is simultaneously universally scorned. Even so, as is the case with most truisms, it is true.

After a comprehensive analysis of American television programming, conservative media pioneer Marlin Maddoux was forced to conclude:

There wasn't a nickle's worth of difference among the *Big Three*—ABC, CBS, and NBC. The stories were basically the same; the bias in their coverage was the same. It became frighteningly clear that the television screen was dominated by the radical left. And opposing views were virtually closed out.[71]

Former Carter administration speech writer Philip Terzian observed:

For the most part, media bias . . . is so obvious, so pervasive, so natural to the press corps, that it is scarcely worth noticing. There is a good reason why journalists react so churlishly to the charge: the evidence is so graphic.[72]

He's right. Most industry insiders do indeed deny any possibility of the taint of bias—even when presented with the dumb certainties of evidence. They persist in maintaining airs of complete objectivity. Loudly and insistently.

New York Post reporter Bill Kantor lashed out that charges of a distinct liberal bias in the media were just "right-wing sour grapes."[73] Lisa McClellan, a Fox network producer, said that such criticisms were "ridiculous" and just "further proof of the right's obsession with conspiracy—more scary neo-fascist hysteria." Mark Lowrey, a liberal syndicated columnist asserted:

The far-right has always had a love-hate relationship with the media: they love to hate us. They feel compelled to find a scapegoat. Well, they're gonna have to find another goat to scape.[74]

U.S. News and World Report editor Harrison Rainie, unnerved by the charge of bias responded:

That's crazy! The media has been, if anything, much more vigilant about fairness and objectivity and sort of explaining issues front to back . . . recently . . . than it ever was.[75]

And Sam Donaldson argued:

The preponderance of the political press corps is very professional and objective. Our own political preferences rarely ever intrude. We just call 'em as we see 'em.[76]

But of course that is precisely the problem.

They "see 'em" through the very peculiar lens of a very particular worldview. Thus, Tom Brokaw quipped that "bias, like beauty, is in the eye of the beholder."[77] Quite so. It is rooted in his or her unique vision of things.

Only God controls events. But the media controls what we know of those events—or even *whether* we know of them. They are indeed the newsmakers—and thus, the culture shapers.

4

FATAL DISTRACTION:
EDUCATION

That I am stolen from myself, this royal tryst to keep.
And though I go there to and fro as child to friendly dark,
A mild and stately seneschal admits me to the park.[1]

SIDNEY MTTRON HIRSCH

M artin Campbell was mad. And well he should have been.

"I thought school was supposed to be a place for kids to go to learn," he fumed. "I thought it was supposed to be a place for kids to get basic skills in things like math, history, and grammar. This kind of stuff is just not supposed to happen. It just isn't right."

Martin handed me a booklet that he'd gotten in school the week before as a part of his "family-life curriculum." Entitled *Values in Sexuality*, the booklet contained a series of role-playing exercises that students are to participate in.

He opened the booklet to one exercise that especially seemed to bother him.

"Look at this. Is this crazy or what?"

In the exercise seven different students are asked to act out a particular predetermined role. All they have to go on is a brief "scene-setting" description of their characters and the situation they find themselves in:

Roommate 1: You have invited a *lover* to spend the weekend with you in your room. You tell your roommates.

Roommate 2: You are a devout Fundamentalist Christian and feel homosexuality is a serious *sin.*

Roommate 3: You feel whatever anyone does sexually is their business, but you feel very *sad* that your friend has closed off lots of options.

Roommate 4: You're a psychology major, and try to *help* by giving advice and diagnosing why your roommate might be gay.

Roommate 5: You feel threatened by the knowledge that your roommate is gay. You try to reason with him and *argue* him into heterosexual good sense.

Roommate 6: You are shocked by the announcement and outraged that a *fag* will be on your dorm floor.

Roommate 7: You already know about your *friend's* gay lifestyle. The two of you have talked some about it. You have no serious difficulties with this and still feel comfortable with him.

After playing their roles, the seven students are then asked to "come to a consensus" about which of the roommates' attitudes is "the most constructive."

Martin had been forced to participate in that very scenario in class two days before.

"After we played our parts," he told me, "we had to de-role and then analyze our feelings in a group discussion. The teacher asked us what stereotypes of homosexuality had emerged in the skit. And then we were supposed to talk about why those stereotypes were wrong and based on ignorance and fear. Well, I was really hacked off by the whole deal. I felt like I was being set up."

When the teacher found that Martin was acting a bit recalcitrant, she began to lecture him about being *open, tolerant, accepting, mature, respectful,* and *honest.*

"I just kept telling her that I didn't agree, and wouldn't agree, but she wouldn't let up on me," Martin said. "It's pretty bad when a teacher isolates one kid like that. I felt like I was getting ganged up on. It wasn't *fair.*"

It may not have been fair, but it was all too typical.

Teaching Values

The opponents of the Christian sexual ethic are well aware of the importance of the family. To change the nature, character, and function of the family in our society is absolutely essential if they are to succeed. That is why it is so important to the homosexual lobby to get their agenda put into the classrooms under the guise of either health or sex education. Congressman William Dannemeyer says:

> Clearly they see the "explicit" and "non-judgmental" sex education as a means of introducing young people to the practices of homosexuals. To "avoid bigotry" the public schools are being enjoined to teach heterosexuality and homosexuality without bias. In fact, since, according to homosexuals, they are victims of widespread "homophobia" as the result of "outmoded religious prejudices," they are demanding that their behavior be defended and their rights affirmed *in American classrooms.* In a curriculum that is supposed to be "value free," they want tolerance of homosexual behavior elevated to the level of a moral imperative.[2]

Many educators believe that the use of classrooms for such blatant *socialization* is not only an illegitimate use of the schools, it is actually the root cause of the educational crisis we face today. Professor Thomas Sowell, in his remarkable book *Inside American Education: The Decline, the Deception, the Dogmas,* writes:

> Like many other people, I have long been appalled by the low quality and continuing deteriorization of American education. However, after doing research for this book, I am frankly surprised that the results are not even worse than they are. The incredibly counter-productive fads, fashions, and dogmas of American education—from the kindergarten to the colleges— have yet to take their full toll. . . . Much has been said about how our young people do not meet the academic standards of their peers in other countries with which we compete economically. While this is both true and important, their academic deficiencies are only half the story. All across this country, the school curriculum has been invaded by psychological conditioning programs which not only take up time sorely needed for intellectual development, but also promote an emotionalized and *anti-intellectual* way of responding to the challenges facing every individual and every society. Worst of all, the psycho-therapeutic curriculum systematically undermines the parent-child relationship and the shared values which make society possible.[3]

Utilizing the educational system to socialize children with a non-Christian worldview actually is nothing new. In fact, it has been one troubling aspect of American education from the very beginning. Recently, however, the perversity of public education has increased so much that more and more parents are hardpressed to overlook it any longer and are searching for viable alternatives.

Homosexuals have been frighteningly effective in gaining control of influential institutions—most notably the public schools. The National Gay and Lesbian Task Force, a lobbying group in the nation's capital, demands that sex education courses that present homosexuality as a "healthy alternative lifestyle" be taught by gays and lesbians. Syndicated columnist Don Feder reports that the National Association for the Education of Young Children, the largest accreditation agency for preschool education, had the Gay and Lesbian Caucus make a presentation on "sexual preference, pride and the early childhood educator" at their 1990 conference.

In Miami, despite a statute mandating that schools teach "abstinence outside of marriage" and "the benefits of heterosexual marriage," the school board has officially approved a call-in phone line for children that in a recorded message tells them that homosexuals are "a non-ethnic, non-racial minority group." Furthermore, students who dial the automated call-in system are assured that "sexual orientation is not a choice. It's a given. It can be compared to being left-handed." The number to this "educational service" is given out by teachers to students and the phone line is partly sponsored by the Florida state government.[4]

In the state of Washington, high school students are give "safe sex" kits at the beginning of each school year. The kits include a variety of condoms, lubricants, and dental dams—a prophylactic device designed for "safe" oral-anal homosexual stimulation—and an instructional booklet advising students how to properly use each item. Additional kits are made available to the students throughout the course of the year "as needs may arise."[5]

In the state of Ohio, several homosexual groups have banded together to provide schools with a "speakers' bureau." According to a promotional brochure, "in 1991, more than 325 schools in the state invited Bureau speakers to explain the facts about homosexual orientation to students in elementary, middle school, and high school students in a non-threatening environment."[6] Additionally, "safe sex instruction, coming-out counseling, and AIDS testing" is made available to the students through this "service."[7]

Although special subversive projects like these are now proliferating in school districts all over the nation, probably the most effective way in which homosexual values are promoted in the public schools is through the typical sex education curriculum.

Part of the reason for that is simply that the homosexual movement is given some help here by other radical groups, such as Planned Parenthood. These groups help homosexuals by desensitizing and acclimating children to perversity and promiscuity. The homosexuals in turn help these groups by lobbying for abortion services and AIDS education programs, which are ostensibly needed to save children's lives.

Anyone who objects to such initiatives is typically portrayed as a lover of ignorance or intolerance. After all, don't children need to be taught the facts about sex?

Connie Marshner, in her excellent guide for parents *Decent Exposure: How to Teach Your Children About Sex,* exposes this fallacy with an example from her own life:

> A boy named Toby used to live around the corner from us. He was a very nice boy, a year ahead of my elder son, Pearse, in school, but interested in similar things. . . . Toby was in the Gifted and Talented program in the Fairfax County Public Schools, however. And in seventh grade he got a whole semester of sex education. Once in that class, he began to talk a lot about sex with my boys. Consequently, my boys began asking me questions that I could tell were inspired by Toby's conversation. Ten-year-old Michael, for instance, strolled into the kitchen one afternoon as I was peeling carrots and casually asked, "Hey, Mom, what's bisexuality?" I decided they needed some facts to counter the impressions Toby was probably giving, so Pearse and I spent a couple of hours during our home schooling one week to go over the facts of life. After those two hours, Pearse said to me, "Well, Mom, I think we've just about covered it. How come Toby has to spend a whole semester on it?" Wisdom out of the mouths of babes. How come indeed?[8]

The answer, of course, is that sex education has little to do with the facts, but a great deal to do with values. In fact, it is loaded with values. Sex educators don't hesitate to say so. But they are not Christian values.

In 1992, The Sex Information and Education Council of the United States (SIECUS), for example, recently came up with national guidelines for sex education. These guidelines, from one of the most prestigious private educational groups in the country, teach:

- No form of sexual orientation or family structure is morally superior to any other.

- The youngest sexually-active children do compensate for unmet emotional needs with sex, but that usually doesn't apply to kids over fifteen.

- Masturbation is physically and psychologically harmless. Alone or with a partner it can be a sensible alternative to risky sexual practices.

- It is healthy to discuss erogenous zones.

- Abortion is legal, and far less risky for developing teens than pregnancy.[9]

Incredibly, this transparent attempt to teach children to accept perversity and hedonism has even received the official endorsement of the American Medical Association.

Oftentimes, parents are the last to learn of what their children are being taught. *Insight* magazine reported:

Five-year-old Johnny fidgets in the back seat of the family Volvo on his way home from school. "Mommy," he finally blurts out, "I think I'm a lesbian." This is how one mother in Washington state discovered that her son was being taught comprehensive sex and AIDS education in kindergarten.[10]

Even outside of the public schools, parents must constantly be on their guard if they care about their child's upbringing. Columnist John Leo has written:

A friend reports that his eleven-year-old daughter came home from school one day and announced that she had put a condom on a banana in her fifth-grade class. My friend was not consulted or even told that the pre-teens were learning how to protect a roomful of tropical fruit from venereal disease. These things have a way of happening without parental input, possibly because the sensibilities of parents, poor yahoos that they are, aren't as good as the sensibilities of enlightened bureaucrats in instructing the young about sex. Besides, you can get a lot more done if parents don't know what's going on. At least my friend had the advantage of dealing with a private school he could yank his daughter out of. At public schools, the stakes are higher.[11]

Indeed they are.

Alternative sexual education curriculums have sprung up such as Teen-Aid and Sex-Respect, that teach abstinence before marriage. The courts, however, are not friendly to such programs. In Jacksonville, Florida, Planned Parenthood, along with some parents, sued the school board to get rid of Teen-Aid. The judge ruled that the curriculum was illegal because it was not "unbiased."[12] A similar ruling was made in Shreveport, Louisiana, about the Sex-Respect curriculum. A state judge ruled that "it violated state laws against teaching religion."[13] Teaching that homosexuality is good, according to the sexual education establishment and the courts, is perfectly appropriate—if not essential. But teaching that one should only have sex with one's spouse is "sectarian."

As far as America's school system is concerned, the homosexual ideology is quickly becoming a mandated dogma and test of orthodoxy.

The Myth of Sexual Education

Even apart from the alien and often prohomosexual values they teach, it should be noted that the sex education courses that are typically taught in the public school system not only don't work in preventing sexually-transmitted diseases (STDs) and teen pregnancies, but they actually do the opposite. For example, Planned Parenthood is probably one of the largest and most well known of the sex education organizations.[14] They claim that sex education is necessary and effective for preventing pregnancies.[15] The truth is such sex education programs have backfired, actually *increasing* teen pregnancies. According to its own survey, conducted by the Louis Harris pollsters, teens who had taken "comprehensive" sex education courses have a 50 percent *higher* rate of sexual activity than their "unenlightened" peers.[16] And yet the courses had no significant effect on their contraceptive usage.[17] The conclusion, one that even Planned Parenthood researchers have been unable to escape, is that sex education courses only exacerbate the teen pregnancy problem.[18] And it takes no immense effort of intelligence to figure out that if teens are getting pregnant in greater numbers, they are also being exposed to more STDs.

In 1970, fewer than half of the nation's school districts offered sex education curricula and none had school-based birth control clinics.[19] Today more than 75 percent of the districts teach sex education and there are more than two hundred clinics in operation.[20] Yet the percentage of illegitimate births has only increased during that time, from a mere 15 percent to an astonishing 51 percent.[21]

In California, the public schools have required sex education for more that thirty years, and yet the state has maintained one of the highest rates of teen pregnancy in the nation.[22]

According to the Harris poll, the only things that effectively and positively impact the teen sexuality crisis are frequent church attendance and parental oversight, the very things that Planned Parenthood has been railing against for three quarters of a century—the very things that sex education courses are designed to circumvent.[23]

The reason sex education doesn't work is quite simple. Children are encouraged to have sex as long as they use some sort of "protection." But by discouraging teenagers from chastity—in which there is no chance of pregnancy or disease—and encouraging them to embrace promiscuity, there is a much greater risk, even if they practice so-called safe sex. As Connie Marshner puts it: "Family planning for children is a euphemism for giving a false sense of security to fornication."[24]

Homoculturalism

Not all forms of education about homosexuality are based on the need for sex or AIDS education; some are based on the dubious notion of multiculturalism. Several new children's books have been written, for instance, that portray homosexual family life as completely normal. *Daddy's Roommate* is about the life of a little boy who lives with his father and his father's male lover. *Heather Has Two Mommies* is about a girl who was conceived by artificial insemination and lives with her lesbian "mommies." Needless to say, both these books present homosexuality as perfectly normal, natural, and healthy.

Of course, one might wonder: apart from a few homosexual parents, who is going to read these books to children? It is hard to imagine even the most liberal of parents looking for such publications in order to "enlighten" their progeny. The fact is, this prohomosexual propaganda is especially aimed at the public education system. It is teachers and educational activists who promote the reading of such books to children for the purpose of effecting social change.

Indeed, *Daddy's Roommate* and *Heather Has Two Mommies* had a great deal to do with a dispute over curriculum in the New York City public schools, which ultimately resulted in the ouster of Joseph Fernandez from his position as School Chancellor.[25] The books were part of a bibliography that was included in the "Children of the Rainbow" curriculum. Among other things, this document reads:

> Teachers of first-graders have an opportunity to give children a healthy sense of identity at an early age. Classes should include references to lesbians and gays in all curricular areas and should avoid exclusionary practices by presuming a person's sexual orientation, reinforcing stereotypes, or speaking of lesbians and gays as "they" or "other." If teachers do not discuss lesbian and gay issues, they are not likely to come up. Children need actual experiences via creative play, books, visitors, etc., in order for them to view lesbians and gays as real people to be respected and appreciated. Educators have the potential to help increase the tolerance and acceptance of the lesbian and gay community.[26]

Though the guide is supposed to represent all cultural groups, it is said to have been authored by Andy Humm, the founder of the Harvey Milk School for homosexual boys.[27]

Interestingly, Fernandez sent the curriculum directly to the schools in the spring of 1992 without sending it to the school board—though it was the board that had legal jurisdiction over any curriculum changes. Fortunately, the schools in Queens gave the guides to Mary Cummins, a member of the school board there. She was able to rally her district against the curriculum, though it involved a long, hard fight with bitter conflict between parents and teachers.[28]

Although many citizens objected to the curriculum and the books it recommended, such as *Heather Has Two Mommies* and *Daddy's Roommate,* few realized just how perverse the curriculum was.

The two books aimed at promoting the acceptance of homosexuality among young children were published by a company that specializes in subversive homosexual works. According to *Lambda Report* editor Peter LaBarbera:

Working out of a seedy, run-down warehouse next to a crime-infested housing project in Boston, Alyson Publications produces and distributes a variety of homosexual literature, from gay travel guides to manuals on the methods of sadomasochistic sex, to erotic lesbian novels, generating one million dollars in annual sales. Alyson is regarded as the top independent gay publisher in the United States.[29]

The Alyson Wonderland series—from which the two childrens' books were originally taken—includes titles such as *Gloria Goes to Gay Pride* and *A Boy's Best Friend*. According to the publisher's catalog, the target audience for the books includes "kids who themselves may later decide they are gay."[30]

Alyson has other books on children and homosexuality with a slightly different angle. In books such as *Pedophilia: The Radical Case, Gay Sex: A Manual for Men Who Love Boys,* and one of Alyson's earliest works, *The Age Taboo: Gay Male Sexuality, Power, and Consent,* the intended audience is child molesters, those who would like to be child molesters, and those who wish to rationalize child molestation. *Gay Sex* goes so far as to provide recommendations from NAMBLA to advise pedophiles on how to avoid outraged parents and police. In *The Age Taboo,* one contributor states:

> Boy-lovers and lesbians who have young lovers . . . are not child-molesters. The child abusers are priests, teachers, therapists, cops, and parents who force their stale morality onto the young people in their custody.[31]

Additionally, *The Alyson Almanac,* a book of homosexual trivia, directs readers interested in pederasty to contact NAMBLA; The *Spartacus International Gay Guide, 1992–1993* is a homosexual travel guide that tells readers where to find boy prostitutes in other countries; *Macho Sluts* is a collection of Pat Califia's allegedly erotic short stories, in one of which a lesbian protagonist "performs sadomasochistic sex on her young daughter, whipping the girl until she bleeds";[32] *One Teenager in 10: Writings by Gay and Lesbian Youth* is a pedophile anthology containing essays celebrating Kinsey's now-debunked estimation that 10 percent of the populace is homosexual.[33]

Of course, homosexual apologists heap scorn on the notion that we should worry about children being recruited into the homosexual lifestyle through the educational system. They act as if there is no rational reason for such suspicions—and thus, that all such reservations spring from "homophobia." Yet here we find that the same publisher who produces books to induce children to accept homosexuality as normal also produces books to help and encourage adults to seduce children.

An old "New Left" slogan claimed, "You don't have to be a weatherman to know which way the wind is blowing." Likewise, you don't have to be a "homophobe" to recognize a child molestation campaign in the school system thinly disguised as multiculturalism. You only have to open your eyes.

The Thought Police

In higher education the situation is as bad as in the elementary and high schools. Almost every major college and university now has enacted restrictive speech codes. Actually, according to James T. Bennett and Thomas J. DiLorenzo, sometimes these rules ban a great deal more than mere speech:

> The lengths to which some universities have gone to enforce ideological conformity range from hilarious to Stalinist. As of early 1991, at least 125 colleges and universities had enacted "speech codes" designed to limit "offensive" speech—that is, politically incorrect speech—on campuses. The University of Connecticut even banned "inappropriate laughter," "inconsiderate jokes," and "conspicuous exclusion from conversation"—the penalty for jokesters (or their insensitive auditors) is expulsion.[34]

They cite as typical the position paper released by the law faculty of the State University of New York at Buffalo entitled "Statement Regarding Freedom, Tolerance, and Political Harassment." The document claimed that promoting "equality and justice" is more important than free speech.[35] Of course, in the minds of the education establishment, "equality and justice" means something far different than what most of us think of when they use the same terms:

> The three areas in which ideological conformity is most ruthlessly enforced are race, sex, and Western culture, broadly defined. Honest people can disagree over the best ways to improve black-white relations, but at many universities anyone who criticizes the use of racial quotas is labeled a racist. End of argument. The same is true of feminist and homosexual politics on university campuses. Those who take issue with any of the scholarship produced in these areas—even if they are not intolerant in any way of

feminists or gays or lesbians—risk being slandered as sexist or homophobic. To criticize "equal pay for comparable worth" proposals, as most
economists do, is to earn opprobrium as a "sexist"—or worse. To advocate
traditional family stability as a partial antidote to poverty, as many social
scientists do, is coming perilously close to committing the most heinous of
. . . crimes: "insensitivity." This is the language of bullies and tyrants, not
men—excuse us, persons—of honor.[36]

Although the damage done to students by such persecution is cause
for concern, the effect it has on scholarship is also frightening. One
Harvard professor has already openly recommended that professors and
scholars censor both their own teaching and research so that no group's
reputation is hurt.[37] No wonder scientists are willing to claim that blatantly bogus research "demonstrates" that homosexuality is genetically
determined!

Christian faculty members are also at risk in today's intolerant climate. In his book *Political Correctness: The Cloning of the American
Mind,* David Thibodaux writes:

> In 1987, the University of Alabama, in response to student complaints,
> fired Phillip A. Bishop, associate professor and director of the university's
> Human Performance Laboratory. The university demanded that Professor
> Bishop "stop injecting religious beliefs into classes" and warned him "to
> stop holding optional classes in which he taught from a 'Christian perspec-
> tive.' . . ." Professor Bishop sued the university in 1988 maintaining that
> his right of free speech had been violated. The court ruled in Bishop's
> favor in 1990, but the Eleventh Circuit Court of Appeals recently rendered
> a decision reversing the lower court's decision and upholding the univer-
> sity's right to so discipline a faculty member.[38]

Indeed, it is interesting that despite all the talk of "acceptance," "tolerance," "diversity," "open-mindedness," "understanding," "sensitivity,"
and "multiculturalism," that institutions of higher learning show very
little interest in open-mindedly accepting, understanding, showing sensitivity toward, or even tolerating Christianity. In fact, they are quite willing to suppress it.

This frightening fact was made perfectly clear in the case of Westminster School in Atlanta, Georgia. Westminster is one of the most
prestigious college-preparatory schools in the South. Near the end of
1992, however, a startling truth was brought to the attention of the Ivy

League schools which had, up until that point, not hesitated to accept Westminster's graduates. Suddenly eight leading universities wrote letters of disapproval to the school, and the admissions dean at Harvard went so far as to say that graduates from Westminster would have a harder time being accepted.

What was the school's problem? Very simple: it was a Christian institution. It hired Christian teachers who specialized in different fields so that they would be able to give their students a Christian perspective on different disciplines of learning. According to the modern world's standards, however, this practice makes the school guilty of sinning against the gods "Diversity" and "Tolerance."

The brouhaha erupted after some thoroughly modernized parents of students and alumni started protesting the school's faith. Despite the fact that Westminster is a private school and that parents are perfectly free to send their children to other schools, these people acted as if a private institution being based on a specific faith was some kind of threat to America's religious diversity.

The position of the universities is even more incoherent. As Chuck Colson observed:

> The real irony is that Harvard has the nerve to accuse Westminster of stifling diversity. Places like Harvard have themselves become straitjackets of political correctness. Does anyone really think students in Harvard classrooms are exposed to much of anything besides secular liberalism?[39]

But then, contradictions are not that important to the education establishment; they treat logic and rationality the way homosexuals treat sex.

Regulating Belief

The way in which perversity is promoted through the government education system should make us reexamine what the public schools are for. An article in *The Advocate* entitled "Why Johnny Can't Learn About Condoms," vilified "fundamentalist minister Robert Simonds" and other Christians for opposing homosexual influence in public education. One prohomosexual journalist perceptively commented:

> Public education epitomizes the religious right's problem with non-Christian society. Public schools serve the function of *mainstreaming* people—

making them into decent, tolerant adults. For Simonds, that makes public schools the enemy, and he has been able to make this case to a lot of fundamentalists.[40]

So there you have it. Your children must be "mainstreamed" by the government through the educational establishment and its attendant bureaucratic machinery. Your taxes are being used to raise your children in values alien to the Christian faith, and if you try to stop it you are guilty of "censorship."[41]

As Bennett and DiLorenzo have said:

Public schools in America are essentially monopolies. They are financed by compulsory taxation, enjoy a captive audience of students thanks to compulsory-attendance laws, and—in most cities—assign students to schools according to where they live. Parents who are dissatisfied with the quality of education their children are receiving must either move to an affluent area, where schools are often better, or send their children to private schools. If they choose the latter, parents must pay twice for their children's education: once in property taxes and again in tuition.[42]

This fundamental incongruity in the American tradition of freedom is not some new development in public education. Horace Mann, who is universally recognized as the father of the American public education system, admitted that public schools were needed "as a means for the state to control people." He said: "Great care must be taken to inform and regulate the will of the people."[43] Newton Bateman, a late-nineteenth-century advocate of public education, echoed Mann's sentiments, claiming:

Government has a right of eminent domain over the minds and souls and bodies of us all; therefore education cannot be left to the caprices and contingencies of individuals.[44]

Thus, the homosexual movement's tactic of getting at children through the public education system is nothing new. It is as old as the public schools are. Indeed, Horace Mann—the "father" of the American public education system—was originally a reformer who wished to "improve" his society through legislation. To his dismay, however, he found adult individuals too resistant and recalcitrant for his designs. Eventually he hit on a new idea: aim for the children. In 1837, he wrote a friend explaining his new strategy:

> I have abandoned jurisprudence, and betaken myself to the larger sphere of mind and morals. Having found the present generation composed of materials almost unmalleable, I am about transferring my efforts to the next. Men are cast-iron, but children are wax.[45]

Contemporary sex education proponents are not merely concerned about passing out information, but wish to instill moral—or, more accurately, immoral—beliefs. As one former Planned Parenthood medical director has forthrightly admitted, "Mere facts and discussion are not enough. They need to be undergirded by a set of values."[46]

Again, this is nothing new. American public education has been driven by moral values. Horace Mann's arguments for the public school had almost nothing to do with reading, writing, and arithmetic, but with inculcating children with his version of morality:

> The germs of morality must be planted deeply in the moral nature of children, at an early period of their life. . . . If we should have improved men, we must have improved means of educating children. . . . Of all the means in our possession, the common school has precedence, because of its universality.[47]

Indeed, Mann wanted religion taught in the public schools. He exhorted teachers:

> Keep children unspotted from the world, that is uncontaminated by its vices; to train them up to the love of God and the love of man; to make the perfect example of Jesus Christ lovely in their eyes; and to give to all so much of religious instruction as is compatible with the rights of others and the genius of our government.[48]

The Advocate argues that sex-education guides that promote abstinence are "sectarian." Teaching children to copulate with condoms, on the other hand, is entirely "nonsectarian."[49]

Sounds absurd doesn't it? But again, this is exactly the same language that Horace Mann used. Though he wanted religion in the public school, he was opposed to orthodox Christianity, and instead wished to promulgate Unitarianism. He did not do this by calling for Unitarianism to be recognized as the official state religion of Massachusetts; rather, he simply called for the religious teaching in the schools to be "nonsectarian."

As the director of Equal Educational Opportunity for the Commonwealth of Massachusetts, Charles Leslie Glenn, Jr., writes:

> Thus, although Mann and the other education reformers may not have intended to promote Unitarianism as a denomination, they were deeply concerned to assure that "liberal religion" would, through the common schools, replace "fanaticism." Were the normal schools some sort of Unitarian conspiracy, then? Only in the sense that they represented the most effective means for the education reformers (themselves mostly but not exclusively "liberal Christians") to develop a supply of teachers who would share their own views about the "pure religion" appropriate to offer as religious instruction in common schools. . . . Orthodox beliefs were not confronted directly, but they were relativized, marginalized. It was by a selective emphasis upon certain elements of Christianity, in a vocabulary familiar from childhood, that the idea was conveyed that these were the *real* essentials of the faith.[50]

Furthermore, according to Glenn, in his book published by the prestigious University of Massachusetts, Mann pioneered subtle methods of centrally controlling education that are still used today:

> The collection and interpretation of educational statistics, ostensibly a perfectly neutral activity, had and continues to have the power to define perceptions of the salient strengths and weaknesses of the schools. The recommendation of reading material—and the banning of other material—had and continues to have the power to shape the range of topics that may be taught or discussed, and the framework in which they will be understood. The training—and eventually the certification—of teachers had and continues to have the power to determine what will occur in the classroom, far more than any system of regulation and prescription.[51]

But if the public education system pioneered by Mann and others was so biased, why did Christians, who ostensibly made up a majority of the country at the time, not resist it? Well, according to Glenn, at first some Christians did resist:

> Those who—more clear-thinking, perhaps—did not fully agree with Mann insisted that what was presented was in fact a false religion, worse than no

mention of religion at all, since it took no account of sin as a corruption of human nature cutting man off from God and from his own happiness, or of God's plan of salvation through Jesus Christ. By retaining only those aspects of Christianity with which Unitarians agreed, the proposed religious teaching was in fact identical with Unitarian teaching. Thus it *was* sectarian in the fullest sense.[52]

The eminent theologian Charles Hodge, for example, strongly questioned the right of the government to interfere in the curriculum decisions of local districts—even in the name of "nonsectarianism."

What right has the State, a majority of the people, or a mere clique, which in fact commonly control such matters, to say what shall be taught in schools which the people sustain? What more right have they to say that no religion shall be taught, than they have to say that Popery shall be taught? Or what right have the people in one part, to control the wishes and convictions of those of another part of the State, as to the education of their own children? If the people of a particular district choose to have a school in which the Westminster of Heidelberg catechism is taught, we cannot see on what principle of religious liberty the State has a right to interfere, and say it shall not be done. . . . This appears to us a strange doctrine in a free country . . . unjust and tyrannical, as well as infidel in its whole tendency.[53]

According to Glenn:

Hodge's view was shared by many of his fellow Presbyterians, and a brief effort was made to establish a system of Presbyterian elementary schools [but] this effort collapsed under the perceived threat of the schools that immigrant Catholics actually *were* establishing.[54]

Roman Catholics saw more readily than the orthodox Protestants—indeed, they blamed the orthodox Protestants—the threat posed by the religiously generic training that took place in the public schools. Though Charles Hodge and other knowledgeable Protestant theologians were admirable exceptions, most Protestants decided that they had more in common with Unitarians than with Catholics—and willingly began supporting public education against Catholic efforts to build their own schools.

One cannot help but think of the saying "What goes around comes around." Or as the Bible states, "We reap what we sow."

Alternative Education

In his remarkable article entitled "The Fraud of Educational Reform," Samuel L. Blumenfeld states: "The more I read what secular educators write these days, the more convinced I become that their grasp of reality has slipped beyond retrieval."[55]

The schools have failed so miserably in accomplishing their basic tasks—teaching our children how to read and write and compute and complete and compete—that Blumenfeld says those educators *know* that they will have to reform their precious system. But what will that reform be like? Blumenfeld tells us:

> We should expect the next phase of educational reform to be dominated by radical ideas disguised in *pedagogic clothes.* Such phrases as *critical thinking, emancipatory pedagogy,* and *master teachers* will sound benign to the public but will convey the right message to the radicals.[56]

Certainly that is what we saw in Lamar Alexander's America 2000 reform proposals during the Bush administration.[57]

Thus, reforming the present educational system is *not* the answer. Radical, prohomosexual educational activists are so deeply entrenched in the public school machinery that reform can only mean *more* of the same: more debauchery, more brazenness, more humanism, and more wickedness.

The early promoters of public, state-controlled education rallied around the slogan "It costs less money to build school-houses than jails."[58] The great patriot-theologian of the South, Robert L. Dabney, responded to this in 1876, saying, "But what if it turns out that the state's expenditure in school-houses is one of the things which necessitates the expenditures in jails?"[59] To which we might add: What if that expenditure also necessitates the expenditure in AIDS hospitals, nationalized child care, and an ever-burgeoning abortion industry?

Certainly, we need to battle the blazing concupiscence of sex and AIDS education programs by sounding the alarms in PTA meetings, community forums, and school board hearings. But, in the meantime, it is essential that we rescue our own children from the flickering flames of promiscuity and perversity.

At all costs.

Conclusion

Nothing illustrates the tragedy of the homosexual agenda for public education better than the frightened letter a teenaged boy wrote to an advice columnist about temptations he was struggling with:

> You've got to help me! I am fifteen and I'm afraid I'm gay. I keep getting interested in guys. I don't even dare take showers after gym because I get aroused. I'm so scared. I don't want this. I try and try not to think this way, but I can't stop. I'm going to kill myself if there's no way to make me straight.

The columnist's reply was a model of "politically correct" thinking:

> You can't change your fantasies, no matter how hard you try. You can control what you do about it, but not what you think. Don't consider suicide! Call a teen hotline and find someone who understands. Many gay teenagers feel desperately lonely and isolated because they know they will be discriminated against and hounded if they come out. An alarming number do take their own lives.[60]

She went on to recommend a homosexual support group that would "help" him—that is, encourage him and train him to give in to his temptations.

There is no way of knowing if this anonymous boy was able to see through the deceptive reply he received and find help, or if he came to accept the message of modern society that is being increasingly promoted in the public education system: "You have no choice. You cannot help yourself. You are not responsible. You must accept yourself the way you are."

But this we do know: The radical transformation of our society's sexual ethics has come in direct contradistinction to the teaching of Scripture. And more, it is in direct contradistinction to the cultural standards that have made Western Civilization what it is. Thus we appear to be treading on treacherous turf.

According to Scripture, the education of children is the responsibility of the parents. Jesus stressed the immensity of this responsibility to our children when He said, "Whoever causes one of these little ones who believe in Me to sin, it would be better for him if a millstone were hung around his neck, and he were drowned in the depth of the sea" (Matthew 18:6).

May we hear and heed.

5

STATUTORY HATE: POLITICS

I am not what my lips explain,
And more devotedly inclined
Than these dry sentences reveal
That break in crude shards from my mind.[1]

DONALD DAVIDSON

A nn Hacklander said she felt as if she "was in China, not in the United States."

The young Wisconsin woman had just been subjected to a four-and-a-half hour session with the Madison Equal Opportunities Commission. Ann was found guilty of a housing-code violation because she turned down a lesbian she interviewed to become her roommate. She, herself, had no problem with the woman's sexual proclivities, but she already had another woman living with her who said she was uncomfortable at the thought of living with a homosexual.

Ann was ordered to pay $500 to the offended lesbian, attend sensitivity-training classes conducted by a homosexual rights group, and submit to monitoring by the commission for two years to make sure her attitude improved.

For what it's worth, the lease was in her name.[2]

Judy Allison, an apartment manager in Atlanta, was sued for violating various civil rights and housing violations as well as discrimination against the handicapped. Her crime? She told an AIDS-infected man

91

who exhibited the disease's characteristic oozing lesions to get out of the apartment complex's swimming pool. Tenant Jerrod Beasley, who had invited the man to the complex, phoned the Lambda Legal Defense Fund and initiated the legal action. In response to Allison's concern for other swimmers, including a pregnant woman, Beasley stated that "everyone knows" AIDS is not transmissible from a swimming pool. But what he failed to mention was that even if catching the Human Immunodeficiency Virus is not a problem, AIDS-infected people, because of their very low resistance to germs and infection, commonly carry a host of other diseases that could easily spread in a swimming pool.

Now Allison can be prosecuted for discrimination against the handicapped because the Americans With Disabilities Act, which recently went into effect, defines people with the deadly disease as "handicapped."[3]

Welcome to the world of "gay rights."

Civil Slaveries

Presently twenty-five of fifty states have antisodomy statutes that prohibit or restrict homosexual practices. One would think that the primary agenda of the homosexual movement would simply involve repealing these laws. Ironically, homosexuals have chosen a different agenda altogether.

Art historian Camille Paglia explains:

> Essentially, gays have two choices. First, if they want to think of themselves as a distinct group worthy of the special protection of civil rights, they should perhaps accept the Judeo-Christian position that homosexuality is against nature (which has tyrannically designed our bodies for procreation) and then celebrate gay love as a seditious and necessary act of human freedom and imagination, in the Sade, Baudelaire, and Wilde way. The scornful term *breeders,* used by some urban gays about heterosexual couples with children, suggests that this strategy is still possible. Another solution is to blur homosexual and heterosexual desire and to see all of eroticism as a dynamic continuum, in constant flux from hour to hour and day to day. This would logically end in withholding legal recognition from gays as a distinct category but would argue instead for protection of all nonconformist sexual behavior on the pagan grounds of pansexuality. In insisting, for political purposes, on a sharp division between gay and straight, gay

activism, much like feminism, has become as rigid and repressive as the old order it sought to replace.[4]

Though homosexuals do claim to be a distinct class, they insist that what they do is "perfectly natural." Thus, we are regularly bombarded with news of alleged findings that prove homosexuality is but an inborn condition.

Sociologist and historian Margaret Cruikshank admits:

> Sexual practices clearly are a private matter; they become politicized when groups or institutions try to stamp them out. If gay people claimed only the right to perform certain sexual acts, however, they would not have been able to create a movement. Their claims rests on sexual identity, which is a sufficient basis for a movement because . . . the sexual identity in question is a minority identity, condemned or discouraged by the dominant heterosexual majority.[5]

Thus, homosexuals do not want to be treated as everybody else; they want to be treated as special. More to the point, they want to force people to live with them and work with them against their will.

Marshall Kirk and Hunter Madsen, in an effort to spell out a "moderate and balanced" homosexual agenda, list five goals they wish to accomplish:

- All sex acts between consenting adults are decriminalized; *no discrimination is permitted between straights and gays in content and application of the laws.*

- Gays are provided, *by special law if necessary,* the same opportunity to speak (including access to mass media) and gather as straights currently enjoy.

- Gays are assured, *by affirmative action if necessary,* equal opportunity and the rights "to work, shelter and public accommodations" which are presently "limited by public intolerance."

- Gays are permitted all the standard rights of marriage and parenthood.

- The public no longer sanctions "the taunting, harassing, or brutalizing of homosexuals, which becomes as socially incorrect, discreditable, and repugnant as overt racism or anti-Semitism."[6]

Notice that the first goal flatly contradicts the second and third goals. Kirk and Madsen claim they want absolute equality before the law; then they claim they want the law to treat homosexuals differently than heterosexuals by coercing landlords and employers—as well as the owners of radio stations, television stations, and newspapers—into accepting homosexuals.

This sort of servile coercion is already eroding basic liberties all across the land. In late 1992, for example, in Washington, D.C., WMZQ, a country radio station, was asked to run an "antibigotry" advertisement which said in part: "Imagine having your love called a crime. . . . Imagine being told your family is not a real family." It was sponsored by the Gay and Lesbian Action League and the Gay and Lesbian Educational Fund. Because the station's policy was to take no "issue advertising," they attempted to refuse the commercial.[7]

The vice-president and general manager of the station, Charlie Oates, told us: "The next day we received a call from the mayor's office." An aide said that the homosexual groups were filing a complaint against him under the Human Rights Act of 1977, which barred him from denying any minority group access to the "cultural life" of Washington, D.C. "The aide told me that they would file a complaint and that I would lose."

Even though Oates viewed the law as "totally unconstitutional," he decided on a "tactical retreat." It was not simply the lawsuit that worried him, Oates told us, but the threat that protestors would demonstrate in front of his office "blocking traffic and marching." He knew that he would be subjected to immense media coverage, which might put him out of business. "I saw my advertiser-base eroding," he said.

One evangelical leader to rise to the defense of the radio station was Gary Bauer, president of the Family Research Council. Bauer described the situation as "tyranny," and stated publicly:

> I worked with President Reagan when we stood up to tyranny behind the Iron Curtain. We won that fight for freedom. But now, we Americans are losing freedom at home.[8]

Ironically, during roughly the same period of time that the station was forced to broadcast homosexual ads, the Clinton campaign was appealing to the Federal Elections Committee (FEC) to prevent their conservative opponents from broadcasting their message.

Martin Mawyer, president of the Christian Action Network, has firsthand experience with the Clinton campaign's attempt to stifle opposition. His organization had managed to get half-hour commercials broadcast in twenty-three different cities. According to Mawyer:

> The commercials exposed Governor Clinton's support of three things: Job quotas for homosexuals, special civil rights protection for homosexuals, and allowing homosexuals in the military. We also exposed Al Gore's support of homosexual couples adopting children and becoming foster parents. We concluded the advertisement by asking the question: "Is this your vision for a better America?"[9]

The Clinton campaign responded swiftly. First, said Mawyer, they used persuasion:

> Ron Brown, the Democratic Party Chairman, has been sending out letters to all the TV and cable operators around the country asking them not to run our ad. And once it gets on the air, he's been trying to yank it off. He has been successful in a couple of instances, but in most cases, they run the full length.[10]

But when persuasion didn't work, says Mawyer, they resorted to political intervention:

> The Democratic National Committee filed a formal complaint against us with the Federal Elections Committee, claiming, of course, that our ad violates FEC laws.[11]

In the name of liberty, openness, fairness, and integrity, Mawyer says, they attempted to stifle liberty, openness, fairness, and integrity. They wanted to have their cake and eat it too.

Similarly, homosexuals claim that all antisodomy statutes are unconstitutional and unfair because they treat homosexuals differently than heterosexuals and thus violate their constitutional liberties. But when private individuals exercise those liberties or choose not to associate with homosexuals because of their moral convictions, the homosexual activists want the state to exact punishments with fines, jail sentences, and—perhaps worst of all—compulsory "counseling."

Even the most "reasonable"—relatively speaking—of the homosexuals do not hesitate to advocate the suppression of free speech and religious liberty. Kirk and Madsen discuss a strategy for promoting gay rights and differentiate between "ambivalent skeptics" and "intransigents."

> Some intransigents . . . feel compelled to adhere rigidly to an authoritarian belief structure (e.g., an orthodox religion) that condemns homosexuality. Our primary objective regarding diehard homo-haters of this sort is to cow and *silence* them as far as possible, not to convert or even desensitize them. . . . The ambivalent skeptics are our most promising target. If we can win them over, produce a major realignment solidly in favor of gay rights, the intransigents (like the racists of twenty years ago) will eventually be effectively silenced by both law and polite society.[12]

Homosexuals attempt to rationalize their desire to use the government to persecute conscience-bound straights and others who do not wish to associate with homosexuals—for whatever reasons. Margaret Cruikshank writes:

> Fundamentalists and others have denounced the few existing laws as special treatment for homosexuals; in fact, special treatment is the status quo, special *discriminatory* treatment. State and city gay rights laws simply treat gay and lesbians like other citizens. They may not be fired from jobs or evicted from housing simply because they are gay. Discrimination in public accommodations occurs when gay groups are not allowed to rent space for their meetings. . . . [F]reedom of speech and freedom of assembly are denied as long as gay people are unprotected from housing and employment discrimination.[13]

Notice that Cruikshank equates the decisions of private individuals who are simply trying to live within the dictates of their consciences with unequal treatment before the law. If "special treatment is the status quo," as she claims, then it is the treatment of free individuals who are facing ethical decisions. Cruikshank doesn't think they should be permitted to make such decisions. That would violate homosexuals' "freedom of speech and freedom of assembly." But what about the freedom of speech and freedom of assembly of Christians—especially Christian landlords and employers? And what about the hiring practices of churches?

Like the plotting piglets in George Orwell's *Animal Farm,* the homosexual rhetoric is clear enough: "All people are equal, but homosexual people are more equal than others."

This was especially obvious in the case of Luethel Tate Green, who was fired from a Washington, D.C.-area hospital. She believed that she was singled out because she complained that lesbians in her department staff were being shown favoritism. She took the hospital to court under a Washington, D.C. "sexual orientation" law and won $140,000 in back pay plus lawyers' fees. She also got her old job back.

Suzanne Goldberg of the Lambda Legal Defense and Education Fund complained:

> To have a heterosexual rely on laws to protect homosexuals really goes against the purpose and reason behind those laws.[14]

Family Affairs

One part of the homosexual agenda is to legally recognize homosexual "marriages" and allow them to "have" children—that is, to adopt them. For the government to recognize heterosexual marriages while refusing to recognize homosexual "marriages," they claim, is a blatant case of inequality before the law.

Interestingly, the homosexual case is bolstered by the fact that, in many situations, the government *does not* recognize heterosexual marriages. As Maggie Gallagher points out, by permitting no-fault divorce, states have made marriage a veritable legal fiction. She uses a couple, Jim and Mary—who are in the throes of divorce proceedings—to demonstrate her assertion:

> When Mary agreed to live in the same house with Jim and accept his financial support and offer her own paid and unpaid labor to the household, to sleep in the same bed and bear his children, she did so because she thought she was married. Had Jim asked her to do these things for him without getting married, she would have slapped his face. Mary knew what marriage meant. The example of her parents, and the teachings of her religion gave her a concrete idea of the unwritten law. It meant the two became one flesh, one family. It was a lifetime commitment. But the state of California informed her that she was not allowed to make or to accept lifetime commitments. No-fault divorce gave judges, at the request of one half a couple, the right to decide when a marriage had irretrievably broken down.

They decided by and large that wanderlust would be a state-protected emotion, while loyalty was on its own. In a cruel display of raw judicial power, the state of California made Mary a single woman again, without protecting her interests and without requiring her consent.[15]

With the advent of no-fault divorce laws, the state no longer obligates couples to fulfill the contractual agreement they made with each other when they got married. As far as the government is concerned, men must have more respect for their credit cards than for their wives.

Yet even with marriage in such a state of disrepair, homosexuals still find it too restrictive. In 1989, for example, homosexual advocates attempted to pass a "domestic partnership" ordinance in San Francisco. This law was to ensure that the city and county governments would not "discriminate against domestic partners" or use "marital status as a factor in any decision, policy, or practice unless it uses domestic partnership as a factor in the same way."[16] The upshot of the bill was that live-in lovers of government employees could get the same benefits as spouses.

The problem with the ordinance is simply that "domestic partners" are *not* the same as married couples. This becomes evident when one looks at how these partnerships can be ended: "A domestic partnership ends when . . . one partner sends the other a written notice that he or she has ended the partnership."[17] The only requirement is that the notice be notarized and turned in to the bureaucracy.

Just as the things homosexuals do are not simply the same-sex equivalent of what heterosexuals do, homosexual "marriage" is not the same-sex equivalent of heterosexual marriage. Although it is good propaganda for homosexuals to claim that "homophobic" marriage laws discourage them from having "stable relationships," there is no convincing evidence that they even want stable relationships. The only thing we do know is that they want spousal benefits for whoever happens to be living with someone.

And when it comes to children, the "family values" of homosexuals become even more disturbing. It is by no means sensationalistic to weigh the impact of the homosexual lifestyle on the emotional health of children in homosexual "families."

Out magazine, for instance, recently published an article containing advice for "queer moms" who need to "get out of the house and into somebody's pants."[18] The writer, Susie Bright, whose latest book is

Susie Bright's Sexual Reality: A Virtual Sex World Reader, mentions that it is extremely important to have lots of baby-sitters because "we are more often than not relying on an extended family of 'aunts,' 'god-mothers,' and friends who are often the very people we'd like to spend an evening with."[19]

The need for baby-sitters raises a problem, however:

> But teenage baby-sitters are often squeamish about sex, not to mention *homosexuality.* Who knows what sort of parents they have, and how much they confide in them? The grim side of a gay mom's social life is that underneath her swinging-single exterior, she is always worried that some-one will try to take her kid away. The law is not on our side. No matter what contracts we've signed with donors, friendly fathers, or sperm banks, the whole area of child custody and gay parenting is up for grabs.[20]

This sounds horrible, of course. Yet when the author of the article tells a prospective baby-sitter what she must be willing to put up with, we get a rare glimpse at the world that children of homosexuals are raised to take for granted:

> I take the out-of-the-closet or out-of-my-house approach. I told my first teenage baby-sitter that I was queer, that I wrote about sex for a living, and that my house was full of erotic art. I said, "If your parents would disap-prove of you working here, or if it's not your cup of tea, then this baby-sit-ting job is not for you."[21]

So the cat's out of the bag. Bright considers it repressive that some people think it is wrong and should be illegal to raise children in the presence of pornography. What wonderful "family values."

Thought Crimes

Supposedly, Americans have the constitutional freedom to hold opin-ions—even if these opinions are immoral, antisocial, or subversive to the government. Though there have been unfortunate exceptions to this tradition of liberty from time to time, it is, nonetheless, a vital part of the American legal heritage.

But now, homosexuals wish to end this legacy. Permanently. They want the state to punish people for holding "wrong" opinions.

In 1990, George Bush signed the "Hate Crimes Statistics Act" in the presence of twenty homosexual rights activists who had been invited to the White House. This law authorizes the United States Attorney General to collect "data on the incidence of criminal acts that manifest prejudice based on race, religion, homosexuality or heterosexuality, ethnicity, or other characteristics as the Attorney General considers appropriate."[22] This law is considered the first step in actually penalizing "hate-crimes."

Of course, it is *already* illegal to commit crimes against people, whether or not they are homosexual. So what this new legislation does is empower the government to look into the hearts and minds of citizens and then punish any and all indiscretions.

As Scott Staley, president of the Council for Responsible Government, writes:

> Perhaps the most serious abuse of legislation, such as the Hate Crimes Statistics Act, is its use of the coercive power of the state to judge motives of the heart. Hate may be a sin, but it is not a crime. The distinction, for civil purposes, between beliefs and actions, is the foundation of the American civil and religious liberty. According to both Biblical law and common law, the state only has jurisdiction over actions—not beliefs. If hate or prejudice is made a crime, the freedom of the conscience is rendered meaningless because our moral obligation to discriminate between good and evil will have been surrendered to the state.[23]

Several states had already written hate-crimes into their law codes. But some of the state courts were overturning the laws on constitutional grounds. In Panellas County, Florida, for example, circuit court judge Robert Beach ruled that the hate-crimes law was too vague to withstand constitutional scrutiny. In that case, five black men beat and robbed a fourteen-year-old white girl. Since they called her a "cracker" while they committed the crime, they were prosecuted under Florida's law, which allowed a judge to impose a stiffer penalty for crimes motivated by hatred of "sexual orientation," race, color, ancestry, ethnicity, religion, or national origin.[24]

In Wisconsin, Todd Mitchel, a black nineteen-year-old, allegedly encouraged several other black youths to assault a white teenager. They were discussing a scene in the movie *Mississippi Burning,* in which a black boy was beaten by a white man. Mitchel pointed to a white fourteen-year-old and said to the others, "There goes a white boy—go get him."[25] He was convicted of aggravated battery, which normally would mean a two-year sentence. But because Mitchell made some antiwhite remarks before the attack, he was sentenced to four years. The Wisconsin Supreme Court ruled that the law had "an unacceptable chilling effect on free expression" and struck it down.[26]

The U.S. Supreme Court overturned another hate-crime law in Minnesota. In this case a white teenager who burned a cross on the lawn of a black family was convicted under the Bias-Motivated Crime Ordinance. The ordinance went farther than the other state laws in that it criminalized displaying any symbol "which one has reasonable grounds to know arouses anger, alarm, or resentment in others on the basis of race, color, creed, religion, or gender."[27] The Supreme Court unanimously ruled against the law, on the obvious grounds that it violated free speech and punished people for expressing ideas. Bear in mind that there are already trespassing and harassment laws that criminalize actions such as burning a cross on a lawn.

But such momentary setbacks have hardly slowed the tidal wave of new hate-crimes legislation at the local, state, and national levels. In October of 1992, for instance, the House of Representatives bowed to gay political pressure and passed a brand new hate-crimes bill that penalized bias-motivated actions.[28] And Florida legislators recently capitulated to the homosexual lobby and passed a law enhancing penalties for crimes "that evidence prejudice based on race, religion, ethnicity, color, ancestry, sexual orientation, or national origin." In addition, the law states that any "person or organization which establishes that it has been coerced, intimidated, or threatened shall have a civil cause of action for treble damages, an injunction or other appropriate relief in law or in equity." This could have an ominous effect on churches that preach and teach the Biblical perspective—that homosexuality is actually sin. One attorney pointed out that the law "creates a completely subjective standard: anyone can prove that he or she was intimidated simply by swearing that was so."[29]

Straight-Bashing

The justification for such legislation is the ever-escalating problem of "gay-bashing"—the supposedly commonplace violence committed against homosexuals by heterosexual bigots. The media trumpets such claims—that homosexuals are continually assaulted by "homophobes," who are no doubt inspired by Christian or right-wing prejudices.

While gay-bashing is often highlighted, the media seems to have somehow overlooked any and all acts of violence committed by homosexuals against heterosexuals.

In the *American Journal of Psychology,* for instance, Dr. Nicholas Groth and Dr. Wolbert Burgess analyzed dozens of cases involving males raping males. They concluded:

> Although we would not expect the incidence of male rape to approach that of female rape in our culture, we believe it is not so rare an event as would appear from reported incidents.[30]

Strangely, besides sexually assaulting their victims, "in half the cases the offender made an effort to get his victim to ejaculate."[31] There seem to be a variety of motives behind this abuse:

> In misidentifying ejaculation with orgasm, the victim may be bewildered by his physiological response to the offense and thus discouraged from reporting the assault for fear his sexuality may become suspect. Such a reaction may serve to impeach his credibility in trial testimony and discredit his allegation of nonconsent. To the offender, such a reaction may symbolize his utter and complete sexual control over his victim's body and confirm his fantasy that the victim really wanted and enjoyed the rape.[32]

Indeed, one of the results of such abuse is coercive induction into the homosexual subculture. Victims of homosexual rape who are induced to ejaculate, as noted, often become confused about their sexuality. This is especially significant since all the victims in the study were young teenagers, "at an age that represents a transition from adolescence into adulthood."[33]

One doesn't need to look at such criminal behavior, however, to see evidence of straight-bashing going on. One need only look at *The Advocate,* the major homosexual news magazine. In an article detailing "How to Seduce a Straight Man," Jason Del Maris claims of homosexuals: "We all dream about the day when we will finally make it with a straight hunk,"[34] and then goes on to recommend the use of deception, alcohol, and manipulation in order to have sex with a heterosexual male.

Del Maris advises homosexuals attracted to a "straight" man to befriend him under false pretenses:

Get close to that stud. . . . Go to the places he goes and do the things he does. "Fancy meeting you here, Bob! Can I buy you a drink?" The guy plays tennis? You play tennis. If he goes surfing, then you go surfing. He plays football; you play football.[35]

Conversation with the less cultured straight man will be difficult, Del Maris counsels his readers, describing the heterosexual man in the most outrageous stereotypes imaginable. To Del Maris all straight men are exactly like the males portrayed in R-rated movies aimed at adolescents and have the intelligence level of a cabbage:

> When things seem darkest, remember that most straight guys actually view their sex life as a long line of faceless bodies. . . . Try not to get glassy-eyed as he rambles on about batting averages, how to fieldstrip a machine gun, or the Three Stooges. A straight man can blather for hours on subjects like these. . . . He doesn't really expect you to carry on a conversation like you would with another gay; he wants someone to listen with an expression of rapt adoration . . . while he talks and talks. Let this bozo think you're his admirer, and he'll repay you with almost doglike devotion.[36]

Del Maris discusses what to do when one is invited into a heterosexual's house (compliment him on his good taste no matter how completely awful it is) and how to win his heart (ply him with food and drink). The article culminates with movement-by-movement instructions for the consumation of the friendship, an event more accurately described as the homosexual rape of the hapless straight man.

Imagine what would happen if a major magazine ran a detailed, step-by-step article on how to seduce a woman, concluding with a virtual rape. How do you think the media would react? What do you think feminists would say? There would be universal outrage, and justifiably so. So why are homosexuals, who claim they want to be treated just like everybody else, not denounced for this sort of "hate-crime"?

And straight-bashing gets worse still.

There is the organized mass violence commonly perpetrated by homosexual groups that never seems to count as "hate-crimes." For example, columnist John Leo wrote in *U.S. News and World Report* about how two activist organizations responded to the production of the movie *Basic Instinct,* which they believed was "homophobic":

ACT-UP and Queer Nation disrupted the filming of *Instinct* in an attempt to censor the script. Paint was splattered on sets, whistles were blown and drivers were induced to honk car horns in an effort to ruin the sound track. Shortly afterward, Ray Chalker, owner of a gay bar and publisher of a gay newspaper was punished for renting the bar to the film company as a site. The bar was picketed, his answering machine jammed with threatening calls; Super Glue was poured into the locks of his home, and his car was vandalized. . . . And in the nasty, anonymous campaign against Chalker during the filming of *Instinct,* "Kill Ray" posters sprouted in gay neighborhoods.[37]

Does the description of this behavior sound as if it was motivated by love? Yet it doesn't count as a hate-crime. If Christians were to even picket a homosexual movie, however—no matter how calm and peaceful they acted—well, *that* would be a hate-crime.

Of course, this sort of behavior, far from being rare, is typical of ACT-UP and Queer Nation—radical homosexual activist groups. Again, John Leo comments:

Among the accomplishments of ACT-UP are the disruption of speeches by New York Governor Mario Cuomo; the harassment of Pat Buckley at an AIDS benefit (she was being punished for what her husband, William F. Buckley, Jr., wrote about AIDS); the disruption of Catholic masses in New York, Washington, Los Angeles and Puerto Rico; the smashing of newspaper boxes to punish an editor in Sacramento and the vilification of a great many AIDS researchers and health workers. A government health official said, rather mildly: "When you listen to ACT-UP describe us as genocidal maniacs, you suddenly start to wonder why you are devoting your life to this problem."[38]

In political battles, threats and intimidation of Christians are constant phenomena. When an ordinance was going to be voted on in Oregon, which would have prohibited any aspect of the government from endorsing or recognizing homosexuality as a legitimate alternate lifestyle, flyers appeared on telephone poles warning people to vote against it. One showed the Christian *ichthus* fish being roasted on a stick over a fire. It read, "YOU BURN US, WE BURN YOU." Another flyer showed the same *ichthus* and warned Christians to vote against the ordinance, "OR WE SHOOT THE FISH." Another said, "CIVIL RIGHTS or CIVIL WAR. Your choice for a limited time only." Finally, another flyer said, with a hint of understatement, that voting against the ordinance "IS A GOOD IDEA." It also clarified what was meant by "civil war," by listing "QUEER KNIVES, QUEER GUNS, QUEER BULLETS, QUEER MISSILES, QUEER TANKS, QUEER TRENCHES, QUEER FIRE, QUEER WARFARE, QUEER PATRIOTS."[39]

But it is not just politicians or civil activists that the straight-bashers target. Dan Doell of Kansas City spends his time caring for AIDS patients at the Samuel Rodgers Community Health Clinic. Yet, despite his work on behalf of homosexuals, he has been denounced as a traitor and a "missionary of hate" by ACT-UP.[40]

Doell's offense is that he has repented of homosexuality. After being seduced as a teenager, Doell spent ten years of his life as a practicing homosexual before leaving the lifestyle. Now he exposes how arbitrary it is to base one's identity on one's sexual proclivities: "People don't stand on a street corner or wear a t-shirt that says, 'I'm greedy,' or 'I'm a gossiper. I was born that way and I'll never change.'"[41]

For his apostasy from the homosexual subculture, ACT-UP in Kansas City started a letter-writing campaign to get Doell fired from his job helping homosexuals. While they attempt to make sure no one can fire them for their own sexual practices, homosexuals seem all too ready to use intimidation to get others fired.

John Freeman, the executive director of Harvest Ministry in Philadelphia, is another person who once engaged in homosexuality but has since repented. His ministry has had great success in ministering to homosexuals and discipling them into a moral lifestyle. According to *World* magazine: "People who follow the 'once gay always gay' belief usually do not look at the choices in life, Freeman said. People are rarely consciously aware of when they started feeling same-sex attractions, but when actions are traced through the years, small choices began to accumulate."[42]

Claiming that homosexuality involves choice causes fury among homosexual activists. The office of Harvest has received numerous bomb threats. The staff has also received other hysterically hostile phone calls. In 1992, sixty demonstrators tried to force their way into the building and take over the offices. But for some odd reason, this doesn't count as a hate-crime.

Conclusion

"I have a vision and you're part of it."

That pledge, made to homosexual activists at a fund-raiser in Los Angeles, may prove to be Bill Clinton's best-kept campaign promise. The president's controversial push to open the US military to admitted homosexuals is just the tip of the iceberg in fulfilling that promise.

Even as President Clinton reneges on key campaign pledges made to much larger, mainstream constituencies, homosexuals are trusting that he will make good on his commitment to their political agenda.

"I have spent the last year of my life telling this community that our agenda will be accomplished through this administration," said gay activist David Mixner, a longtime Clinton friend and advisor who turned down a job in the Clinton administration so that he could lobby the president to fulfill his promises "in a timely manner."[43]

"There's a lot of support from the administration for the efforts of the gay and lesbian community," said Romulo "Romy" Diaz, Jr., the newly appointed deputy chief of staff and counselor to Energy Secretary Hazel O'Leary.[44]

Indeed, the president has made dozens of promises to the homosexual movement. In addition to lifting the ban on gays in the military, the president has pledged:

- He will issue an order barring "discrimination based on sexual or affectation orientation" in the federal government—effectively giving homosexuals protected "minority" status in the two-million-member federal bureaucracy.

- He will support a national "gay rights" bill. In fact, Clinton supports the bill to amend the Civil Rights Act by adding "sexual orientation" to the list of protected classifications. The bill would make homosexuals a protected "minority" akin to racial minorities and the disabled.

- He will implement affirmative action policies for homosexuals.

- He will support condom distribution programs.

- He will increase federal funding on AIDS research as part of a "Manhattan Project" to wage a real "war" on the disease.

- He will appoint an "AIDS czar" to implement all the recommendations of the president's National Commission on AIDS.

- He will oppose content restrictions for the National Endowment for the Arts, the Public Broadcasting Service, and National Public Radio.

- He will demand that the Justice Department crack down on "hate crimes" against gays and lesbians.

- He will oppose mandatory HIV testing in *all* circumstances.[45]

Making good on those promises, according to the *Washington Blade,* a homosexual tabloid in the nation's capital, he has already appointed more than two dozen homosexuals to high level positions in the administration.[46]

Thus, the movement is stronger than ever before, with more influence than ever before, and more opportunities than ever before.

But even amid such dismal news, there is yet reason for hope. As James Dobson of "Focus on the Family" has said:

One thing is absolutely certain: The withering wave of secular humanism we are now seeing will eventually collapse of its own weight. It always does. Why? Because it violates the basic laws of God. A nation *cannot* be blessed while killing its babies, destroying its families, "de-moralizing" its teenagers, and promoting perversion. Since we cannot immediately change the policies that distress us, our task for the moment is to engage actively in this great democratic system and then hold onto our convictions and our resolve until the turnaround occurs. That day *will* come—unless we are entering the final events of human history. Even in that eventuality, we are commanded "to occupy until I come" (Luke 19:13).[47]

And so we will. And so we must.

6

DEAD CERTAINTIES: MEDICINE

This is the man who classified the bits
Of his friends' hells into a pigeonhole.
He hung each disparate anguish on the spits
Parboiled and roasted in his own withering soul.[1]

ALLEN TATE

F ounded in 1639 by the antinomian followers of William Cod-
dington, the picturesque Aquidneck Island town of Newport has
from its earliest days been a center of antisocial dissent and counter-cul-
tural insurrection. Forcibly joined to the Providence and Warwick settle-
ments to form Rhode Island in 1649, the maverick town was known for
its fierce independence and its frequently ribald escapades.

Throughout the seventeenth and eighteenth centuries it was renowned as a haven for subversives and revolutionaries of any and every
stripe. Black market commerce thrived there as exiled Jewish merchants, vagabond pirates, and ambitious social subversives traded in
slaves, rum, prostitution, and opium. Though it developed as a fashionable vacation site for the rich and famous during the nineteenth century—it wasn't long after Cornelius Vanderbilt occupied his palatial
"Breakers" there that the names gracing the manors along Cliff Walk
and Ocean Drive began to read like a who's who of the American
elite—the community retained its radical flavor.

In 1919, several enlisted men were sent from the nearby Newport Naval Training Station to investigate reports of rampant immorality in the bustling resort town. According to George Cauncey, an assistant professor of history at the University of Chicago, they "found evidence of a highly developed and varied gay subculture in this small seaport community."[2]

Interestingly, not all of the participants in this subculture defined themselves as homosexuals:

> Relatively few of the men who engaged in homosexual activity, whether as casual participants in anonymous encounters or as partners in ongoing relationships, identified themselves or were labelled by others as sexually different from other men on that basis alone. The determining criterion in labelling a man as "straight" or "queer" was not the extent of his homosexual activity, but the gender role he assumed. The only men who sharply differentiated themselves from other men, labelling themselves as "queer" were those who assumed the sexual and other cultural roles ascribed to women; they might have been termed "inverts" in the early twentieth-century medical literature, because they not only expressed homosexual desire but "inverted," or reversed, their gender role.[3]

Thus, the subculture we would today define as homosexual was actually made up of two distinct groups. One group played roles culturally defined as feminine in sexual contacts—that is, "they allowed themselves to be penetrated."[4]

> The second group of sailors who engaged in homosexual relations and participated in the group life of the gang occupied a more ambiguous sexual category because they, unlike the queers, conformed to masculine gender norms. Some of them were heterosexually married. None of them behaved effeminately or took the "woman's part" in sexual relations, they took no feminine nicknames, and they did not label themselves—nor were they labelled by others—as queer. Instead, gang members, who reproduced the highly gendered sexual relations of their culture, described the second group of men as playing "husbands" to the "ladies" for the "inverted" set.

Not only were the masculine participants not considered "queer" by the homosexual subculture, but officials had no ready label for such people either:

The Navy, which sometimes grouped such men with the queers as "perverts," found it could only satisfactorily identify them by describing what they *did*, rather than naming what they *were*.[5]

One list of suspects, for example, labeled the men as "fairies" and other names, except for one who was simply reported to have penetrated the others.[6] Incredibly, the sailors who investigated and ultimately infiltrated the subculture actively engaged in penetrative sexual acts with the effeminates and then testified against them in court. Neither they themselves, the Navy, or the court thought that their sexual entrapment methods had compromised either their morals or the law:

> Navy officials never considered prosecuting the many sailors who they fully realized were being serviced by the fairies each year, because they did not believe that the sailors' willingness to allow such acts "to be performed upon them" in any way implicated their sexual character as homosexual. Instead, they chose to prosecute only those men who were intimately involved in the gang, or otherwise (as the Navy sought to prove in court) that homosexual desire was a persistent, constitutional element in their personalities, whether or not it manifested itself in effeminate behavior.[7]

Until defense attorneys accused the sailors of being just as perverse as the "queers" they were testifying against, no one ever thought to question their actions.

Several local ministers were outraged—testifying that there was no moral or legal difference between the sins of the accused and those of the accusers.

But apparently the Navy and the court saw it differently:

> The charges reflect the difference between the ministers' and the Navy's understanding of sexuality and human sinfulness . . . first, the ministers condemned the Navy for having instructed young enlisted men—the decoys—in "the details of a nameless vice," and having ordered them to use that knowledge. The naval authorities had been willing to let their agents engage in sex acts with the "queers" because they were primarily concerned about people manifesting a homosexual disposition rather than those engaging occasionally in homosexual acts. The Navy asserted that the decoys' investigative purpose rendered them immune from criminal prosecution even though they had committed illegal sexual acts. But the ministers viewed the decoys' culpability simply "as a moral question . . . not a technical question at all"; when the decoys had sex with other men,

they had "scars placed on their souls," because, inescapably, "having immoral relations with men is an immoral act." The sin was in the act, not in the motive or disposition.[8]

Sadly, the clergymen found that their view of sex was not accepted by very many others:

> The ministers' preoccupation with the moral significance of genital sexual activity and their fear that anyone could be entrapped may reflect the continued saliency for them of the Christian precept that *all* people were sinners subject to a variety of sexual temptations, including those of homosexual desire. According to this tradition, Christians had to resist homosexual temptations, just as they resisted others. . . . The fact that the ministers never clearly elucidated this perspective and were forced increasingly to use the Navy's own terms while contesting the Navy's conclusions may reflect both the ministers' uncertainty and their recognition that such a perspective is no longer shared by the public.[9]

Though the homosexual ideology as we understand it today did not yet exist, the Navy's concern with "dispositions" instead of sins demonstrates that a shift in worldview was already taking place—from a Christian to an Enlightenment paradigm.

The Disease Model

Under the guiding influence of Christianity, sexual "identity" was actually not ever an issue in Western civilization until very recently. Camille Paglia observes:

> Before the late eighteenth century, identity was determined internally by moral consciousness and externally by family and social class.[10]

But the Enlightenment began to change all that with its emphasis on the state of nature. Citing the early Enlightenment philosopher Michel Eyquem de Montaigne, Paglia writes:

> He lists his sexual habits as casually as his menus or bowel movements . . . The sex act is rhetorically equivalent to his taste in wines or reluctance to use silverware. . . . Montaigne's identity is not shaped by sex.[11]

By the time of Rousseau, however, that casualness had hardened, not only legitimizing sexual perversion, but alleging that such proclivities were actually inescapable. As Paglia puts it:

> The sexual revolution he has wrought is evident in the emergence of homosexuality as a formal category. From antiquity there were homosexual acts, honorable or dissolute, depending on culture and time. Since the late nineteenth century, there is homosexuality, a condition of being entered after searching or "questioning," a Rousseauist identity crisis. Modern psychology, following Rousseau, pessimistically roots sex deeper than does Judeo-Christianity, which subordinates sex to moral will. Our sexual "freedom" is a new enslavement to ancient necessity.[12]

Maggie Gallagher, in her brilliant postfeminist manifesto, likewise notes that until relatively recent times the homosexual did not exist as a category of being:

> We have not always been so woefully dependent on the sexual act itself. Two hundred years ago, for example, homosexuality did not exist. There was sodomy, of course, and buggery, and fornication and adultery and other sexual sins, but none of these forbidden acts fundamentally altered the sexual landscape. A man who committed sodomy may have lost his soul but he did not lose his gender. He did not become a homosexual, a third sex. That was the invention of the nineteenth-century imagination.[13]

Of course, the old moral standards were not immediately displaced by Enlightenment novelties. In fact, there was much grass roots resistance to such ethical anarchy. To counter this recalcitrance, proponents of the Enlightenment instituted a series of intermediary steps based on the emerging "human sciences."

The romantic philosopher and adamant atheist Friedrich Nietzsche—anticipating the emphasis of much contemporary psychology—explained the expansive humanist position on morality in his typically candid style:

> Today we no longer have any pity for the concept of free will: we know only too well what it really is—the foulest of all theologians' artifices, aimed at making mankind responsible. . . . Wherever responsibilities are sought, it is usually the instinct of wanting to judge and punish which is at work. The doctrine of the will has been invented essentially for the purpose

of punishment, that is, because one wanted to impute guilt. The entire old psychology, the psychology of will, was conditioned by the fact that its originators, the priests at the head of ancient communities, wanted for themselves the right to punish—or wanted to create for themselves the right to punish—so that they might become *guilty*: consequently, every act had to be considered as willed, and the origin of every act had to be considered as lying within the base consciousness. . . . Christianity is a metaphysics of the hangman.[14]

Most of the church's opponents were not as honest about their intentions at first. They did not attempt to openly contradict Christian teaching, as much as subtly work to undermine its foundations. Societal norms that had long been based on the Christian world-and-life view, were not necessarily altered but offered a new "more scientific" basis.

This "bait and switch" tactic was successfully accomplished to a substantial degree through the work of Sigmund Freud. Freud invented a bizarre Darwinian explanation for sexual behavior that "medicalized" sex and said that homosexuality "is assuredly no advantage, but it is nothing to be ashamed of, no vice, no degradation."[15] His great professional achievement was to make sex a scientific, rather than a moral problem, a biological issue of sickness and cure rather than sin and redemption. He essentially invented a therapeutic system designed to help people adjust to their perversions so that they could somehow function normally—all the while defying the standards of basic morality.

Thus, homosexuality, though still considered aberrant, was no longer considered a sin, but a sickness. Until as recently as 1970, the American Psychiatric Association's official publication, the *Diagnostic and Statistical Manual of Psychiatric Disorders,* listed homosexuality as a mental illness.[16]

From Disease to Dignity

By the beginning of this century modern psychology, sociology, and anthropology—having substituted science for Scripture as the authoritative basis for sexual morality—had secured their cultural tenure sufficiently to actually attack the Christian ethic directly. To a great degree this dramatic shift was the direct result of the work of Alfred Kinsey. In his 1948 *Report on Male Sexuality* he made many shocking claims— that some 37 percent of American men had at least one homosexual experience between adolescence and old age and that a full 10 percent were constitutionally homosexual. Though his findings have since been utterly repudiated—new studies show that actually less than 3 percent experiment with homosexuality and less than 1 percent persist in that lifestyle—Kinsey's findings were, for the most part, accepted by the scientific establishment and the dominant media culture.[17] That popular acceptance profoundly undermined the previously undisputable Christian notion that homosexuality is a deviant behavior.

Kinsey asserted that all forms of copulation—whether heterosexual, homosexual, or other—were essentially equal. All that mattered was the mechanical achievement of an orgasm. How it was achieved was substantially irrelevant. Since Kinsey's data showed that "everyone was doing it," he was able to make a convincing case that our society's ethical norms should be revised to match our society's actual practices. Homosexuality began to gain acceptance as a normal alternative lifestyle.

Despite the fact that his work was anything but scientific or ethical, Kinsey's research remains a cornerstone in the modern medical matrix of science and ethics. Dr. Judith Reisman of the Institute for Media Education, for instance, has demonstrated beyond any shadow of a doubt that Kinsey's methods were at best flawed, at worst entirely fraudulent, but that academic institutions have attempted to ignore the evidence and have thus steadfastly refused to revise their presuppositional assumptions.[18]

Apparently, by using carefully selected volunteers, Kinsey knowingly skewed his findings. When his coworker, the esteemed psychologist Dr. Abraham Maslow, pointed this out, Kinsey simply ignored the data, dismissed his friend, and removed all his works from the report's bibliography.[19]

In fact, according to Reisman, Kinsey's data was replete with intellectual dishonesty. For instance:

> The problem with Kinsey's "statistically common behavior" (or statistical morality), is that it was defined by using data from a sample of interviewees that was unrepresentative of society—that contained, in the case of the male sample, for example, a high percentage of prisoners and sex offenders. Present and former prison inmates made up as much as twenty-five percent of the group of men Kinsey used to find out what "normal" male sexual behavior was.[20]

In addition, many of Kinsey's experiments involved outright pedophilia in direct violation of laws against the sexual molestation of children. According to Dr. Reisman, Kinsey knowingly utilized experiments in the molestation of children of all ages, including babies. Kinsey's own narrative raises serious suspicion:

> Data on pre-adolescent climax come from the histories of adult males who have had sexual contacts with younger boys and who, with their adult backgrounds, are able to actually recognize and interpret the boys' experiences. . . . Nine of our adult male subjects have observed such orgasm. Some of these adults are technically trained persons who have kept diaries or other records which have been put at our disposal. . . . Orgasm has been observed in boys of every age from five months to adolescence. . . . In five cases of young pre-adolescents, observations were continued over periods of months or years, until the individuals were old enough to make certain that true orgasm was involved.[21]

How fortunate for him that Kinsey *just happened* to find "technically trained" child molesters who had kept detailed records of their activities and the responses of the children. No doubt most pedophiles go around with a notebook so that they can keep precise records of their criminal encounters in the hope that they might meet an interested sexologist who can use the information.

Sure they do.

In Kinsey's study of males there is a table that gives figures on the "speed of pre-adolescent orgasm." Readers are told that observations of how long it took children ranging "from five months of age to adolescence" to climax were "timed with second hand or stop watch."[22] So not only were these pedophiles carrying notebooks but they had stopwatches as well—or else they paid careful attention to their wristwatches while molesting these children.

Dr. Paul Gebhard, who was the coauthor with Kinsey of *Sexual Behavior in the Human Female,* later described the ethics and legality of Kinsey's studies:

> We have always insisted on maintaining confidentiality, even at the cost of thereby becoming amoral at best and criminal at worst. . . . An example of criminality is our refusal in cooperating with authorities in apprehending a pedophile we had interviewed who was being sought for a sex murder.[23]

Despite all this, Kinsey's research is still cited by the scientific community and the popular media as if it were divine revelation.

Cozy Accommodations

Joseph Schumpter once said, "The first thing a man will do for his ideals is lie."[24] Kinsey proved that.

Apparently the second thing he will do is accommodate. The American Psychiatric Association proved that.

In 1973, the organization removed homosexuality from its list of abnormal behaviors and mental illnesses. It did so not because it had made some new scientific discoveries or had found compelling clinical documentation of Kinsey's thesis. Rather, it merely capitulated to direct political pressure. Uncomfortable with the rather bizarre "lobbying" tactics of gay activists, the members of that esteemed professional association determined to yield to expediency rather than adhere to truth.

Thus the association ceased to define homosexuality as a mental illness simply and solely because, beginning at the 1970 convention, the activists launched an intense campaign involving disruption and intimidation to coerce doctors to change their diagnosis. Instead of standing their ground, the leaders of the association tried to placate the homosexuals with concessions. Within three years, the homosexuals gained enough clout to completely alter the long-standing designation. Ronald Bayer, in his *Homosexuality and American Psychiatry*—which is very sympathetic to the homosexual lobby—is surprisingly forthright about their methods in confronting the psychiatric profession:

> There was a shift in the role of demonstrations from a form of expression to a tactic of disruption. In this regard gay activists mirrored the passage of a confrontation politics that had become the cutting edge of radical and antiwar student groups. The purpose of the protest was no longer to make public a point of view, but rather to halt unacceptable activities. With ideology seen as an instrument of domination, the traditional willingness to tolerate the views of one's opponents was discarded.[25]

The activists were not concerned with convincing anyone; they were only interested in coercing everyone. They had, after all, given up any hope in "willfulness" and had adopted a philosophy of Darwinian determinism in both biology and social relations. This is seen in their abandonment of the term "sexual preference" for "sexual orientation."

Congressman William Dannemeyer explains:

> Soon the phrase "sexual preference" began to get in the way of the agenda. One of the arguments that had proven most successful in the political arena was the idea that homosexuality was inherited, that it was the result of genetic or hormonal factors that were beyond the control of the individual, that homosexuals had sex with one another because they had to. Thus it was "natural" and "normal" for them. . . . Sexuality could no longer be a "preference," since "preference" implied "choice," and the new line of argument was narrowly deterministic. So they came up with "sexual orientation."[26]

The modern homosexual movement desperately wants us to believe that homosexuality is no more subject to a person's control than eye color or skin pigmentation. Thus, they want to reinterpret the prohibiting of homosexual *acts* as the oppression of *persons* who they claim are "by nature" homosexual. Anyone who says otherwise is portrayed as an unscientific imbecile.

The Third Sex?

But what does the scientific evidence say?

Since science deals with the study of observable phenomena and providing them with objective explanations, its message is always in flux. Between the time we write this book and the time that you read it, who knows what "new evidence" will suddenly get broadcast on every news show and slapped on the cover of every newsmagazine in America? Even so, some phenomena are so self-evidently documentable that even the most compromised of observers have to concede their veracity.

Kinsey, for instance, for all his dishonesty, was forced to admit that there was scanty evidence for biological or genetic causes for homosexuality. As his partner Dr. Wardell Pomeroy stated, "Kinsey was confident that there was absolutely no evidence of inheritance" of homosexuality.[27] Dr. Pomeroy himself stated that "there is little or no evidence of the existence of such a thing as innate perversity."[28] Even Masters and Johnson, long known for their research in sexuality, have written that "the genetic theory of homosexuality has been generally discarded today."[29]

Nevertheless, recently some reports have appeared claiming to prove that one's "sexual orientation," is determined by one's biology. For example, a couple of years ago, papers carried headlines about genes being linked to homosexuality. A study of 115 homosexual men with twins and 57 with adopted brothers found that 52 percent of the homosexuals' identical twins were also homosexual, 22 percent of homosexuals' fraternal twins were also homosexual, and 11 percent of homosexuals' adopted brothers were homosexual. Psychiatrist Richard Pillard of Boston University, who performed the study with Northwestern University psychologist J. Michael Bailey, summed up the findings, saying that "the closer the genetic relationship, the more likely the relative is to be a gay male."[30] Dr. Gregory Carey of the University of Colorado agreed, saying, "Some of the earlier evidence suggested there was genetic effect, but the studies were not well done. This is something that really sort of clinches it."[31]

But as a student at Cornell University Medical College pointed out:

The study's findings support a genetic theory only if one accepts the premise, buried deep in the original article which appeared in *Archives of General Psychiatry,* that "because all types of relatives studied . . . were reared together they are all perfectly correlated for shared environment."[32]

But, as everyone knows, siblings are commonly treated quite differently by parents and others. It is easily conceivable that identical twins are more likely to be treated similarly and lead similar lives than adopted brothers. In fact, the study also found, though it was never publicized, that just over 9 percent of non-twin brothers of homosexuals were also homosexual.[33] If genetics is the factor then there should have been far more biological brothers who shared homosexuality than there were adopted brothers.

Recently, Bailey and Pillard released a similar study of lesbians— with predictably similar findings. The study consisted of 108 lesbians with identical and sororital twin sisters and 32 lesbians with adoptive sisters. Almost half of the identical twins were both homosexual, whereas 16 percent of the nonidentical twins and only 6 percent of the adopted sisters were both homosexual.

Newsweek reported:

Each pair grew up in the same home which neutralized the significance of parental influence on their sexuality.[34]

But again, this assertion is not only false, but exactly the opposite of the truth. Intriguingly, *Newsweek* didn't report on what percentage of lesbians' non-twin sisters were also lesbians.

Another much-reported study also appeared recently collaborating the first two. Dr. Simon LeVay claims he found a difference in the brains of homosexuals and heterosexuals—the homosexuals apparently have a smaller neuron group, called INAH3, next to the hypothalamus—using tissue from forty-one autopsies:

> Nineteen subjects were homosexual men who apparently died of complications of Acquired Immunodeficiency Syndrome—and one bisexual man was also included in this group. Sixteen subjects were presumed heterosexual men: six of these subjects were presumed heterosexual women. One of these women died of AIDS and five of other causes.[35]

To say that this experiment is exceedingly dubious is a gross understatement. LeVay is attempting to tell us that he has found a difference between the brains of homosexuals and heterosexuals when he actually has no idea if there are really any heterosexuals in his group. Even members of the homosexual movement found this to be too much to swallow. As an article in the *Bay Area Reporter* observed:

> It turns out that LeVay doesn't know anything about the sexual orientation of the control group, the 16 corpses "presumed heterosexual." A sloppy control group like this is . . . enough by itself to invalidate the study. LeVay's defense? He knows the controls are heterosexual because their brains are different from the HIV corpses. Sorry, doctor; this is circular logic. You can use the sample to prove the theory or vice versa, but not both at the same time.[36]

But it gets even worse. Dr. Paul Cameron has written:

> Three out of nineteen homosexuals had a larger INAH3 than the mean size for "heterosexuals" (the second largest INAH3 belonged to a gay) and three of sixteen "heterosexuals" had smaller INAH3 than the mean size for homosexuals . . . According to LeVay's theory, three of the "heterosexuals" *should* have been homosexual, and three of the "homosexuals" *should* have

been heterosexual. When you completely misclassify six of thirty-five, you don't have much of a theory.[37]

Nevertheless, this report was touted in the media as evidence that homosexuality is determined by birth—that people are "born gay" or "born straight."

Of course, everyone seems to want to forget that homosexuality is commonly practiced in prison by both men and women. As Charles Tittle wrote in *Society of Subordinates*:

> Graphic excerpts from interviews seemed to suggest that social organization among women prisoners had an institutional origin, since most of the participants had not been involved in homosexual liaisons prior to the prison experience and were evidently unlikely to continue homosexuality after leaving prison.[38]

Likewise, Tittle says, male inmates often indulge in this kind of homosexual activity while incarcerated. But it is a temporary aberration. Upon release they return to "normal" heterosexuality:

> For males, homosexual activity seemed to focus primarily on physical gratification; in many instances it represented a commodity for economic exchange; and it was likely a transitory act.[39]

Furthermore, while homosexual practices are common all over the world and throughout history, exclusively innate homosexuals are another matter. After noting the worldwide acceptance of pederasty, Camille Paglia notes:

> Exclusive sex or love affairs between adult males is another matter. This phenomenon is so rare, when we consider history as a whole, that it requires explanation.[40]

Perhaps the most compelling evidence of the erroneous logic of the determinism argument is the proliferation of associated homosexual groups organized around a myriad of other proclivities.

Time magazine, for example, recently ran an investigative piece entitled "Bisexuality: What Is It?" After three pages of blathering psychobabble and political correctness the article asks:

In the waltz of love, where do bisexuals fit in? Are they straight or gay, or a category unto themselves?[41]

According to *Time,* bisexuality is "a disturbing challenge," "a riddle," "a discomfort," and a "puzzle." That is because the homosexual ideology's doctrine of biological determinism and sexual classification ultimately means that either bisexuals are perverse heterosexuals who are willing to experiment against their nature, repressed homosexuals who just can't bring themselves to entirely break away from the opposite sex, or their own classification.

Thus, bisexuals, *Time* asserts, are caught in the middle of the homosexual-heterosexual polarization. One bisexual is quoted as saying, "Your feet are in both camps, but your heart is in neither. You have the opportunity to experience a kind of richness, but you constantly feel you have to make a choice."[42] But psychologist William Wedin, the director of New York City's Bisexual Information and Counseling Service, warns that bisexuals must not conform to either classification:

You create a sexual neuter if you attempt to wipe out one set of feelings over the other.[43]

In order to escape such an unthinkable fate, self-avowed bisexuals have formed their own self-help and political groups:

Fearful of stigma and discrimination, bisexuals across the U. S. and Europe are becoming more organized and politically active, networking in such groups as BiNet and BiPac. They are also challenging gay organizations, with which they have had an uneasy alliance, to focus more on bisexuality.[44]

Well, why stop with bisexuals? The homosexual "community" already includes any number of individuals who have variant tastes—sadomasochists, urinophiles, coprophiles, pedophiles, and zoophiles. And there is no reason to stop there. The article breezily informs us that our "sexual orientation" is a mixture of heredity and environment that is fixed by the age of five.[45]

The sad truth is that *Time* magazine feels free to lift the lid on pagan Pandora's Box to let bisexuality out into the open, apparently incognizant of what will follow it out of the darkness into the daylight. This is a common blindness among the proponents of various sexual liberation movements. Camille Paglia saw a similar myopia in a recent report on human sexuality commissioned by an independent American ethics commission:

> We are told that "those of us with varying degrees of social power and status must now move away from the center, so that other, more marginalized voices . . . may be heard." But the report picks and chooses its marginalized outcasts as snobbishly as Proust's Duchesse de Guermantes. We can move tender, safe, clean, hand-holding gays and lesbians to the center—but not, of course, pederasts, prostitutes, strippers, pornographers, or sadomasochists. And if we're going to learn from the marginalized, what about drug dealers, moonshiners, Elvis impersonators, string collectors, Mafiosi, foot fetishists, serial murderers, cannibals, Satanists, and the Ku Klux Klan? I'm sure they'll all have a lot to say. The committee gets real prudish real fast when it has to deal with sexuality outside of its feminist frame of reference: "Incest is abhorrent and abhorred," it flatly declares. I wrote in the margin, "No lobbyists, I guess."[46]

Ultimately, this is the question we must ask ourselves: in order to be enlightened and caring do we really have to ascribe *every* personality quirk—whether innocent or perverse—to genes and early childhood upbringing?

The Plague of Plagues

While the homosexuals' insistence that their estate is either the result of a natural inclination or an inherited disease is more than a little suspect, one thing is certain: their estate results naturally in an inclination for disease.

Most people immediately think of the Acquired Immune Deficiency Syndrome (AIDS) when the subject of disease is brought up in relation to homosexuality. But AIDS is only one of many diseases destroying the lives of homosexuals. Dr. Paul Cameron writes:

> The median age of homosexual men dying from AIDS is thirty-nine. The median age of homosexual men from all other causes is 42 (compared to seventy-five for married men generally and fifty-seven for unmarried men generally). Only one percent of male homosexuals die of old age, compared to seventy-three percent of men in general who live to be sixty-five or older. Less than three percent of all homosexuals are over the age of

fifty-five. The median age of lesbians at death is forty-five compared to seventy-nine for married women and seventy-one for unmarried women generally.[47]

The very nature of the homosexual lifestyle is destructive of health and hygiene. Besides the fact that gay socializing revolves around drinking, drugs, and late-night carousing, gay sexuality inevitably involves brutal physical abusiveness and the unnatural imposition of alien substances into internal organs—orally and anally—that inevitably suppresses the immune system and heightens susceptibility to disease. In fact, gay sex is a veritable breeding ground for a panoply of diseases. Among them are colonitis, an excruciating inflammation of the mucus membrane; mucosal ulcers in the rectum; and Kobner's phenomenon, a psoriasis of the rectum and genitals.[48] In addition, a group of rare bowel diseases, previously considered tropical, are now epidemic in urban gay communities.[49] Popularly dubbed "Gay Bowel Syndrome," these afflictions include:

- Amebiasis, a colon disease caused by parasites, causing abscesses, ulcers, and diarrhea;

- Giardiasis, a parasitic bowel disease, again causing diarrhea and sometimes enteritis;

- Shigellosis, a bacterial bowel disease causing severe dysentery;

- Hepatitis A, a viral liver disease, which its victims can spread to others through handling food, and even through the water splashed on toilet seats.[50]

Even the more conventional sexually transmitted diseases are especially acute among homosexuals. Tony Marco writes that male homosexuals are "fourteen times more likely to have syphilis than heterosexuals, eight times more likely to have had hepatitis A or B," and "hundreds of times more likely to have had oral infection by STDs through penile contact."[51] Furthermore, female homosexuals are "nineteen times more likely to have had syphilis than their heterosexual counterparts, twice as likely to have had genital warts, four times as likely to have had scabies, seven times more likely to have had infection from vaginal conflict, twenty-nine times more likely to have had oral infection from vaginal contact, and twelve times more likely to have had an oral infection from penile contact" than female heterosexuals.[52]

This prevalence of venereal disease has been admitted by homosexuals. As Marco points out:

> In an April 21, 1976 article in *The Advocate,* homosexual author Randy Shilts stated the following: One half of America's syphilis carriers are gay. Gays are five times more likely to have syphilis than straights. Shilts estimated that 150,000 gay men at that time were syphilitic. Using Kinsey's dubious ten percent of the population figure for gay presence in American society, Shilts' estimate was that a gay man would "contract gonorrhea" every thirty seconds of that year.[53]

Not only do the perversity and promiscuity of the homosexual life make the average homosexual much more likely to be infected by any one of a number of conventional STDs, it also makes him extremely susceptible to AIDS.

As Camille Paglia comments:

> The first medical reports on the disease killing male homosexuals indicated men most at risk were those with a thousand partners over their lifetime. Incredulity. Who could such people be? Why, it turned out, everyone one knew.[54]

Indeed, Paglia is forthright in placing blame for the rise of AIDS and other sexually transmitted diseases on the pansexual left:

> I, like, hit the wall. All of us did, I think, in some way, from the sixties, either from the drugs or from the sex, which led to the sexually transmitted diseases of today. People don't want to talk about this. They want to say, "No, there's no connection between behavior and the sexual diseases of today." But please, let's not be stupid. Let's not rewrite history. There is a terrible reality which we must face. I've said it again and again: "Everyone who preached free love in the Sixties is responsible for AIDS." And we must accept moral responsibility for it. This idea that it was somehow an accident, a historical accident, a microbe that sort of fell from heaven is absurd. We must *face* what we did.[55]

Dr. Luc Montagnier of Paris' Pasteur Institute, who first isolated what is now called the Human Immunodeficiency Virus, that is generally supposed to be the retro-viral cause of AIDS, has come up with a theory that backs up Paglia's assertion. He thinks that promiscuity among homosexuals may have created the disease in the first place. *Time* magazine revealed:

> Montagnier supported a controversial theory that mycoplasma, a bacterium-like organism, is the trigger that turns a slow-growing population of AIDS viruses into mass killers. According to Montagnier, the explosion of sexual activity during the 1970s fostered the spread of a hardy drug-resistant strain of mycoplasma. HIV, meanwhile, lay dormant in Africa. The AIDS epidemic began, Montagnier speculates, when the two microbes got together, perhaps in Haiti.[56]

Furthermore, homosexuals, for the most part, are still engaging in such dangerous behaviors. A study of 655 homosexual men in San Francisco found:

> Knowledge of health guidelines was quite high, but this knowledge actually had no relation to sexual behavior.[57]

In fact, the idea that homosexuals should limit their promiscuous encounters has proven to be entirely untenable to homosexuals:

> The recommendation that gay men limit themselves to committed monogamy was discussed and found to lack creativity . . . and to reflect the simple insensitivity of an outsider approaching the gay world.[58]

At the 1990 International Conference on AIDS, researchers concluded that "simply being informed about the AIDS virus does not make people any more likely to practice safe sex."[59] Though there appeared to be a brief increase of "safe sex" precautions during the previous four years, there was evidence it was only temporary. It was revealed that men under the age of thirty were twice as likely to engage in unprotected anal sex as older men. Furthermore, nineteen percent of homosexuals and bisexuals who practice "safe sex" admitted backsliding into even more unsafe behavior over a four-year period.[60]

One jarring example of this kind of promiscuity continuing in the face of AIDS and other diseases, was cited by homosexual author and journalist, Frank Browning:

Any residual doubts about the place of sex—hot, sweaty, raunchy sex—in the AIDS-prevention campaign disappeared at the fifth global conference on AIDS in Montreal. For five days the discos were packed with gay doctors, nurses, activists, and researchers shamelessly cruising one another. A nearby bathhouse was doing a land-office business. A *%&#-off club posted promotional fliers in the conference exhibit hall. And in the middle of the hall a monitor was showing a "safe sex" video sponsored by a West German health agency. The video was played and replayed all day long for two days, and there seemed never to be fewer than twenty-five or thirty viewers—men, women, straight, gay—gathered about the screen in a fidgety semi-circle. Two men who, except for their blondness, might have been Michelangelo's models were demonstrating a wide array of "safe" erotic possibilities.[61]

Far from being concerned, however, Browning actually defends the debauchery that took place:

Most of my straight friends have told me that they cannot fathom how an AIDS conference can also be a sex carnival. My standard, flip response has frequently been "But what else could it be?" The lust of men for other men has not evaporated just because funerals and memorial services have become nearly as ordinary as an evening of theater. To a considerable degree, those gay men who have committed themselves to trench duty in the battle against AIDS have done so exactly because they would not and, perhaps, could not relinquish passion to death. Simple survival as whole human beings forced them to face AIDS squarely and to determine how much they would permit it to control them.[62]

Homosexuals not only are notorious for exposing unknowing partners to the dangers of getting AIDS, but some show absolute scorn for doctors who tell them that they must stop having sex. Homosexual journalist Randy Shilts writes of Gaetan Dugas, an airline attendant who many believe to be "patient zero," the person who first brought AIDS to America:

Gaetan Dugas' eyes flashed but without their usual charm, when Selma Dritz bluntly told him he must stop going to the bathhouses. The hotline at the Kaposi's Sarcoma Foundation was receiving repeated calls from people complaining of a man with a French accent who was having sex with people at various sex parlors and then calmly telling them he had gay cancer.

It was one of the most repulsive things Dritz had heard in her nearly forty years in public health:

"It's none of your *&#@%#! business," said Gaetan. "It's my right to do what I want with my own body."

"It's not your right to go out and give other people disease," Dritz replied, keeping her professional calm. "Then you're making decisions for their bodies, not yours."

"It's their duty to protect themselves," said the airline steward. "They know what's going on there. They've heard about this disease."

Dritz tried to reason further but got nowhere.

"I've got it," Gaetan said angrily. "They can get it too."

Gaetan Dugas was not alone among AIDS patients at the bathhouses. Bobbi Campbell, who had made his self-avowed role as a Kaposi's Sarcoma Poster Boy into something of a crusade, was also going to bathhouses, although he denied having sex with people. Gay doctors had told Dritz that several other patients went as well.[63]

Indeed, throughout his massive work on AIDS, *And the Band Played On,* Shilts shows that time and time again homosexuals have lashed out at those who have called attention to their inherently unhealthy lifestyle. In fact, they have even become incensed at concerned fellow homosexuals who try to warn them. Back before AIDS was more positively identified, homosexual author and playwright Larry Kramer attempted to spread the word about the prevalence of certain diseases:

By late December 1981, Larry was embroiled in controversy over the outspoken role he had assumed in trying to alert New York gays to Kaposi's Sarcoma. "Basically Kramer is telling us that something we gay men are doing—drugs or kinky sex or both—is causing Kaposi's Sarcoma," wrote Robert Chesley, a Manhattan gay writer, in one of his several letters attacking Kramer in the *New York Native.* "Being alarmist is dangerous. We've been told by such experts as there are that it's wrong and too soon to make any assumptions about the cause of Kaposi's Sarcoma, but there's another issue here. It is always instructive to look closely at emotionalism, for it so often has a hidden message which is the *real* secret of its appeal. I think the concealed meaning of Kramer's emotionalism is the triumph of guilt: that gay men *deserve* to die for their promiscuity. . . . Read anything by Kramer closely. I think you'll find the subtext is always: the wages of gay sin is death. . . . I am not down-playing the seriousness of Kaposi's Sarcoma. But something else is happening here, which is serious: gay homophobia and anti-eroticism."[64]

Shilts writes that Kramer's urgent warnings were thus universally scorned by the prevalent homosexual community:

The antipathy, Larry Kramer knew, surrounded the book he had written about gay life in New York. . . . Everything, from its title, *Faggots,* to its graphic descriptions of hedonism on the Greenwich Village-Cherry Grove axis had stirred frenzy among both gay reviewers and the people whose milieu Larry had set out to chronicle. Manhattan's only gay bookstore had banned the novel from its shelves while gay critics had advised readers that its purchase represented an act inimical to the interests of gay liberation.[65]

To make matters worse for Kramer, he turned out to be something of a prophet. At the climax of his novel, his protagonist told an unfaithful lover that his profligate promiscuity needed to stop "before you %*#@ yourself to death."[66] Once AIDS began to break out among homosexuals and Kramer tried to warn them, they ridiculed him. As Marshall Kirk and Hunter Madsen write:

For trying to get gay men to believe what they preferred doggedly to ignore—that AIDS is, indeed, spread sexually, and that promiscuity had become a guarantee of early death—he was denounced by large numbers of New Yorkers as "alarmist" and "sex-negative"; he was also accused of saying "I told you so." The fact that he had every *right* to say it cut no ice.[67]

The fact is that hostility to basic health guidelines is quite common among homosexuals. This is understandable to a certain degree since homosexual behavior is so unhealthy—to follow such guidelines means to give up the lifestyle altogether. Instead, homosexuals contend that the doctors are being "sex-negative"—a terrible sin according to what passes for ethics among homosexuals. In Frank Browning's *The Culture of Desire: Paradox and Perversity in Gay Lives Today*—a book praised as "absolutely cutting edge," "honest," "provocative and intensely personal," and "engrossing" by numerous prominent homosexual activists—the author evaluates the medical advice given about avoiding AIDS:

Though the scientists were too considerate, too worldly to charge homosexuality outright as a violation of nature, they offered a variant: If you press the body beyond its limits *as an organism,* you will violate the rules of self-preservation. It was within that *"bionormative"* context that "safe sex"—as a slogan, as an approved list of behaviors—was born.[68]

Browning goes on to rail against "repressed" physicians who advise homosexuals to cease to practice certain "sexual indelicacies." He finds their warnings against "fisting" especially repugnant:

By 1984, it was clear that AIDS was the result of some microbe—HIV, and possibly other agents as well—that could be transmitted via blood and semen. Yet what, it was asked, could possibly be transmitted from the fist to the rectum so long as the fist was clean or, at least, gloved in rubber? Researchers answered that inappropriate objects inserted in the rectum could cause abrasions or fissures through which HIV could later gain entry. But by the same logic, a mishap during *any* anal sex could also result in cuts and abrasions that, if the area were later exposed to blood or semen, could lead to HIV infection.[69]

It is simply unimaginable to Browning that shoving a fist and forearm up into a man's rectum could be relatively more dangerous than other practices. Instead, he has to come up with a psychological explanation for the advice of these scientists:

Dr. Joseph Sonnabend, a long-time and controversial researcher on the epidemic, believes the confusion about anal penetration is the result of heterosexual anxiety over the use of the rectum as a site of sexual pleasure: "The rectum is a sexual organ, and it deserves the respect that a penis gets and a vagina gets. Anal intercourse is a central activity, and it should be supported, it should be celebrated." Instead of having instructed people to repress anal sexual desire, Sonnabend argues, AIDS advisers and public-health officials ought to have taught them how to explore that desire within hygienic, HIV-prophylactic constraints.[70]

Here then is the inverted paradox of the "safe sex" myth. Not only is it not safe, it isn't even sex.

The Myth of Heterosexual AIDS

The message to the public on AIDS has been mind-bogglingly contradictory. On the one hand, we are told that "AIDS isn't a gay disease" since it is caused by a contagious virus that will infect anyone, whether or not he is homosexual. On the other hand, any attempt to quarantine those infected with the Human Immunodeficiency Virus—or HIV—has been condemned as somehow "homophobic." It is almost as if treating AIDS like any other contagious, deadly disease is just a disguised attack on homosexuals.

Although AIDS never actually became a widespread epidemic as originally predicted—infection and mortality rates apparently were vastly overestimated and in fact the "epidemic" crested as long ago as 1988—it has nevertheless been an effective tool for promulgating the homosexual agenda in the public schools, the political arena, and the popular media.[71]

But the question remains: can "anyone" *really* get AIDS? Are we all at risk? Will the AIDS epidemic soon spread to the population at large?

In a word, no.

The fact is, this disease—or as Dr. Franklin E. Payne has argued, this "spectrum of diseases"—is undeniably "lifestyle-specific."[72] In other words, it is almost exclusively contained within identifiable and behaviorally predicated at-risk communities.

What that means is simply that AIDS is fundamentally a lifestyle disease.

Of course, the publicity surrounding the disease has given quite the opposite impression. In their book on governmental and institutional misinformation, *Official Lies: How Washington Misleads Us,* economists James Bennett and Thomas DiLorenzo write that, at first, AIDS was recognized for what it was—a homosexual disease. In fact, the original name given to it was GRID—Gay Related Immuno-Deficiency:

By 1986, the party line had changed. Talk of the "gay cancer" was stifled. AIDS, we were told, was no longer a disease of promiscuous homosexuals, drug addicts, and an occasional unlucky hemophiliac or recipient of tainted blood. It could happen to anyone. As *Cheers* star Ted Danson lectured the folks out in TV-land in one of numerous government-sponsored commercials, "Anyone. Any type can get it." Such taxpayer-financed television and radio commercials were furnished free of charge to thousands of stations. In one, a blond young man says, "If I, the son of a Baptist minister, living in a rural area, can get AIDS, anybody can." Well, yes, if that son of a

Baptist minister shared a needle with an infected person, or got a transfusion of infected blood, or engaged in receptive anal intercourse with an infected person. But the commercial implied that AIDS was rather like lightning: it is as likely to strike a ninety-two-year-old virgin maiden as a twenty-four-year-old promiscuous homosexual junkie.[73]

Of course, heterosexuals *have* occasionally been infected by AIDS. Kimberly Bergalis, for example, was apparently infected by her homosexual dentist, David Acer. Her tragic death is especially sinister since a close friend of Acer's later claimed that he purposefully infected some of his patients in order to raise concern about homosexual AIDS.[74]

Nevertheless, as Dr. Robert Root-Bernstein, the associate professor of physiology at Michigan State University writes:

We are left with the observation that apparently 1,700 of his other patients walked out of his office HIV free.[75]

And then there is the strange case of Earvin "Magic" Johnson. The star of the Los Angeles Lakers and the Olympic Dream Team has gone from being a basketball celebrity to being an AIDS celebrity. When Johnson announced he was HIV-positive, he was immediately heralded as proof-positive that "typical" heterosexuals could get AIDS. Even if Johnson was infected by heterosexual contact, however, it is hard to imagine how his case could be considered "typical." As one writer commented:

How curious to be told that, if a man who apparently had thousands of sex partners can get AIDS, we are all at risk.[76]

But a heterosexual "epidemic," by definition, must involve the infection of more than just occasional isolated individuals. Michael Fumento, the author of *The Myth of Heterosexual Aids,* has written:

Infection data collected from military applicants and blood donors continue to show that infections from heterosexual transmission remain extremely low.[77]

To make his point, Fumento points out:

More white males are diagnosed with breast cancer each year than the number who have been diagnosed with heterosexually transmitted AIDS during the entire epidemic.[78]

According to Dr. Root-Bernstein, figures from the Center for Disease Control show:

The number of AIDS cases attributed to heterosexual contact is only six percent (10,011 cases as of June 1991) in the United States and slightly less in Canada and Great Britain.[79]

And even those numbers may be grossly inflated. Dr. Joyce Wallace of the Foundation for Research on Sexually Transmitted Disease in New York testifies:

In my experience, many men will go so far as to say they've had sex with a dog before they'll admit to sex with another man.[80]

In New York she and others have had much experience with men who have to be interviewed repeatedly before admitting to receptive anal intercourse or drug abuse.

Michael Fumento writes that in Florida a CDC re-evaluation of "heterosexual cases" found:

At least thirty percent belonged to other categories and most of the remaining seventy percent were Haitian, leaving almost no room for native born homosexuals.[81]

Since all the CDC's statistics on heterosexual AIDS only tell us that the victims *claim* to have been infected through heterosexual practice, it is likely that the numbers are substantially lower.

Furthermore, it is often questionable whether discussion of heterosexual AIDS is adequately understood. It often turns out that the man and woman involved in transmission were involved in other high-risk behaviors such as anal intercourse.

Victor Lorian, a physician at the Bronx Lebanon Hospital Center in New York has stated:

The risk of AIDS has more to do with sexual practice than sexual orientation. Homosexual men are singled out as being at high risk. Indeed they are, but not because of homosexuality per se, but because they practice anal sex. Heterosexuals who practice anal sex are at the same high risk. . . . Warnings that anal intercourse is dangerous are valid, can be understood by most lay people, and could save many lives.[82]

Partner studies over the years have only confirmed such conclusions. Again, Fumento writes:

These are studies of couples in which one member is HIV-positive and the other originally is not, and they reveal that, over a period of years, about twenty percent of all women sleeping with HIV-positive men eventually become positive themselves. The only study of partners in which the woman was already infected indicates that of sixty-one infected women and their seventy-one originally uninfected male partners, only one male ever became infected—in what can only be termed a wild relationship, with over a hundred bouts of penile and vaginal bleeding between them.[83]

Though a number of women continue to face a serious risk from HIV-positive men—and undoubtedly many have already suffered great personal tragedy—the fact is that there is virtually no possibility of a heterosexual epidemic. As Fumento points out:

For an epidemic to spread, each case—be it of influenza, bubonic plague, or HIV—must generate at least one new case. Otherwise, the epidemic will slowly die off with its individual victims. Where it takes five old cases to equal one new case, as in male-to-female transmission of HIV, you don't have epidemic spread. Where it requires about fifty old cases to equal one new case, as in female-to-male transmission of HIV, you don't have epidemic spread.[84]

The HIV Confusion

It is taken for granted by the vast majority of the populace that the so-called Human Immunodeficiency Virus—or HIV—causes AIDS. Indeed, the consensus seems so overwhelming that to question whether the virus actually causes the disease appears tantamount to questioning whether Galileo was right about the sun being the center of the universe—which it isn't.

All the current AIDS research we hear about in the mass media appears to be aimed at protecting the body from this virus. All the "safe sex" advertising we see is aimed at preventing a person from getting infected with the virus. The viral cause of AIDS is not considered a theory—it is a dead certainty.

But it's not.

Despite all the campaign rhetoric, the research emphasis, and the standard treatment focus, there are a large number of medical scientists who have their doubts.

In fact, there have been prominent researchers who have had their doubts from the beginning. Randy Shilts reveals that when the immunodeficiency syndrome was first identified, many in the Food and Drug Administration were skeptical of the allegations made about the disease by the Center for Disease Control:

> Many at the FDA did not believe that this so-called epidemic of immune suppression even existed. Privately, in conversations with CDC officials, FDA officials confided that they thought the CDC had taken a bunch of unrelated illnesses and lumped them into some made-up phenomenon as a brazen ruse to get publicity and funding for their threatened agency. Bureaucrats have been known to undertake more questionable methods to protect their budgets.[85]

Though the CDC was eventually able to create a public consensus that HIV is the sole cause of AIDS, for many in the scientific community, those serious doubts remain.

How can reputable scholars in the field question the consensus of the majority? Or conversely, how could so many experts actually be so far off the mark?

According to Dr. Robert Root-Bernstein, the answer is found in an ironic combination of professional pride and professional gullibility. He recounts how Dr. Carl Djerassi, the so-called father of the birth control pill, Dr. Gordon Burns Woodward, a Noble Prize winner, Dr. Gilbert Stork, and Dr. Lewis H. Sarett created a counterfeit research paper in 1952. At that time, there was much interest in cortisone research, leading one of the medical scientists to joke that any paper with the words "synthesis of cortisone" was certain to be published. This comment lead them to concoct an elaborate practical joke in the form of a counterfeit research paper which claimed to have synthesized cortisone from "neohamtogenin," a fictitious substance supposedly derived from New Hampshire maple syrup:

The fictitious cortisone paper was attributed to two non-existent chemists and was replete with fake literature citations. At the crucial synthetic step—a step that would have revolutionized chemistry—they used the dodge that details (which they did not have) would be given in a subsequent paper. In other words, "take the proof of our assertion that this chemical reaction has been carried out on faith"—something no scientist should do. The trap was laid; the clues were placed; and on the last day of the conference, Woodward read his non-sensical communication to his audience of chemical experts.[86]

What was the response of these experts? Did they laugh at this joke? Did they accuse Woodward of fraud? On the contrary, they took it deadly seriously. In fact, "at one point a Swiss chemist actually stood up to claim priority for the non-existent discovery."[87]

The paper was read at Harvard only a few days later. Once again, the audience fell for the joke, hook, line, and sinker:

> Not a single graduate student or research fellow doubted the reality of Woodward's presentation. Stork, one of the co-authors of this farce, was so irritated by the gullibility displayed by his colleagues that he attempted to point out the fraud to a group of the Harvard attendees—without success. Djerassi and the others were taken aback by this turn of events and did not submit their article for publication for fear that it might actually be taken as a serious contribution to the literature.[88]

On April 23, 1984, HIV was declared to be the cause of AIDS before any scientific paper had established that fact. At the same press conference, Margaret Heckler, then secretary of Health and Human Services, announced government funding for research on HIV.[89] Shortly thereafter, AIDS was defined by the CDC as "an amalgamation of any number of conventional immuno-repressive diseases in addition to the presence of antibodies to HIV."[90]

But contrary to the CDC's definition, it eventually became obvious that the disorder in the immune system could occur without the presence of HIV. According to *Time* magazine, at the Eighth International AIDS conference:

> Scientists reported cases of people who have an AIDS-like condition but have not been found to be infected with HIV.[91]

Though they caused furor in the media, these cases were not new. As Dr. Franklin E. Payne has said:

> Over the last three years, the . . . CDC had identified six cases. The Amsterdam conference was just the first time that these findings had been made public—not by the CDC, but another researcher.[92]

And that is just the half of it. Not only can people get AIDS without contracting HIV, but those exposed with HIV do *not* always get AIDS. Dr. Root-Bernstein, for example, points out that initially many predicted huge outbreaks of AIDS among prostitutes and their clients. It simply never happened.[93]

Interestingly, from at least 1872, there have been documented cases of mysterious diseases that we now recognize as AIDS.[94] Why was there no "epidemic" until just recently?

The Duesberg Hypothesis

Perhaps the most outspoken critic of the HIV-AIDS consensus has been Dr. Peter Duesberg. A member of the National Academy of Sciences, a pioneer in cancer-gene research, and the first to map the genetic structure of retro-viruses—of which HIV is one—Dr. Duesberg is certainly no quack.

On the contrary, Dr. Robert Gallo, the famed National Institutes of Health virologist, once called Duesberg "brilliant and original" and said he had "a rare critical sense which often makes us look twice, then a third time, at a conclusion that many of us believed to be foregone."[95] Of course, that was before Duesberg started proclaiming medical heresies about HIV and AIDS. Now Gallo refers to his opinions as "baloney," saying, "He does not know what he is talking about."[96] Indeed, Gallo admits that he cannot respond to Duesberg without "shrieking."[97]

It is not surprising that Dr. Gallo is so jumpy on the subject. Shortly after he publicly claimed credit for discovering the allegedly deadly HIV retro-virus, an international brouhaha erupted. It seems that a certain Dr. Luc Montagnier and his coworkers in France had previously isolated the retro-virus. The good doctor had repeatedly consulted with Gallo concerning the discovery, supplying his colleague with the full details of his as yet unpublished research. Apparently Gallo then stole the idea and took credit for the work. After a brief investigation—realizing that he'd been caught with his hand in the cookie jar—Gallo admitted that Montagnier had "discovered the virus first." Thus, according to medical reporter Lane Cochrane, the powerful and influential Gallo had "lied for the sake of yet greater fame and fortune."[98]

But these scandalous goings-on were just the tip of the iceberg. Root-Bernstein writes:

> Moreover, the Gallo team has revealed other unsavory characteristics. Salahuddin has been found guilty of business fraud, and Gallo and several other team members are under investigation by the U.S. government for possible frauds of various types including improper business practices, creating false data, and claiming priority for a discovery that rightly belonged to the French.[99]

Thus, it is not surprising that when Dr. Duesberg began to debunk even more of the Gallo orthodoxy, that he was met with stiff opposition. His former admirer became his archnemesis. Before he even realized what was happening, his research grant from the National Institutes of Health was allowed to expire.

"It was a sanction, clearly," Duesberg told Tom Bethell of *The American Spectator*:

> NIH couldn't say, "Here's one of our star scholars and he's saying we are wasting three billion dollars on HIV research."[100]

So is the medical establishment really wasting 3 billion dollars on HIV research? According to Duesberg's theory: probably so.

His research indicates that AIDS is in fact not caused by this powerful new retro-virus but by a host of new lifestyle behaviors—lifestyle behaviors that have become widespread since the seventies. People who are diagnosed with AIDS, he argues, are always engaged in immunosuppressive behaviors. These include heavy alcohol and drug use as well as oral-anal ingestion, anal intercourse, and fisting—all prevalent practices among urban homosexuals.

He cites the fact that throughout the seventies and early eighties, homosexuals commonly used amyl-nitrite inhalants, or "poppers," in bathhouses for their aphrodisiac and stimulant effect:

> This use declined when homosexuals themselves recognized their danger, and the incidence of Kaposi's has since declined likewise.[101]

Additionally, continual bouts of venereal disease repeatedly fought off with antibiotics can lead to immuno-suppression. So can regular and prolonged malnutrition. These are common ingredients in the lifestyles of "fast-lane" homosexuals.[102]

Other groups susceptible to AIDS are often subject to similar immuno-suppressive factors apart from any virus, Duesberg asserts. Surgery is commonly immuno-suppressive due to the trauma, the anesthesia, and the transfused blood. Obviously, he maintains, transfusions also greatly affect hemophiliacs, who must then use blood clotting agents— which in turn further exacerbates their level of immuno-suppressive stress. And of course, he says, the great majority of so-called AIDS babies are born to drug addicts and prostitutes, persons whose lifestyles would have resulted in immuno-suppression of their babies when they were still in the womb.

Even AIDS treatment programs have proven to be immuno-suppressive, according to Duesberg. AZT, for example, is highly toxic and specifically destroys the body's remaining immune system.[103] Thus, people who are treated with the drug typically die of opportunistic infections associated with AIDS.[104]

Though not in complete agreement with all the details of Duesberg's hypothesis, Dr. Root-Bernstein challenges the scientific community and public policy experts to reconsider the commonly held view of AIDS. In his remarkable book *Rethinking AIDS: The Tragic Cost of Premature Consensus,* he argues that the disease has largely been misunderstood—and that adamant pronouncements are premature at best, dangerous at worst. He writes:

> AIDS did not suddenly appear out of nowhere among otherwise completely healthy young men and women whose only immuno-suppressive risk was HIV. This is a myth. The people who developed AIDS during the initial phases of the epidemic, like the people who continue to develop AIDS today, were and are, virtually without exception, unhealthy, immuno-compromised people even before they contract HIV and long before they develop AIDS. The evidence for this statement existed in 1980. It is, if anything, even more apparent today.[105]

We know that AIDS is a lifestyle disease. We know that it is fairly well contained within certain behaviorally predicated communities. We know that HIV is usually present but sometimes not. We know that it has not spread to epidemic proportions. And we know that it is more often than not deadly.

Beyond that though, we know very little whatsoever. All the rhetoric, all the lobbying, and all the media hype in the world cannot change that.

Thus, Dr. Root-Bernstein offers a passionate plea for medical and moral sanity:

> I could not care less whether AIDS is caused by HIV, by HIV with appropriate co-factors, or by non-HIV causes. I do care that we investigate all of these possibilities and reject all but one of them. Until research is done on the alternatives, we do not know and we cannot know for certain, the cause or causes of AIDS. Assurance in science comes only through elaborating as many possible explanations as can be imagined for a phenomenon and eliminating all that can possibly be eliminated. That process has not been employed in AIDS research. The door on alternative possibilities was prematurely closed before anyone had a chance to see how many rooms there were, let alone explore their treasures. We must research them now or risk basing our AIDS policies, prophylactic measures, and medical treatments on incomplete and ineffective knowledge.[106]

Conclusion

Looking at how medical science is used to understand the alleged causes of homosexuality as well as the many health problems associated with it, one finds a common thread: rationalization.

We are told that homosexuality is an inborn condition, not a chosen lifestyle. Likewise, we are told AIDS is the result of a random virus, not a behaviorally related disease. The former proposition is absolutely false; the latter, probably so.

In the medical realm—as in the cultural, the educational, and the political realms—the debate over homosexuality has tended to ignobly transcend the facts.

Perhaps it was a similar kind of calumny that provoked H.L. Mencken, the pundit of the last generation, to comment:

> All the durable truths that have come into the world within historic times have been opposed as bitterly as if they were so many waves of small pox, and every individual who has welcomed and advocated them, absolutely, without exception, has been denounced and punished as an enemy of the race. In that kind of atmosphere, with that kind of

publicity, the connoisseur of the higher political mountebankery cannot fail to gain the upper hand.[107]

If that be the case, may we be ever vigilant to rectify the situation—lest lives be lost needlessly, heedlessly, lest our culture be torn asunder by the blind impulses of a bacchic orrus.

7

TROOP IMMORALE: MILITARY

What country shall we conquer, what fair land
Unman our conquest and locate our blood?
We've cracked the hemispheres with careless hand!
Now, from the Gates of Hercules we flood.[1]

ALLEN TATE

I n 1945, a young naval recruit was sound asleep during his first night aboard ship when he was abruptly disturbed. "The awakening was sudden and panic-filled. A hand was caressing my leg, running up the inside of my thigh. A dim figure ducked away as I lashed out, kicking, swinging a fist and striking the air. There was no more sleep that night."[2]

Kevin McCrane, now a retired businessman living in New Jersey, had been drafted into the navy at the close of World War II. In January he was assigned with four others to the USS *Warrick,* a cargo carrier. The day after McCrane was sexually harassed, the ship set sail for Honolulu. "But the excitement was gone, at least for me. At the end of a long day riding the sea's rolling swells, I took a twelve-inch, box-end wrench from the engine room and retreated to my berth. Hanging onto the wrench under my pillow, I slept."[3]

Had this been the only incident, McCrane's voyage would have been bad enough. But it only got worse. On his fourth day at sea, he went to the *Warrick's* post office. There he was "warmly" received by the second-class petty officer in charge. Perhaps too warmly: "Grinning broadly, he stepped back from the counter, dropped his dungarees, fondled himself and made an obscene invitation. I walked away."[4]

He went to the third-class petty officer on his watch to report the sexual harassment. "He laughed at what I told him," remembers McCrane. "He told me to watch out."[5]

The new recruits aboard the *Warrick* soon compared notes and discovered that all of them had recently been "accosted, patted," and "propositioned." They soon learned that there was only safety in numbers: "Though we were in different divisions, we flocked together for meals, averting our eyes when one of *them* leered in our direction."[6]

Avoiding "them" became a constant struggle for sexual survival aboard the ship:

> There were five such aggressive homosexuals that we knew of on board this ship with almost 250 men. They were all petty officers. Their actions were enough to poison the atmosphere on the *Warrick*. Meals, showers, attendance at the movies, decisions about where you went on the ship alone—all became part of a worried calculation of risk.[7]

The consequences for failing to evade these officers and getting caught by them alone were quite severe. McCrane received news from a tearful fellow recruit that "the smallest and most vulnerable" of the recruits had been caught in the paint locker and forcefully sodomized.

At the end of the voyage the ship was given a new executive officer who summarily transferred each of the homosexual officers off his ship. This caused the crew to break out into spontaneous cheering.[8]

Even in the Military

Sadly, McCrane's awful experience was not entirely unique. Despite the historic ban on homosexuals in the military, there have been a number of homosexual rape incidents through the years in all four branches of the American armed forces. Try as it may, the military simply has been unable maintain absolute immunity from the forces of moral disruption infecting the society at large. Though the men and women who have served our nation with courage and distinction in the military have more often than not been among the best America has to offer—paragons of virtue, discipline, and uprightness—they have sometimes also been among the worst America has to offer. Though the recruitment process has always been designed to screen out those less desirable elements, like everything else in this poor fallen world, it is a fallible process.

That process has proven to be particularly fallible when it comes to identifying and disqualifying homosexuals from military service. And it appears that the evidence is not merely anecdotal. A decade ago the *American Journal of Psychiatry* reported on a study of homosexual assaults in the military, several of which were carried out by more than one attacker.

For example:

One sailor was referred for a psychiatric evaluation two weeks after being physically and sexually abused when he was given a "blanket party" the first day he reported on board his ship. A blanket party consists of several men forcibly wrapping the victim in blankets so that he is unable to determine exactly who is sexually abusing him.[9]

After that attack, the sailor was subjected to an even more humiliating and perverse assault:

One week later he was given a "greasing" by three shipmates. A greasing involves stripping the individual naked and massaging him with a thick black grease used to lubricate heavy machinery. In some cases a flexible tube is forced through the victim's anus and into his rectum. The tube is connected to a cylindrical reservoir filled with the lubricating grease. The reservoir and tube resemble a large hand-driven pump. The contents of the piston-driven reservoir are then pumped into the victim.[10]

Unlike the blanket party, this time the victim clearly knew who his assailants were. He reported them and judicial action was taken. This did not end his torment, however. The sailor began to get threats from other shipmates that he would be physically hurt, raped again, or even thrown overboard once the ship was sent out to sea. Finally, he went to the ship physician and begged him to get him off the ship. "Get me to my dad and out of here, away from this," he pleaded. "My dad can help me."[11]

Another sailor was also assaulted twice:

He was overpowered by three shipmates, beaten, and dragged to a secluded food storage area on the ship. Although he resisted, his attackers undid his pants and attempted anal intercourse, but he was able to escape. He was threatened if he reported the incident. He then left his duty station without authorization. This broke a one-and-a-half-year record of excellent adjustment to the Navy. He returned after a few weeks and was again attacked by the same three in the same area. This time he was beaten, stripped of his clothing, held down by two of the three, and raped anally by the third. He again left on unauthorized leave.[12]

The sailor found it almost impossible to deal with the homosexual assault. His state of mind became increasingly worse:

His service adjustment continued to deteriorate. He was frightened about returning to the ship for fear he would be assaulted again. When he did return, he carried a wrench for protection wherever he went. He was afraid to tell anyone of the assault for fear of being labeled "queer" and being discharged from the navy for homosexuality. When he did inform his superiors, no one believed him. Since the initial attack, he reported being increasingly angry and experiencing insomnia with nightmares and dreams reliving the assault.[13]

Other studies have revealed similarly shocking incidents. One soldier was held down by three sailors while a fourth one raped him. Fear deterred him from reporting the incident. Afterwards he wrote: "I feel so uncomfortable around anyone in the military. I can't sleep. Mostly, I don't feel like a man no more. . . . I would like to get away from these people. Help me please."[14] Another serviceman, trapped on a ship out at sea, was sexually assaulted by three crewmen. He attempted suicide afterwards, and after the cruise was over, he left the military without permission.[15] Still another naval serviceman was raped by five U.S. marines. As a result, he developed a fear of sexual molestation as well as a passionate hatred for the navy.[16]

Though certainly isolated and extreme, these incidents offer evidence of a kind of ongoing covert homosexual counterculture within the military.

Making the Military Safe for Homosexuality

What is amazing about these incidents is that they all occurred while the ban on homosexuals in the military was in full force. Indeed, Dr. Peter Goyer and Dr. Henry Eddleman wrote that they became interested in studying homosexual rape in the military because they were surprised at the number of such cases:

> For the past few years we have worked in a psychiatric outpatient clinic serving a predominantly male population of active-duty Navy and Marine Corps personnel. In our work with this unique population we became aware that we were evaluating more adult male victims of male assault than had been suggested in the medical literature.[17]

But it could have been worse. Much worse.

In fact, despite the surprising frequency of homosexual incidents that such studies have recently uncovered, they are still very much the exception rather than the rule. Dr. James Gilmore, another researcher who has studied the problem of sexual assaults in the military, has said:

> There is no doubt that in a semi-closed community like the armed forces, tragic incidents like these can and do occur—sometimes more often than we'd like to admit. But there is also no doubt that they are ameliorated in both their frequency and intensity by an enforced code of conduct. The very fact that homosexual activity within the four branches of the service has always been forced underground is testimony to the efficacy of the ban—in both inhibiting that activity and protecting innocent parties from libertine unrestraint. Without such a code, violations of persons, property, and propriety would undeniably escalate beyond bearable limits—and commanding officers would be left without appropriate disciplinary recourse. The ban is a necessary hedge of protection against any further moral or strategic erosions.[18]

But now it appears that Bill Clinton wants to do away with that "hedge of protection" altogether. In fulfillment of his campaign pledge to lift the ban on homosexuals in the military, he announced in the first full week of his presidency plans to bring gays in the military out of the closet.[19] Past presidents have expressed their desire to use the military to make the world safe for democracy. President Clinton apparently wants to use democracy to make the military safe for homosexuality.

Needless to say, the president's position has provoked a fire storm of protest including a deluge of irate letters, phone calls, and telegrams—more than at any other time in recent memory. According to one national survey, nearly 82 percent of Americans opposed lifting the ban.[20] Another poll determined that 89 percent of the military community was opposed the president's plan and more than 45 percent said that they would consider leaving the military altogether if it were actually implemented.[21]

A number of prominent military leaders even began to speak out boldly against their new commander in chief's intentions—a real rarity in the disciplined world of the armed forces.

Brigadier General Richard Able asserted:

> Privacy. Freedom of association. Sexual preference. Individual rights. All these and many, many, more are freedoms near and dear to every American. They should be. They've been paid for dearly, in civil and military conflicts over the past 200 years. Here's the rub: Each of them also happens to be a privilege at least partly set aside by every man and woman who voluntarily chooses to enlist or accept a commission in the armed services of the United States. Take sexual preference. Sexual preference, by definition, is a matter of choice—clearly unlike race or gender, which are matters of birth. Sexual preference is a choice civilian Americans are free to make, but a choice set aside under current law and regulations by all those who choose military service. There are reasons for that—good and well-thought out reasons rooted in military law and time-proven fundamentals that make for battlefield effectiveness. These fundamentals still are valid today and for the days to come.[22]

He went on to assert:

> Yes, Uncle Sam is looking for more "proud, brave, loyal and good Americans" who are willing to serve our nation and honestly put its interest first. America has many needs for truly selfless, tireless servants. Those who answer the call, but who also have chosen an open homosexual lifestyle can, and clearly would, serve our nation best outside the military services.[23]

Likewise, Lieutenant Commander Gerry Carroll has said:

> I can imagine few things more destructive to the military—upon which we have depended for two hundred years for the safety and security of our way of life—than to try to integrate homosexuals into it. Forcing young servicemen and women to live in the close contact of others with a chosen lifestyle that is utterly repugnant to them will ultimately put this nation in the position of countries like France or the Netherlands, who speak loudly but carry no stick at all.[24]

Debunking the "civil rights" aspect of the issue the Chairman of the Joint Chiefs of Staff, General Colin Powell has asserted:

> Skin color is a benign, non-behavioral characteristic. Sexual orientation is perhaps the most profound of human behavioral characteristics. Comparison of the two is a convenient but invalid argument.[25]

Once the president's advisors and handlers began to realize the magnitude of the opposition arrayed against him, they suggested that he offer a "compromise," in which he promised not to lift the ban by immediate executive order, but would wait six months and then remove it only if warranted. In the meantime, he would direct the military to disregard the ban on homosexuals.

Not surprisingly, that kind of transparent dodge did not make anyone too terribly happy. Indiana's conservative senator Dan Coates declared:

> Given the president's fixed position, it appears that any compromise or negotiation on this issue is doomed before it starts. A six-month period of study when the conclusion is foregone is simply a political cover.[26]

Meanwhile, liberals were disappointed that the president caved in—however insincerely—to political pressure. Massachusetts Congressman Gerry Studds, himself an avowed homosexual complained:

> The administration needs to decide whether or not it has the courage to lead, to decide to do right, even when the decision is unpopular or difficult. I fear for this administration should the president break his promise.[27]

But such a fear is likely unfounded. After all, throughout his campaign for the White House, Bill Clinton not only promised to lift the ban on homosexuals in the military, he promised the passage of hate crimes legislation, preferential hiring codes, and massive increases in AIDS funding.[28] And although he has shown absolutely no qualms about breaking his promise of a middle class tax cut, he knows that he must appease the homosexual activists if he has any hope of holding his tenuous coalition together. Besides that, the president has no desire to see—in the words of one homosexual columnist who apparently doesn't mind resorting to base stereotypes when it serves his purposes—"upwards of one million raging queers storming the White House."[29]

Martin Mawyer, the president of the Christian Action Network, is convinced that Clinton will do everything he can to keep his promise to the homosexual community because:

> There is a tremendous activism behind it, whereas middle-class America that wants that tax-cut is not organized. They don't do kiss-ins, tie-ins; they don't break into buildings like the militant homosexuals do. And I don't think President Clinton wants to draw attention anymore than he's already getting from the gay-rights activists by breaking this pledge.[30]

Activists rarely have the ability to translate their concerns into actual votes—the movement's attempt to flood Washington with a million gays and lesbians in April 1993 was an embarrasing failure—but they continue to wield a tremendous amount of influence anyway.[31] Thus says Mawyer:

> When President Clinton made these pledges to the homosexual community, it was for money and it was for activism because that's what these individuals can bring. They never could bring votes.[32]

Details, Details

The fact that Clinton's position was from the beginning ideologically driven rather than pragmatically informed means that the inherent problems involved in lifting the homosexual ban were never really taken into consideration. Such "meddlesome details" as the disposition of military housing, spousal benefits, pensions, health care, and on-base social clubs have simply been delegated to Defense Secretary Les Aspin.

Robert Morrison, a lobbyist on Capitol Hill for the Family Research Council, has said that even Washington Democrats have complained about the nagging but neglected complications involved in lifting the ban:

> Senator Sam Nunn has raised a number of questions, such as: What are you going to do about formal military dress balls? Are you going to allow military officers to come and dance with homosexual dates?[33]

It seems that ideological pronouncements rarely take such mundane practical concerns into account.

"The next thing you have to face," Morrison said, "is quotas for advancement, promotion, and retention."[34] Though the military does not have an official quota system, it does have something perilously close to it. When a minority member of the armed forces is turned down for a promotion, the promotion board must be prepared to defend that decision, perhaps several times. In contrast, promotion boards generally do not have to answer to anyone if they bypass a white male. Since lifting the ban on homosexuality has already been compared to ending discrimination against minorities, there is every reason in the world to expect homosexuals would get that same kind of preferential treatment.

Even if all these problems were resolved, Clinton would still face a huge obstacle. He originally promised to overturn the ban by executive order. As columnist Jeffrey Hart has argued:

> Nothing can be more fundamental to the Constitution than its first article, which defines the powers of the president and the Congress. Article 1, Section 8, says, "Congress shall have power . . . to make rules for the government and regulation of the land and naval forces." It is spelled out quite clearly. . . . Thus Congress, by law, enacted the homosexual ban. It was Clinton's delusion that he can overturn such a law "with the stroke of a pen." . . . It makes one wonder what they have been teaching at the Yale Law School.[35]

If the president attempts to issue an executive order he will be flatly violating the Constitution's separation of powers. Nevertheless, not one to be hampered by such extraneous legal technicalities as the Constitution's mandated separation of powers—we've got to get rid of gridlock after all—Clinton is determined to pursue his goal of an omni-sexual army. Regardless of the details.

Making the Argument

Lieutenant Colonel John Eidsmoe, a renowned military historian and constitutional scholar has said:

> Those who believe homosexuals should be allowed into the armed forces present their arguments in many forms. But essentially their arguments boil down to three: First, homosexuals have a right to serve in the armed forces without discrimination. Second, the ban is unenforceable since homosexu-

als serve "undercover" anyway. Third, the ban deprives the armed forces of a valuable manpower resource.[36]

According to Eidsmoe, all three arguments are self-evidently erroneous. Of the first, he says:

Military service has never been regarded as a constitutional right. Serving in the armed forces is a privilege which the government may grant or withhold, and sometimes a duty which may be required, but not a right which the citizen can claim as absolute. The privilege may be terminated when the best interest of the military and the best interest of the nation so require. Many long-term soldiers are discovering this today as reductions in force go into effect.[37]

Similarly, he argues that "unenforceability" is a fallacious argument:

The fact that homosexuality persists does not mean the ban is unenforceable or should be repealed. The same reasoning could be applied to other problems: Murder is against the law, but people still commit murders; therefore the ban on murder is unenforceable and should be repealed. Theft is against the law, but people still commit theft; therefore the ban on theft is unenforceable and stealing should be made legal. Child abuse is against the law, but people still abuse children; therefore the ban against child abuse is unenforceable and should be repealed. In a more serious vein, the same argument is made for legalization of drugs. Obviously, our criminal laws have not eliminated all murders, thefts, or abuse of children or drugs. That does not mean these laws are failures. The real question is, how much more murder, theft, child abuse and drug abuse would take place if these practices were legalized?[38]

Finally, he says, the manpower issue is moot as well:

Undoubtedly, the armed forces will lose some good performers if the ban is retained. Undoubtedly, the cost of replacing these people will be substantial, though not as high as the General Accounting Office has estimated. However, these costs might be more than offset by the other increased costs that could result from legalizing homosexuality. One of these might be increased cost of health care through an AIDS epidemic and other prevailing risk-correlated diseases.[39]

Despite the fact that each of these arguments has been publicly dissembled—in testimony before Congress, in military court hearings, in public debate, and in the press—the advocates of lifting the ban persist in cloaking them with respectability.

Thus, just as he has avoided dealing with the administrative details, Les Aspin—the president's point-man on the issue—has steadfastly avoided facing the facts.

According to Morrison, Aspin is not much better connected to reality than his erstwhile boss:

> He was one of Robert McNamera's so-called whiz kids. That's how he got his start in Washington. Described in the sixties by author David Halberstand as "The Best and The Brightest," these are the people who were so convinced of their own brilliance that they moved ahead quite arrogantly, some think, to put this country into Vietnam. Well into that debacle they continued to offer us computerized projections of how and when we would win.[40]

There was certainly an element of that same arrogance, observed Morrison, in Aspin's testimony before the Senate Armed Services Committee concerning the gay ban:

> He said, among other things, that we would have problems with this ban even if Bush had been re-elected. The courts, he asserted were giving us trouble about it.[41]

But the fact is, the military has never lost a case in court on this issue. Never. Not once.

According to Eidsmoe, that remarkable record—maintained against innumerable tests—has stood for good reason:

> It is due to the fact that homosexuality does not involve a "fundamental" constitutional right. As the Supreme Court noted in *Bowers v. Hardwick,* certain rights are considered more "fundamental" or "preferred" than others; such rights are entitled to "heightened judicial protection."[42]

Which rights are "fundamental"? Justice White, speaking for the 5–4 majority in *Bowers v. Hardwick,* offered the following explanation:

> Sodomy was a criminal offense at common law and was forbidden by the laws of the original thirteen States when they ratified the Bill of Rights. In 1868, when the Fourteenth Amendment was ratified, all but 5 of the 37 States in the Union had criminal sodomy laws. In fact, until 1961, all 50 States outlawed

sodomy, and today, 24 States and the District of Columbia continue to provide criminal penalties for sodomy performed in private and between consenting adults. . . . Against this background, to claim that a right to engage in such conduct is "deeply rooted in this Nation's history and tradition" or "implicit in the concept of ordered liberty" is, at best, facetious.[43]

Thus, Eidsmoe concludes:

Since homosexuality does not involve fundamental rights or suspect classifications, a state does not need to show a compelling interest that cannot be achieved by less restrictive means in order to win in court. All the state needs to demonstrate is that its policy on homosexuality has a *rational basis*. Furthermore, the Armed Forces is in an even stronger legal position on this issue than are the state governments, because of the unique demands of military discipline. In *Goldman v. Weinberger, Greer v. Spock*, and many other cases, the Supreme Court has recognized that the armed forces have an interest in maintaining good order and discipline; and when the military insists that a certain policy is necessary to maintain order and discipline, the Court generally defers to that military determination even where fundamental rights are involved—and as noted earlier, no such fundamental rights are involved here. Despite all of the media publicity surrounding court cases, the plain fact remains that every court of final jurisdiction that has ever ruled on the armed forces' exclusion of homosexuals has upheld the basic policy as constitutional.[44]

Of course, if at first you don't succeed, try, try again. And try the homosexual advocates do.

Courting Disaster

In fact, one convenient way liberals have always found to get around the inconvenient details of legal precedent and political reality is an activist use of the courts. Thus it came as no surprise when just as Clinton seemed hopelessly mired in his quixotic crusade to lift the homosexual ban, he received a big boost from the judicial branch. Federal District Judge Terry Hatter, a Carter appointee, suddenly ruled that the longstanding—and oft court-tested—ban was actually unconstitutional. Without even a hint of complicity, White House press secretary Dee Dee Myers told reporters that she did not expect the ruling to be appealed by the Justice Department.[45]

Tom Jipping, the Director of the Center for Law and Democracy of the Free Congress Foundation, said he is not surprised that the decision is not being appealed:

> It fits the administration's policy preference, after all. And political expediency wins out over legality every time at the White House.[46]

Even so, the battle is hardly over. Because the ruling only applies to the district under the current presiding judge's jurisdiction—which includes only portions of California—it does not directly affect national policy-making standards. At least not yet.

William Carson, a legal scholar at the Kellogg Institute, believes that the administration may attempt to string together several such precedents and thus fabricate a "legal necessity" argument that would effectively neutralize public opinion and political opposition. "The courts can be used as a kind of trump card," he says.

> If the president can somehow showcase a few manipulated test cases—and no one in the higher courts calls his hand—he may actually be able to win this battle by default. He just needs a handful of cases to turn the tide in his favor—and despite twelve years of conservative appointments, enough liberal judges are still out there to deliver sufficient precedents.[47]

Colonel Ronald Ray, a Marine Reserve Judge Advocate, has pointed out that such limited court precedents are often maneuvered onto the books as "sweetheart suits."[48] These were quite common, he says, during the Carter years when litigators involved in public-interest suits were "actually in sympathy with the plaintiffs."[49] As a result, the government's attorneys deliberately lost their cases as a means of bypassing the more laborious political process. "They were using the courtroom to legislate minority positions that they couldn't win in the legislature."[50]

Politicalization

G. K. Chesterton, the great English journalist during the first half of this century, used to quip, "There are very few things in life that a little politics can't make worse."[51] It seems that is more true today than ever before.

Mark Jefferson, a highly decorated Vietnam veteran, "became aware of several" homosexual incidents during his twenty years of service in the Air Force. "I am strongly opposed to lifting the ban," he says:

> It is not because I think the present system is perfect—not at all. I think much can be done to improve the fairness and consistency of enforcement.[52]

He argues that politicizing the military—whether in campaigns, cabinets, or courts—does little to either solve the grave moral crisis of our times or meet the strategic needs of our world:

> It is more than just a little imprudent to usher in sweeping changes in the nature and the character of the military community merely to satisfy the political whims of the moment. You don't have to go very far or look very hard to find something in America today that politics has irreparably harmed. Surely we're not foolish enough to inflict that kind of dystopic social engineering on the armed forces too.[53]

Surely not.

Even if the American people were inclined to make sweeping changes in the nature of American life, the fact is, they would not trust the government to make them. It is not that the American people believe that politics is insignificant. It is just a recognition that in the end, there are any number of things in life that are *more* significant. And effective.

Most of us would have to agree with the astute political axiom of commentator George Will:

> Almost nothing is as important as almost everything in Washington is made to appear. And the importance of a Washington event is apt to be inversely proportional to the attention it receives.[54]

Eugene McCarthy, once the darling of the New Left, also said it well:

> Being in politics is like being a football coach; you have to be smart enough to understand the game, and dumb enough to think it's important.[55]

Intuitively, we know that is true. Thus, according to political analyst E. J. Dionne:

Americans view politics with boredom and detachment. For most of us, politics is increasingly abstract, a spectator sport barely worth watching.[56]

He says that since the average voter "believes that politics will do little to improve his life or that of his community, he votes defensively," if at all.[57] As odd as it may seem, that kind of robust detachment and nonchalant insouciance is actually close to what the Founding Fathers originally intended. They feared ongoing political passions and thus tried to construct a system that minimized the impact of factions, parties, and activists.[58] Citizens of the Republic were expected to turn out at the polls to vote for men of good character and broad vision—and then pretty much forget about politics until the next election.[59] Gouvenor Morris—who actually wrote the first draft of the Constitution and was instrumental in its acceptance—said:

The Constitution is not an instrument for government to restrain the people, it is an instrument for the people to restrain the government—lest it come to dominate our lives and interests.[60]

Similarly, Patrick Henry stated:

Liberty necessitates the diminutization of political ambition and concern. Liberty necessitates concentration on other matters than mere civil governance. Rather, whatsoever things are true, whatsoever things are honest, whatsoever things are just, whatsoever things are pure, whatsoever things are lovely, whatsoever things are of good report; if there be any virtue, and if there be any praise, freemen must think on these things.[61]

Suspicious of professional politicians and unfettered lobbyists as well as the inevitable corruptions of courtly patronage and special interests, the founders established a system of severe checks and balances designed to de-politicize the arena of statecraft and its attendant statesmanship.[62]Though there was disagreement between various factions about how much "energy," or "lack thereof," government ought to exercise, there was universal agreement about what John DeWitt called the peripheral importance of institutional action to the actual liberties of daily life.[63] Thus the founders worked together to insure that the republican confederation of states was free from ideological or partisan strife.[64] Though they were not entirely successful, for much of our history American life has been marked by the distinct conviction that what goes

on next door is of greater immediate concern than what goes on in
Washington.

To politicize military life by imposing alien standards not only con-
travenes the essence of "the doctrine of military necessity," but of the
essence of the American covenant as well.[65]

Legislating Morality

The question of admitting open homosexuals into the military has to do
with fundamental moral principles; debate on the subject necessarily
must focus on the ideas that underlie the governmental system of the
United States. The great mastermind of Prussian military dominance,
Carl von Clausewitz, once asserted:

> Moral elements are among the most important in war. It is a paltry philoso-
> phy if, in the old fashioned way, one lays down rules and principles in total
> disregard of moral values.[66]

Sadly, that is an argument that the new military theorists in the homosexual movement would like to ignore. David Mixner, the head of
ANGLE, the powerhouse behind the "Lift the Ban" lobbying effort and
the organizer of the homosexual March on Washington, believes that all
such arguments are "irrelevant in modern America."[67]

He and his high-dollar comrades argue that to impose such standards of honor, discipline, and decency in the military—or anywhere else
in American life—is "a violation of the spirit of American democracy"[68]
and a "contradiction of our most basic constitutional tenets."[69] Any attempt to do so is instantly dubbed as "bigotry,"[70] or "zealotry and insensitivity,"[71] or "the excesses of religious fundamentalism."[72] You simply
"can't legislate morality," they say.[73]

Not so. Morality is, as pastor and statesman Dr. D. James Kennedy
has so often asserted, precisely "the only thing you *can* legislate."[74]
That's what legislation *is*. It is the codification in law of some particular moral concern—generally so that the immorality of a few is not forcibly inflicted on the rest of us.

Murder is against the law because we recognize that the premedi-
tated killing of another human being is a violation of a basic, fundamental moral principle—a moral principle traditionally held dear in this
country: the sanctity of human life. Theft is against the law because we

recognize that taking someone else's belongings without permission is a breach of another one of our most basic and fundamental ethical standards: the inviolability of private property. The fact is, *all* law is some moral or ethical tenant raised up to social enforcabilty by the civil sphere.

Thus, the question in the debate on lifting the ban on gays in the military is not "*Should* we legislate morality?" Rather, it is "*Whose* morality should we legislate?" Or, put another way, "*What* moral standard will we use when we legislate?"

There was no ambivalence among the founders of this nation on that question. The standard of morality that they unhesitatingly codified into law was the Bible. The Declaration of Independence was a document carefully informed by a scriptural notion of law.[75] The Articles of Confederation were thoroughly entrenched in the biblical worldview.[76] The Constitution was undeniably a Christian legal document.[77] The Federalist Papers were born out of the great verities and profundities of liberty found only in the Bible.[78] The Bill of Rights would have been inconceivable apart from the moral standard wrought by God in His Word.[79] Every major document, every major consultation, and every major institution the Founding Fathers forged from the fires of freedom to create and guide our remarkable legal system was a conscious affirmation and imitation of Biblical ideals, values, standards, ethics, and morals.

Now to be sure a number of other historical and philosophical influences helped to shape the course of American law: Justinian's Roman Civil Law, Alfred the Great's *English Common Law,* Charlemagne's Rule of the Franks, William Blackstone's *Commentaries,* and John Locke's *Second Treatise on Civil Government.* However, each of these, in turn, was itself derived, at least in part, from the Biblical standard.[80]

Robert Goguet, in his authoritative history of the development of judicial philosophy in this country, argued that the Founding Fathers' legislation of biblical morality was more than simply a reflection of their personal faith or cultural inheritance. It was a matter of sober-headed practicality:

> The more they meditated on the Biblical standards for civil morality, the more they perceived their wisdom and inspiration. Those standards alone have the inestimable advantage never to have undergone any of the revolutions common to all human laws, which have always demanded frequent amendments; sometimes changes; sometimes additions; sometimes the re-

trenching of superfluities. There has been nothing changed, nothing added, nothing retrenched from Biblical morality for above three thousand years.[81]

The Framers were heavily influenced by the writings of Thomas Hooker, founder of the city of Hartford in the Connecticut colony and learned Puritan divine, and thus they agreed wholeheartedly with his oft-quoted maxim on the wellspring of law and order in society:

> Of law there can be no less acknowledged than that her seat is in the bosom of God, her voice in the harmony of the world. All things in heaven and on earth do her homage; the very least as doing her care, and the greatest as not exempt from her power. Both angels and men, and creatures of what condition soever, though each in a different sort of name, yet all with one uniform consent, admire her as the mother of their peace and joy.[82]

John Jay was one of the most influential of the Founding Fathers and the first Chief Justice of the Supreme Court. He too affirmed the necessity of virtue for the proper maintanence of civil stability and order:

> No human society has ever been able to maintain both order and freedom, both cohesiveness and liberty apart from the moral precepts of the Christian Religion applied and accepted by all the classes. Should our Republic ere forget this fundamental precept of governance, men are certain to shed their responsibilities for licentiousness and this great experiment will then surely be doomed.[83]

James Madison, our fourth president, primary author of the Bill of Rights, and champion of liberty throughout the founding era, echoed that sentiment:

> We have staked the future of all our political institutions upon the capacity of each and all of us to govern ourselves, to control ourselves, and to sustain ourselves according to the Ten Commandments of God.[84]

Again and again that same refrain was repeated. The men who framed our nation had a particular goal in mind: building a free society of responsible and morally upright men and women. They wanted to build a "city on a hill," a "light to the nations," and a godly legacy. They were willing to give sacrificially—often giving their very lives and livelihoods—to achieve those ends.

As a result, America became a *great* nation. It became great because its character was rooted in Christian morality. As Alexis de Toqueville asserted, "America is great because America is good."[85]

Rights and Responsibilities

A brash and cavalier attitude to America's goodness and moral stalwartness is perhaps the single most distressing trait of the current assault on the military ban on homosexuals. In the name of civil liberties, the gay activists have pressed forward a radical agenda of moral corruption and ethical degeneration.

Ironically, their brazen disregard for decency and their passionately undeterred defense of perverse impropriety has actually threatened our liberties because it has threatened the *foundation* of those liberties.

Homosexual activists want the privileges of America bestowed upon the citizenry as an unearned, undeserved, and unwarranted *entitlement*. Apart from the grace of God, though, there simply cannot be any such entitlement in human societies. Great privileges bring with them great responsibilities. Our remarkable freedom has been bought with a price. And that price was diligence, sacrifice, and moral uprightness. The homosexual agenda—driven and supported by America's fanatically twisted fringe—is a pathetically self-defeating crusade that has confused liberty with license.

Gardiner Spring, the eloquent pastor-patriot during the early nineteenth century in New York, persuasively argued that the kind of free society America aspired to be was utterly and completely impossible apart from moral integrity:

> Every considerate friend of civil liberty, in order to be consistent with himself must be the friend of the Bible. No tyrant has ever effectually conquered and subjugated a people whose liberties and public virtue were founded upon the Word of God. After all, civil liberty is not freedom from restraint. Men may be wisely and benevolently checked, and yet be free. No man has a right to act as he thinks fit, irrespective of the wishes and interests of others. This would be exemption from all law, and from the wholesome influence of social institutions. Heaven itself would not be free, if this were freedom. No created being holds any such liberty as this, by a divine warrant. The spirit of subordination, so far from being inconsistent with liberty, is inseparable from it.[86]

Similarly, Aleksandr Solzhenitsyn, the exiled Russian novelist, historian, and Nobel laureate, stated:

> Fifty years ago it would have seemed quite impossible in America that an individual be granted boundless freedom with no purpose but simply for the satisfaction of his whims. The defense of individual rights has reached such extremes as to make society as a whole defenseless. It is time to defend, not so much human rights, as human obligations.[87]

Homosexual activists and their sundry supporters desire to divorce rights from responsibilities. The danger is that if they ever do entirely succeed, rights will become extinct:

> There is a way that seems right to a man, but its end is the way of death. (Proverbs 14:12)

Conclusion

The modern homosexual activists desperately want to legislate morality. *Their* morality. Or should we say, their *immorality*. Despite all their high-sounding civil rights rhetoric—limiting majorities to protect minorities—they are intent on remaking American culture in their own image, beginning with the military.[88] They are intent on holding the majority captive to the fancies, follies, and foibles of the minority.

Freedom is a rare and delicate thing—as the last five thousand years of recorded human history readily attest. It can only survive in an ecology of Christian morality. Our Founding Fathers knew that only too well.

Therefore, if we genuinely desire Lady Liberty to kiss our land with her fresh fragrance and lush bounty, we had best turn from promiscuity and perversion and fully embrace the values and virtues that our framers embraced: the values and virtues of the Bible.

It was the opinion of one of early America's most distinguished statesmen and jurists, Fisher Ames, that "no man can be a sound lawyer in this land who is not well read in the ethics of Moses and the virtues of Jesus."[89]

That is as true today as it was then—regardless of what the homosexual activists and their cohorts may or may not believe.

8

AN IMPURITAN ETHIC: CHURCH

I've lived in half-way houses all my life,
Known nature half-way, half-way shared the art
Of bending flowers, or words; with half a heart
Have served my business; through religious strife
Kept half-way faith; without the drum and fife
Of certitude and triumph, or the smart
Of abject failure, played a paper part
With half-known facts with which my mind is rife.[1]

JESSE WILLS

John and Linda Ahlstrom were utterly astonished. They had just heard that a committee designated by their denomination to reexamine the church's stand on sexual morality had abandoned traditional and Scriptural values. Instead, it had embraced the prevailing morality of the surrounding culture—affirming the "compatibility" of premarital sex, extramarital sex, and homosexuality with "Christian faith and practice."

"Who would have ever dreamed that these kinds of behaviors would one day be condoned by the church?" John asked incredulously. "By the world, sure. By a few fringe groups, maybe. But by the church? No way. I've been a Presbyterian all my life. My parents and grandparents were faithful members of the church before me. Through the years, I've seen a lot of crazy things. But this beats all."

"I'm not really sure why they even want to call what they believe *Christian* anymore," added Linda. "Just where is the line of distinction between faith and faithlessness? If a church ceases to believe Christian doctrine, if it denies Christian tradition, if it rejects Christian values, and if it denounces Christian behavior, can we continue to legitimately call it *Christian?* I have to admit: I have my doubts."

"We're supposed to be the place where the world turns for answers to the toughest questions in life," said John. "But instead, we've turned that completely backwards. Here we are in the midst of some of the most difficult days ever, and the church almost appears to be in worse shape than even the world."

"It seems to me that the church has walked out on a limb this time," Linda agreed. "It is really in trouble."

This Present Crisis

Indeed, the modern church is in trouble. Real trouble.

Though its attendance is growing, its influence is diminishing. Though its giving is up, its impact is down. Though its profile is heightened, its vitality is lessened. And that is not even the worst of it. The church today is divided against itself—locked into a fierce conflict over the most basic questions of ethics and morality.

"I am more worried about the evangelical faith in this country than ever," says author and pastor Michael Scott Horton. "I wonder if evangelical Christianity can survive another era of being tossed back and forth with every wind and doctrine."[2]

And he is not alone. Recently, innumerable voices have joined together in a chorus of concern:

Theologian R. C. Sproul characterizes the church as "continuing to slide into the morass of theological relativism and subjectivism."[3] Renowned social commentator Charles Colson refers to American Christianity as "a church in exile."[4] Church historian Martin Marty laments that "the church today may be in more difficulty and travail than at any other time in its long history. Scandals on every side, divisions, schisms, conflicts, avarice, and simple greed have very nearly made the Church a laughingstock."[5] The newly installed Archbishop of Canterbury, George Carey, confides, "I fear for the future. The church seems to have lost its way."[6] Evangelist Billy Graham concurred, saying, "I'm not certain what the future holds for the institutional church, but at the moment it looks grim."[7] Presbyterian leader D. James Kennedy argues that "there is little hope for the world if the church cannot agree on the simplest of things—like what is right and what is wrong." And the respected leader of mainstream evangelical renewal during the last three decades, the late Francis Schaeffer, evaluated the state of the American church in our day as "the great Evangelical disaster."[8]

Without a doubt, the church is in trouble. Or rather, with a *great many* doubts the church is in trouble. In fact, doubts are just about all the church is known for raising. Not doctrinal truth. Not the level of debate. And certainly not the dead. Just doubts. For the church—which is supposed to be the discipler of the nations (Matthew 28:19), the voice of authority in the world (Matthew 16:19), and "the pillar and ground of the truth" (1 Timothy 3:15)—no longer proclaims a common confession, but speaks with a "scattered voice."[9] Every day seems to bring headlines of new ethical scandals, divisions over doctrine, and revisions of revelation. Many of the long-accepted verities of the Christian faith are being rejected for the vagaries of the contemporary consensus of confusion.

Though this crisis in the church directly affects many modern issues, perhaps the most visible and certainly the most volatile is the debate over the church's teaching on and treatment of homosexuals. The fact is the division within the visible church over homosexuality is representative of almost all that is troubling Christianity today. It inescapably involves the issue of biblical authority, the nature of church ministry, the scope of church discipline, and the church's responsibility and relationship to the civil sphere.

War in Heaven

Skirmishes and full-fledged battles in this civil war of values seem to constantly break out within the church. Three recent major denominational struggles especially demonstrate the crisis facing the modern church.

The United Methodist church for instance has been torn asunder by a controversy over traditional Christian sexual morality. In 1988, a proposal was brought before the denomination's General Conference to remove from the church's long-standing official statement of social principles that homosexual orientation or practice is "incompatible with Christian teaching." After three years of debate, eighteen members of a twenty-four-member panel released a report calling for the elimination of the traditional statement on homosexuality. Four other members released a dissenting report calling for the statement to remain. The two remaining refused to sign either report.

Both sides agreed that there is disagreement among medical and sociological "experts" over the "causes" of homosexuality. Both agreed that the church must urge the recognition and protection of "basic rights and civil liberties" of homosexuals. Both agreed that the church should be a place of acceptance for homosexuals—after all, United Methodists already practice some level of acceptance because two of the members of the study committee were themselves self-professing homosexuals. The only substantial difference between the two reports was that the majority claimed that current scientific, philosophical, and theological knowledge "does not provide a satisfactory basis upon which the church can responsibly maintain the condemnation of all homosexual practice," whereas the minority claimed that same current lack of expert consensus "does not provide a satisfactory basis upon which the church can responsibly alter its previously held position."

Both reports have been met with the ire of rank-and-file Methodists. Should either be sent to the next General Conference, a fire storm of controversy is sure to erupt. Opposing battlements are already in place.

When a recent straw poll showed that the committee favored codifying the majority report, the denominational office was deluged with mail—almost 95 percent of which supported the church's traditional stand that homosexuality is entirely incompatible with Christian teaching. Additionally, thirty-five of fifty regional conferences debating the issue of homosexual practice rejected any ethical exemptions for homosexuality.[10] Conservatives have been optimistic about their chances of maintaining a clear biblical affirmation of sexual morality. James Heidinger, executive secretary of Good News, a conservative caucus within Methodism, contends that "we have indicators from annual conferences that we will see the strongest Evangelical delegation going to General Conference that we have seen in thirty to fifty years."[11]

However, liberal groups are also preparing for an upcoming General Conference. A special interest group within the denomination, the Methodist Federation for Social Action, has resolved to ask delegates at the Conference to remove any prohibitions of the ordination of homosexuals. Another group, Affirmation, recently changed its name to reflect the heightened tensions. The group is now called Affirmation: United Methodists for Lesbian, Gay, and Bisexual Concerns.[12]

Whatever the ultimate outcome, this conflict over basic sexual morality has already taken its toll. The church lost more than 60,000 members last year alone. And since 1968, the once powerful church has shrunk from 11 million members to under 9 million.[13]

Sadly, this modern crisis of creedal identity has not been limited to the United Methodists. The Episcopal church is also reeling from internal division over the issue of homosexuality.

At their July 1991 triennial convention, the Episcopalian leadership was unable to resolve the debate over homosexuality. While on the one hand a resolution was passed "affirming the teaching of the Episcopal church that physical sexual expression is appropriate only within life-long monogamous marriage," on the other hand, the resolution claimed there is "discontinuity" between this teaching "and the experience of many members of this body."[14] Conservatives proposed canon law requiring clergy to abstain from all unbiblical sex, while liberals tried to pass a measure affirming homosexual practice and allowing the ordination of gays. Both attempts failed.[15]

This "discontinuity" effectively destroyed all attempts to enforce the "teaching of the Episcopal church." The proposed censure of two bishops for ordaining noncelibate homosexuals as a violation of the church's 1979 resolution, which declared such ordinations "not appropriate," was refused in favor of a declaration that they had caused "pain and damage to the credibility of this house and to parts of the whole church."[16] In light of the fact that many bishops openly admitted ordaining homosexuals and some priests gave public testimony about their homosexual practices, the failure of the church to censure its errant clergy established a debilitating precedent—essentially, Episcopal bishops can simply do as they please.

Seven hundred sixty-five Episcopal church members at the triennial convention, who were mostly from the evangelical, charismatic, and Anglo-Catholic wings of the fragmenting denomination, signed a "statement of conscience" protesting the unwillingness of the church to take a stand.[17] In addition, the conservative Episcopal Synod of America, which claims two hundred chapters throughout the church, declared that Episcopalians were divided into "two religions," and further stated: "A church which affirms Biblical truths but cannot discipline those who reject them has descended to the level of any other human institution and thus cannot win the world for the Gospel."[18] One conservative wrote, "Both sides recognize they are patronized by an amorphous, cowardly center that idolizes a false sense of unity."[19]

And so the battle rages.

Mainline Presbyterians—like the Methodists and the Episcopalians—are also fractiously divided over the issue of homosexuality and sexual fidelity. In 1991, a special task force on human sexuality appointed by the Presbyterian Church, United States of America, produced a startling report that has garnered tremendous interest nationwide. Because it completely rejects twenty centuries of Christian consensus on sexual mores, the report has been more than a little controversial. Most of the national media reported that the committees's recommendations—presented in a report titled *Keeping Body and Soul Together: Sexuality, Spirituality, and Social Justice*—were, after much debate, rejected by the General Assembly of the denomination. Actually though, the delegates merely instructed another committee to construct a plan to present at the next annual Assembly "to assist the church in exploring significant Biblical, theological, and ethical issues raised in the church around human sexuality during this past year," and told them to use the controversial report as one of their resources along with a dissenting minority report and other denominational pronouncements.[20]

The General Assembly also voted to send a pastoral letter to all their congregations assuring members that "we have affirmed in no uncertain terms the authority of the Old and New Testaments and have strongly reaffirmed the sanctity of the marriage covenant between one man and one woman to be a God-given relationship to be honored by marital fidelity."[21]

In fact, an attempt to affirm that monogamous marriage is *"the only* God-ordained relationship for the expression of sexual intercourse" was rejected in favor of simply stating that marriage was *"a* God-given relationship" for sexual intercourse.[22]

Both sides of the tortured debate were frustrated by the General Assembly's decision. Homosexuals want to know why they cannot be ordained if they are welcome in the church, and others wonder, if homosexuality is a sin that keeps practitioners from being ordained, why are they not subject to church discipline.[23]

According to Elisabeth Hannon of Presbyterians for Gay and Lesbian Concerns:

Every proposed action that would have represented progress to gay and lesbian people failed. But so did every proposed action that would have made us more fundamentalistic on sexuality. At least, individuals will have access to this very important document. I think we can claim a victory in that.[24]

The disputed document was two-hundred pages long with forty-eight recommendations. It advocated reversing the long-standing prohibition of homosexual ordination and supported developing "resources" for "recognition" of same-sex relationships; it also requested the denominational Board of Pensions to change its programs to allow same-sex couples to receive medical and retirement benefits.[25]

The document was written by the Task Force on Human Sexuality, which had drawn criticism from its inception some five years ago. Critics have argued that the group's membership was not at all representative of the church at large. Indeed, a poll found that 90 percent of mainline Presbyterians oppose the ordination of homosexuals, as do 95 percent of ruling elders and lay officers.[26]

Surprisingly, critics of the paper who despised its lack of fidelity and integrity were by no means restricted to "fundamentalist" or "traditionalist" Christians. Camille Paglia, for instance, vociferously criticized it in her scathing essay "The Joy of Presbyterian Sex."

> *Keeping Body and Soul Together* dramatically demonstrates the chaos and intellectual ineptitude in the fashionable liberal discourse on sex that now fills the media and the academic and political worlds. All human problems are blamed on an unjust social system, a "patriarchy" of gigantic and demonized dimensions, blanketing history like a river of molasses.[27]

Furthermore, Paglia argues that, despite the report's abandonment of the Bible's teaching on sex, "it is in fact a repressive, reactionary document" that "reduces the complexities and mysteries of eroticism to a clumsy, outmoded social-welfare ideology."[28] Although the liberal clerics and laypeople disdain Scripture's rules for sexual practice, they have replaced these with regulations of their own:

> Mainline American Protestantism, *outside the Evangelical movement,* systematically repressed both sex and emotion as part of the Puritan bequest. That repression continues in current American liberalism, which is simply Protestantism in disguise. The Presbyterian report tries to paper over with words the raw elemental experiences and conflicts of our mortality. "Eros,"

says the report's glossary, is "a zest for life." Is this a soap commercial? . . . The report gives us vanilla sex, smothered with artificial butterscotch syrup. In its liberal zeal to understand, to accept, to heal, it reduces the grand tragicomedy of love and lust to a Hallmark card. Its unctuous normalizing of dissident sex is imperialistic and oppressive. The gay world is stripped of its outlaw adventures in toilets, alleyways, trucks, and orgy rooms. There are no leathermen, hustlers, and drag queens. Gay love is reduced to a nice, neat, middle-class couple moving in next door on *Father Knows Best*. It's *Guess Who's Coming to Dinner?* all over again, with Sidney Poitier, Mr. Smooth and Perfect, recast in gay form. This is censorship in the name of liberal benevolence.[29]

As a committed pagan, Paglia is able to see through the fog bellowing out of the liberals who lauded the Presbyterian report and raise a simple question that every committed evangelical has been wanting to ask:

The report is so eager to argue away the inconvenient facts of Christian morality about sex that one has to ask the committee members, Why remain Christian at all? Why not leave Judeo-Christianity for our other great Western tradition, the Greco-Roman, in which philosophic discourse about ethics is possible without reference to a transcendent deity? As a lapsed Catholic of wavering sexual orientation, I have never understood the pressure for ordination of gay clergy or even the creation of gay Catholic groups. They seem to me to indicate a need for parental approval, an inability to take personal responsibility for one's own identity. The institutional religions, Catholic and Protestant, carry with them the majesty of history. Their theology is impressive and coherent. Efforts to revise or dilute that theology for present convenience seem to me misguided.[30]

Sadly, the Methodists, Episcopalians, and Presbyterians are not alone in this kind of "misguided dilution." The Christian Church—or the Disciples of Christ—is another denomination losing members over the issue of homosexuality.[31] The United Church of Canada's recent sharp decline in membership can be attributed to its decision to make the ordination of practicing homosexuals possible.[32] The size of the World Council of Churches may soon be reduced by a fourth because Eastern Orthodox communions may leave in protest over the acceptance of homosexuality by member communions as well as the Council's dialogue with the Metropolitan Community Church, an almost exclusively homosexual denomination.[33]

And it appears that the epidemic will soon become pandemic.

There are a host of prohomosexual organizations claiming to represent legitimate minorities within Protestant and Anabaptist denominations and lobbying for dramatic changes in their churches' polity and practice. Besides Methodism's group, Affirmation, there is American Baptists Concerned; there is the Brethren and Mennonite Council for Lesbian and Gay Concerns; there is the Disciples of Christ group, GLAD; there is the Southern Baptist group, Honesty; there is the Episcopalian group, Integrity; there is the Presbyterians for Lesbian and Gay Concerns; there is the Seventh-Day Adventist group, Kinship; and there is the the United Church of Christ group, United Church Coalition for Lesbian and Gay Concerns.

Virtually no denomination has escaped unscathed. Even the Roman Catholic and Eastern Orthodox communions have been brought into the fray. Axios is a Greek Orthodox advocacy group for homosexuals. Dignity and the Catholic Coalition for Gay Civil Rights are both aimed at the Roman church.

In addition, there are several powerful nondenominational organizations focusing their attentions on softening the commitments of evangelical, Reformed, and charismatic churches: Evangelicals Concerned, Evangelicals Together, Lambda Christian Fellowship, and the National Gay Pentecostal Alliance.[34]

The bottom line is that in nearly every sector and in every arena, the issue of homosexuality is tearing the church apart.

The Court Prophets

Laboring night and day, the forces advocating the complete abandonment of traditional values have raised up several key spokesmen—who by virtue of their prominence and influence have successfully dominated the debate thus far.

Probably the loudest and most tenacious advocate of homosexual orientation and practice in the church is the Episcopal Bishop of Newark, John Shelby Spong. Though his best known book is *Rescuing the Bible from Fundamentalism: A Bishop Rethinks the Meaning of Scripture*[35]—an unabashed tract for liberalism and humanism that stridently derides the orthodox standard of the authority of Scripture—an earlier work was *Living in Sin: A Bishop Rethinks Human Sexuality,*[36] written to justify the acceptance of homosexuals by the church. Spong gained national notoriety when he defied church canons and ordained a homosexual priest, Robert Williams, who later embarrassed the bishop by publicly blasting monogamy and denigrating the historic faith.[37] Nevertheless, at the triennial conference of the Episcopal church, Bishop Spong announced he would soon ordain another gay priest.[38]

Interestingly, Robert Williams's undoing is reminiscent of Camille Paglia's remark that liberal Protestants, for all their pretensions of tolerance and acceptance of diversity, have real hang-ups with the homosexual lifestyle as it exists in reality—its "outlaw adventures in toilets, alleyways, trucks, and orgy rooms." Before ordaining Williams, Spong had him carefully screened and believed Williams was in his fourth year with an exclusive relationship with a man he called his "spouse."

Apparently, though, they had an "open marriage." According to *Newsweek* magazine:

> A month after his widely publicized ordination, Williams was invited to address an Episcopal symposium on gay and lesbian marriage. To the surprise of his audience, Williams declared that celibacy is unnatural and spiritually inhibiting, and monogamy is just as bad. "If people want to try, OK. But the fact is, people are not monogamous," he declared. "It is crazy to hold up this ideal and pretend it's what we're doing, and we're not," When a priest challenged him by asking whether he thought Mother Theresa would be better off taking a lesbian lover, Williams testily replied: "If you're asking me do I think Mother Theresa ought to get #%*&, my answer is 'yes'."[39]

In the evangelical camp, there are also voices calling for "rethinking" homosexuality—as with Bishop Spong though, their "rethinking" is merely an euphemistic cover for "rejecting" traditional moral standards.

Virginia Ramey Mollenkott and Letha Scanzoni, for instance, are both prominent academic evangelicals. Their book, *Is The Homosexual My Neighbor? Another Christian View,*[40] is an attempt to argue that homosexuals should be accepted. Instead, they dance around the issue with the grace of a three-legged elephant. Starting with the title—which equates perversity with ethnic identity by alluding to Jesus' parable about the Good Samaritan—the authoresses go on to raise all sorts of silly questions about the traditional Christian position, which are supposed to raise doubts about it in the minds of their readers.

Following the argument that is implicit in their title, Scanzoni and Mollenkott do everything they can to equate aversion to sodomy with unchristian intolerance. The Nazi's are quoted as being antihomosexual;

Christians opposed to homosexuality are compared to white supremacists and chattel slaveholders of the antebellum South; they are compared to Judaizers who wanted to circumcise Gentiles; and homosexuals are compared to left-handed people. The book constantly harps on the problem of "homophobia"—reducing ethical principle to a psychological problem.

Discussing the biblical text—or, more to the point, subverting it—Scanzoni and Mollenkott state:

> A careful examination of what the Bible says about issues relating to homosexuality still leaves us with many unanswered questions. For one thing, the idea of a lifelong homosexual orientation or "condition" is never mentioned in the Bible. . . . Since the Bible is silent about the homosexual condition, those who want to understand it must rely on the findings of modern behavioral science research and on the testimony of those persons who are themselves homosexual.[41]

Yes, and in Nazi Germany, Christians who believed that Jews could be baptized into the church were considered superstitious. After all, the highly "scientific" discipline of eugenics had "proven" that Jews were of a different and inferior race. Since the Bible assumed that there was only one race—the human one—we're sure many German Christian leaders decided that they needed to look at eugenic research in order to truly understand "the Jewish problem."

Having denied the sufficiency of Scripture, the authoresses go on to trot out "the assured results of science," though it is obvious from their survey that they are choosing their "experts" carefully. If homosexuals have any psychological problems at all, we are told, it is because of homophobia.

In their conclusion, Scanzoni and Mollenkott draw back from actually advocating homosexual practice as normal and instead pretend the Christian view of homosexuality is some great mystery the church must work through. They present two views of homosexuality, the "traditional" and the "alternative," and act as though both are equally viable possibilities. At the same time, however, they come down solidly on the side of accepting homosexuality as moral, while avoiding saying so directly. As a piece of subversive propaganda, *Is the Homosexual My Neighbor?* is brilliant.

A more evangelical voice calling for Christians to rethink their attitudes toward homosexuals is Tony Campolo, a professor of sociology at Eastern College, an ordained Baptist minister, and a popular speaker. Campolo argues that not all people with "homosexual orientations" are "perverting their original nature." At a meeting of the Evangelical Round Table he stated: "Paul, in Romans 1, condemned *one kind* of homosexual behavior which is a perversion resulting from an insatiable sexual appetite yielded to the demonic."[42]

Campolo went on to suggest that homosexual lovers ought to live together in a lifelong covenant without having sex. He explained: "There are Christians who might disapprove of this arrangement, claiming that the Bible implies a condemnation of even romantic feelings between members of the same sex. However, these critics are hard-pressed to build a Biblical case for their complaints."[43]

Spong, Mollenkott, Scanzoni, and Campolo have had a tremendous impact on the shape and tenor of the debate over sexual ethics in general and homosexuality in particular. That is clear enough. What is astonishing is that more and more people—people who claim to believe and follow the Bible as the sole standard for faith and practice—are calling on Christians to reconsider the attitude of the church toward homosexuality. Such a revolution does not bode well for the future of the faith. It does not bode well in the least.

Turning a Deaf Ear

When Balak, regent of the ancient kingdom of Moab, was confronted by the advancing armies of Israel immediately following the Exodus sojourn, he began to cast about for a strategy to defeat them (Numbers 22:2–3). Military confrontation seemed hopeless. Diplomatic appeasement seemed suicidal. And defensive alliances seemed delinquent (Numbers 22:4). So in desperation, he sent for Balaam, a conjurer and diviner, who was thought to have the power to bless and bind through spells and incantations (Numbers 22:5–6).

Balak wanted to hire Balaam to curse Israel.

At first the magician was reluctant to take part in Balak's ploy—despite his generous offer (Numbers 22:15–35). But eventually he gave in and delivered four oracles (Numbers 22:36—24:25). Much to Balak's chagrin, however, each of the oracles predicted that Israel was invincible from without. No army, no king, no nation, and no empire would be able to stand against it. The only way God's chosen people could be defeated was if they defeated themselves from within—through disobedience and moral defilement.

That was all Balak needed to know. He didn't need an army. He didn't need diplomats. He didn't need allies. And now, he didn't even need diviners. All he needed was something to tempt Israel away from its fidelity.

He chose sex. He sent the most beguiling sexual enticements in all of Moab down into Israel's camp at Peor (Numbers 25:1–3,6). Enticing the people to play the harlot, sexual immorality was able to do what no warrior or general ever could: tempt and trap Israel. And not a sword was drawn. Not an arrow was unsheathed. Not a javelin was hurled.

The people were dragged off into captivity by their own lust. They were defeated by the compromise of their biblical standards.

The disintegration of the authority and influence of the modern church is more the sad consequence of the church's rueful recalcitrance than humanism's proud proficiency.

Under the influence of romantic and existential sentiment, all too many professing Christians have absolutized the intuitions of individual conscience rather than the certainties of revealed external standards. Under the barrage of a latitudinarian and modernist prevarication a large portion of the church has begun to confuse *the moral faculty*—the ability to make choices—with *the moral good*. Subjective whims and fashions have thus been given the weight of objective authority and truth. The Balak temptation has once again done its work.

City Under Siege

According to the Bible, the spiritual state of the church is the most important factor influencing the course of history. The prophet Azariah recognized this truth:

> For a long time Israel has been without the true God, without a teaching priest and without law; but when in their trouble they turned to the Lord God of Israel, and sought Him, He was found by them. And in those times there was no peace to the one who went out, nor to the one who came in, but great turmoil was on all the inhabitants of the lands. So nation was destroyed by nation, and city by city, for God troubled them with every adversity. (2 Chronicles 15:3–6)

Notice the cause and effect relationship. The apostasy of God's people resulted in world turmoil and distress. As the New Testament makes abundantly clear, we must apply this lesson to the church (Matthew 21:43; 1 Peter 2:9). If the church is a faithful "city on a hill," then it will enlighten the entire world (Matthew 5:14). But, switching to another metaphor, if the church commits infidelity it will become like flavorless salt and be "trampled underfoot by men" (Matthew 5:13).

It is all too common for believers to point outside the church to other institutions as evidence that Christianity is declining in America. Attempts to address the situation are commonly aimed at those other institutions as well. We often speak of "family values" and "political action" as being the solution to our problems. Although it is certainly true that Christians must defend the family and bring our values into the civic arena, perhaps our highest priorities should be to promote *Christian* values and *ecclesiastical* action.

Indeed, it seems doubtful that we are going to make much positive progress in our culture until God's house is in order. Therefore, if we wish to win the cultural war in society, we must fight the spiritual war in the church. As Paul promised the church in Rome, "Do you want to be unafraid of authority? Do what is good, and you will have praise from the same" (Romans 13:3).

Conclusion

The church is supposed to stand united. Jesus' last prayer was that His disciples "might be one." Unity is absolutely essential for the church's witness to the world. Our unity actually demonstrates to unbelievers that God sent Jesus into the world (John 17:20). A church publicly at odds over any issue is a terrible contradiction that sends a mixed message to the world. But a church divided against itself over such basic ethical standards is an unconscionable tragedy.

Even so, Christ did not pray for unity at any cost. He also prayed that His people be kept in truth: "Sanctify them by Your truth. Your word is truth" (John 17:17). He prayed that truth might be a means of protecting His disciples from becoming merely part "of the world." After all, the church is supposed to be *in* the world, not *of* it.

To pursue unity at the expense of truth is an exercise in futility. To compromise the truth does not lead to unity with the church, but to unity with the world.

"I hate all the squabbling and fighting," John Ahlstrom said. "But I hate the complete abandonment of our faith—which was once and for all delivered to the saints—even more. At some point you just have to take a stand."

"And we're taking our stand here," his wife Linda asserted. "For the sake of our church, for the sake of our children, and for the sake of the future of our civilization. Right here. On the truth. That is where we'll stand."

PART III

ALTARS AND ARSENALS

But when, the last crust gnawed, the last word said,
You stand on these, I on the other shores,
I'll be the lonelier then, I think, to see
You so disdainful of eternity,
How soon you open expectant doors
To clink your cup once more with dying men,
And you not caring to be born again.[1]

ALEC BROCK STEVENSON

9

REVEALING NOTIONS:
TRUTH

What requisitions of a verity
Prompted the wit and rage between his teeth
One cannot say. Around a crooked tree
A moral climbs whose name should be a wreath.[2]

ALLEN TATE

"What is truth?" asked Pontius Pilate before he sent an innocent man to be tortured to death. Thus did Pilate indicate that he was very much a modern man. Indeed, his question lies unspoken behind much of the mad modern quest—including the current societal debate over homosexuality.

Jesus said, "I am the way, the truth, and the life" (John 14:6). Although some deign to reduce the Lord's statement to mere mysticism, He meant for it to be much more than that.

The fact that Jesus *is* the Truth means that He *speaks* the truth—tangibly, propositionally, and specifically. Throughout the Gospels, Jesus prefaces His instruction saying, "Truly, truly, I say to you." Again, He said, "My Word is truth." He made clear to His hearers that His Word was more enduring than all creation: "Heaven and earth will pass away," He said, "but My words will never pass away" (Luke 21:33).

Furthermore, Christ affirmed that His Word included even the books of the Old Testament—and thus they were likewise true in every way, shape, and form. He highlighted the fact that "the Scripture cannot be broken" (John 10:34). And He did not hesitate to appeal to the whole of the Word of God as a seamless absolute standard for all behavior: "Why do you also transgress the commandment of God because of your traditions" (Matthew 15:3).

So strong was His emphasis on the Word that He divided humanity into two classifications: Those who heard, believed, and obeyed His Word, and those who did not hear, disbelieved, and disobeyed His Word. Christians—that is, followers of Christ—are, *by definition,* those who respond obediently to His Word and are gathered into His church (John 10:1–18).

The bottom line for Him was the fact that the Bible is the Word of God and true in all that it contains.

This is, in fact, an inescapable presupposition woven throughout all of the Scriptures:

- Your righteousness is an everlasting righteousness, and Your law is truth. (Psalm 119:142)

- The entirety of Your word is truth, and every one of Your righteous judgments endures forever. (Psalm 119:160)

- And he who has seen has testified, and his testimony is true; and he knows that he is telling the truth, so that you may believe. (John 19:35)

- These words are faithful and true. (Revelation 22:6)

But, the Bible is not merely true, it is also useful, important, and necessary as guidance for daily living:

- You shall therefore keep His statutes and His commandments which I command you today, that it may go well with you and with your children after you, and that you may prolong your days in the land which the LORD your God is giving you for all time. (Deuteronomy 4:40)

- I have more understanding than all my teachers, for Your testimonies are my meditation. (Psalm 119:99)

- All Scripture is given by inspiration of God, and is profitable for doctrine, for reproof, for correction, for instruction in righteousness, that the man of God may be complete, thoroughly equipped for every good work. (2 Timothy 3:16–17)

In addition, the Bible provides a check on our own waywardness and perversity. It convicts us of our sins in thought, word, and deed, which—otherwise—we would not recognize as sin:

- Your word I have hidden in my heart, that I might not sin against You. (Psalm 119:11)

- There is a way that seems right to a man, but its end is the way of death. (Proverbs 14:12)

As Christians, all our opinions must be in line with the teachings of Scripture. As philosopher Cornelius Van Til asserted:

The Bible is thought of as authoritative on everything of which it speaks. And it speaks of everything. We do not mean that it speaks of football games, of atoms, etc., directly, but we do mean that it speaks of everything either directly or indirectly. It tells us not only of the Christ and His work but it also tells us who God is and whence the universe has come. It gives us a philosophy of history as well as history. Moreover, the information on these subjects is woven into an inextricable whole. It is only if you reject the Bible as the Word of God that you can separate its so-called religious and moral instruction from what it says, e.g., about the physical universe.[3]

The Purpose of the Word

According to Jesus, we are to obey the precepts and statutes of God's Word *because* we have been justified. We do not obey them *in order to be* justified. Obedience to the Bible is the *effect* of salvation, not the *cause* of salvation. In other words, the Scriptural fealty is designed to be a tool of sanctification, not the *means* of justification and redemption. It is a way of *life,* not a way of *salvation.*

Thus, Jesus constantly upheld the validity of even the moral standards of the Law as a guide for living and an expression of the unchanging standards of His holy character:

- Man shall not live on bread alone, but on every word that proceeds out of the mouth of God. (Matthew 4:4)

- It is easier for heaven and earth to pass away than for one stroke of a letter of the Law to fail. (Luke 16:17)

- Whoever then annuls one of the least of these commandments, and so teaches others, shall be called least in the Kingdom of Heaven; but whoever keeps and teaches them, he shall be called great in the Kingdom of Heaven. (Matthew 5:19)

Again and again He affirmed the truth that "all Scripture is God breathed" (2 Timothy 3:16) and it "cannot be broken" (John 10:35). Clearly then, He did not come to do away with the Law—to abolish or abrogate it. On the contrary, He came to fulfill it—to confirm and uphold it (Matthew 5:17). He reiterated the fact that every one of "His righteous ordinances is everlasting" (Psalm 119:160) and that "the Word of our God shall stand forever" (Isaiah 40:8).

Jesus was affirming that unlike human lawmakers, God does not change His mind or alter His standards: "My covenant I will not violate, nor will I alter the utterance of my lips" (Psalm 89:34). When the Lord speaks, His Word stands firm forever. His assessments of right and wrong do not change from age to age: "All His precepts are trustworthy. They are established forever and ever, to be performed with faithfulness and uprightness" (Psalm 111:7–8).

Jesus did not hesitate to appeal even to Old Testament case law to bolster His teaching (John 8:17). He used it to vindicate His behavior (Matthew 12:5). He used it to answer His questioners (Luke 10:26), to indict His opponents (John 7:19), to identify God's will (Matthew 19:17), to establish kingdom citizenship (Matthew 7:24), to confront Satan (Matthew 4:1–11), and to confirm Christian love (John 14:21). He was, in short, a *champion of the law.*

But He also put Law in its place. He showed us that Law is not designed to effect salvation for men. Instead, it is designed to effect sanctification for men. It is designed to enable men to submit to and evidence the rule of God.

This is what the apostle Paul meant when he said that we are no longer "under the Law" (Romans 6:14–15), that in fact we are "dead to the Law" (Romans 7:4; Galatians 2:19). Instead, we are under the sacrificial covering of Christ's blood fulfilling the death sentence of the law against us (Romans 8:1–2). But Law is not made void; its curse is

(Galatians 3:13). In fact, when Law is put in its proper place, it is "established" (Romans 3:31).

The Bible is the Word of God. It is His revelation of wisdom, knowledge, understanding, and truth. It is not simply a splendid collection of inspiring sayings and stories. It is God's message to man. It is God's instruction. It is God's direction. It is God's guideline, His plumb line, and His bottom line.

Thus, as Christians it is absolutely essential that we take every single aspect of God's Word to us very seriously—and then attempt to live in accord with its authority in every detail of our lives.

Beginning at the Beginning

So what does the Bible teach about homosexuality?

Whenever Jesus addressed issues of human sexuality, He used the original creation of man as a point of reference. The creation account demonstrates the importance of human sexuality: "So God created man in His own image; in the image of God He created Him; male and female He created them" (Genesis 1:27). Interestingly, the creation of both sexes is treated as essential for humanity to bear "the image of God." But notice, after God created the first man, Adam, He decided that he needed a companion:

> And the LORD God said, "It is not good that man should be alone; I will make him a helper comparable to him." . . . and then the LORD God caused a deep sleep to fall on Adam, and he slept; and He took one of his ribs, and closed up the flesh in its place. Then the rib which the LORD God had taken from man He made into a woman, and He brought her to the man. And Adam said: "This is now bone of my bones and flesh of my flesh; she shall be called Woman, because she was taken out of Man." Therefore a man shall leave his father and mother and be joined to his wife, and they shall become one flesh. (Genesis 1: 18, 21–23)

From the beginning of time, God's design for sexuality has been a one man, one woman, lifelong, covenantal commitment. Nineteenth-century theologian James Bricknell Houston Greg asserts:

> The creation of gender—and thusly, sexual—differentiation by God from the beginning of the Genesis account clearly established chaste heterosexuality as normative for sexual impulses and acts. God the Creator gives the

things of the earth their essential identity and function and He thusly define's man's proper relationships. Mankind's natural function in sexuality has been defined by God as male-female behavior.[4]

And according to pastor William Brandt:

The Biblical perspective of sexuality simply cannot be comprehended apart from the bounds of holy matrimony—that of one man and one woman.[5]

The Seventh Commandment

God spoke from Mt. Sinai in a thunderous voice, "You shall not commit adultery" (Exodus 20:14; Deuteronomy 5:18). Thus did He prohibit all sex outside of the holy bounds of marriage.

This clearly enunciated standard was elaborated in the various case laws He gave Moses—laws that applied the Ten Commandments to specific issues in the life of God's people. For instance, "You shall not lie with a male as with a woman. It is an abomination" (Leviticus 18:22).

Strong words. But the Bible does not hesitate to use strong language when appropriate. Thus, it compares male homosexuals to brutish animals:

There shall be no ritual harlot of the daughters of Israel, or a perverted one of the sons of Israel. You shall not bring the hire of a harlot or *the price of a dog* to the house of the Lord your God for any vowed offering, for both of these are an abomination to the Lord your God. (Deuteronomy 23:17–18)

In fact, this kind of covenantal violation is so serious in God's eyes that He actually declared it subject to capital punishment:

If a man lies with a male as he lies with a woman, both of them have committed an abomination. They shall surely be put to death. Their blood shall be upon them. (Leviticus 20:13)

Again and again, the absolute invariability and inescapability of the prohibition is underscored. Through the years though, many have tried to avoid the obvious significance of such passages. They have argued, for example, that the case laws were only intended for the nation of Israel, and thus have no additional application whatsoever. This, despite the fact that God repeatedly indicates that the other nations were by no means exempt. That is the very reason they fall under divine judgment:

And you shall not walk in the statutes of the nation which I am casting out before you; for they commit all these things, and therefore I abhor them. (Leviticus 21:23)

Indeed, once the Hebrews had settled in the land, God told them that they were to be a witness to the nations around them, which would be attracted by their laws (Deuteronomy 4:5–8). Plainly, God intends His prohibition of homosexuality to apply to the people of all cultures because God is the creator and sustainer of them all and His Word is eternal and inviolate—it "will by no means pass away" (Matthew 24:35).

Therefore God's condemnation of same-sex perversions is absolute and categorical—even homosexual partners who may be "committed and faithful" fall under His immutable bar of justice. There is no hint in Scripture that there are exceptions or aberrations to this standard—thus in the case laws, whereas any form of extramarital sex was a capital offense, premarital heterosexual offenses were adjudicated with an option of covenantal marriage (Exodus 22:16–17; Deuteronomy 22:28–29). There is no such option for homosexual offenses because God does not recognize covenantal marriages between people of the same sex.

Even apart from the case laws, God's blanket condemnation of homosexuality is evident in numerable passages throughout Scripture—not the least of which is the story of His destruction of Sodom and Gomorrah. Though the cities were judged for several sins, rampant unchecked homosexuality ensured their fate (Ezekiel 16:49–50). According to Scripture, the divine judgment poured out on the cities was meant to be "an example to those who afterward would live ungodly" (2 Peter 2:6). Later, the entire Hebrew tribe of Benjamin was almost wiped out for behaving like Sodom (Judges 19–20). Still later, whenever the prophets of the Old Testament accused Israel of severe apostasy they would compare the nation to the city of Sodom (Isaiah 3:9; Jeremiah 23:14).

The Gospel

Many today would contend that there is a vast gulf of differentiation between the harsh teaching of the Old Testament and the fresh forgiveness of the New Testament—particularly when it comes to the issue of homosexuality. Jesus, for instance, is silent on the question, they say. But that is simply not the case. Not only did Christ repeatedly endorse the teachings and commandments of the entire moral law of Old Testament—He said that "heaven and earth would pass away" before the statutes of the Word passed away—He appealed directly to the creation account of one man and one woman as the sole model for covenant marriage (Matthew 19:14–16). Additionally, He used the example of Sodom's sin as a warning to Israel of divine wrath in the same way the Old Testament prophets did. Christ was not the least bit ambivalent about this. In fact, He went so far as to assert that the only option for those who do not marry is celibacy (Matthew 19:11–12).

As the Christian faith began to penetrate into the surrounding promiscuous and perverse pagan culture, the apostles were forced to deal more directly with the issue of homosexuality. In Romans, Paul, under the superintendence of the Holy Spirit, condemned homosexuality as he discussed the consequences of suppressing God's revelation in creation:

> For this reason God gave them up to vile passions. For even their women exchanged the natural use for what is against nature. Likewise also the men, leaving the natural use of the woman, burned in their lust for one another, men with men committing what is shameful, and receiving in themselves the penalty of their error which was due. (Romans 1:26–27)

And, furthermore, he wrote, "Knowing the righteous judgment of God, that those who practice such things are worthy of death," they, nevertheless, "not only do the same but also approve of those who practice them" (Romans 1:32).

Notice here that the Scriptures condemn not only homosexual acts but homosexual desires. This principle takes what Jesus said about heterosexual lust at the Sermon on the Mount and applies it to homosexuality: "You have heard that it was said to those of old, 'You shall not commit adultery.' But I say to you that whoever looks at a woman to lust after her has already committed adultery with her in his heart" (Matthew 5:27–28).

Indeed, the Bible assumes that, contrary to popular opinion, men and women are responsible for their desires and are capable of controlling them (Job 31:1,9; Proverbs 6:25).

Again and again throughout the New Testament, homosexuality is listed among those unacceptable sins of the flesh from which the Gospel has liberated us:

- Do not be deceived. Neither fornicators, nor idolaters, nor adulter-ers, nor homosexuals, nor sodomites, nor thieves, nor covetous, nor drunkards, nor revilers, nor extortioners will inherit the kingdom of God. (1 Corinthians 6:9–10)

- But we know the law is good if one uses it lawfully, knowing this: that the law is not made for a righteous person, but for the lawless and insubordinate, for the ungodly and for sinners, for the unholy and profane, for murderers of fathers and murderers of mothers, for manslayers, for fornicators, for sodomites, for kidnappers, for liars, for perjurers, and if there is any other thing that is contrary to sound doctrine, according to the glorious gospel of the blessed God which was committed to my trust. (1 Timothy 1:8–11)

- And the angels who did not keep their proper domain, but left their own abode, He has reserved in everlasting chains under darkness for the judgment of the great day; as Sodom and Gomorrah, and the cities around them in a similar manner to these, having given themselves over to sexual immorality and gone after strange flesh, are set forth as an example, suffering the vengeance of eternal fire. (Jude 6–7)

Furthermore, the apostle Paul follows the example of Jesus in his discussion of how to deal with sexual temptation. He makes clear that heterosexual marriage or celibacy are the only two options for Christians (1 Corinthians 7:1–40).

The Divine Image

Although such passages make clear *that* homosexuality is an abomination, they do not explain *why* homosexuality is an abomination. Some might suppose that the reason is simply that homosexuality is a threat to the family. This may be partly true, but it only leads to another question: Why is the Bible so concerned about the family?

The answer may be found in Paul's admonitions concerning marriage:

Wives, submit to your own husbands, as to the Lord. For the husband is head of the wife, as also Christ is head of the church; and He is the Savior of the body. Therefore, just as the church is subject to Christ, so let the wives be to their own husbands in everything. Husbands, love your wives, just as Christ also loved the church and gave Himself for her, that He might sanctify and cleanse her with the washing of water by the word, that He might present her to Himself a glorious church, not having spot or wrinkle or any such thing, but that she should be holy and without blemish. So husbands ought to love their own wives as their own bodies; he who loves his wife loves himself. For no one ever hated his own flesh, but nourishes and cherishes it, just as the Lord does the church. For we are members of His body, of His flesh and of His bones. "For this reason a man shall leave his father and mother and be joined to his wife and the two shall become one flesh." This is a great mystery, *but I speak of Christ and the church.* (Ephesians 5:22–32)

Notice that the apostle Paul can barely produce two sentences about husbands and wives without overflowing with descriptions of Christ and the church. The relationship between Jesus Christ and His bride, the church, is the model for human sexual relationships.

Clearly then, God did not just make up a sexual code at random and then impose it on us. Rather, by making mankind—both male and female—in His image (Genesis 1:27), God gave us an analogy of the relationship between the Creator and His creatures. The norm of heterosexuality within the covenantal bounds of marriage is in essence based on the nature of reality.

That is why apostasy from the worship of the true God is often called adultery or harlotry in the Old Testament (Isaiah 1:21; Jeremiah 2:20; Ezekiel 16:15; Hosea 9:1). Jesus likewise characterized His apostate countrymen as "an evil and adulterous generation" (Matthew 12:2, 16:4). Similarly, the apostles also used the same metaphor (2 Corinthians 11:1–3; James 4:4; Revelation 17:5).

This correspondence between the relationship of the Creator and His creatures and the relationship of men and women helps us understand why the apostle Paul discusses homosexuality early in his letter to the Romans. In the context of the passage, Paul is dealing with idolatry:

For the wrath of God is revealed from heaven against all ungodliness and unrighteousness of men, who suppress the truth in unrighteousness, because what may be known of God is manifest in them, for God has shown it to them. For since the creation of the world His invisible attributes are clearly seen, being understood by the things that are made, even His eternal power and Godhead, so that they are without excuse, because, although they knew God, they did not glorify Him as God, nor were thankful, but became futile in their thoughts, and their foolish hearts were darkened. Professing to be wise, they became fools, and changed the glory of the incorruptible God into an image made like corruptible man—and birds and four-footed animals and creeping things. Therefore God also gave them up to uncleanness, in the lusts of their hearts, to dishonor their bodies among themselves, who exchanged the truth of God for the lie, and *worshipped and served the creature rather than the Creator,* who is blessed forever. Amen. (Romans 1:18–25)

By worshiping the creature rather than the Creator, people begin a descent deeper and deeper into depravity. Whereas Paul lists many sins that result from not worshiping the true God, he spends the most time describing both male and female homosexuality (Romans 1:26–27). His point is clear: religious inversion ultimately leads to sexual inversion.

In a very real sense then, homosexuality represents the culmination of apostasy.

At War with the Word

Given the intensity of the conflict over this issue, many today may be laboring under the false impression that Scripture is unclear in its pronouncements on homosexuality. Indeed, many homosexuals and their apologists claim that fundamentalists, traditionalists, or members of the "religious right" have grossly misinterpreted the Bible in this regard.

Under the provocative headline "Does God Hate Gays," a writer in one homosexual magazine claimed:

The Old and New Testament Scriptures used by the religious right to condemn gays have been taken out of context, mistranslated, and misinterpreted. These Scriptures never were intended to address consenting love between two people of the same sex—homosexuality as we know it today. They focus instead on 1) the practice of having anal intercourse with call boys, 2) pagan or cultic worship and fertility practices, and 3) rape.[6]

There is in fact, no exegetical evidence to support any of these notions. None whatsoever. Even so, homosexual apologists persist.

In the best-selling book *The Gay and Lesbian Liberation Movement* we are confidently told:

After scholars who scrutinized the Bible passages thought to condemn homosexuality found that these passages had been misinterpreted, religious leaders who based their opposition to homosexuality on the Bible lost credibility.[7]

What scholars? What leaders? Where? When?

Again, there is no substantive support for such assertions. Yet with a brash and haughty don't-confuse-me-with-the-facts aplomb, the apologists press on.

Perhaps the most brilliant of all the nay-saying apologists is John Boswell, an assistant professor of history at Yale University. He argues against the clear teaching of Scripture utilizing the time-honored tack of textual criticism.

For instance, he asserts that Sodom was not destroyed for homosexual practice, but "for inhospitable treatment of visitors sent from the Lord."[8] He bases this dubious claim on the fact:

The Hebrew verb "to know" . . . is very rarely used in a sexual sense in the Bible: in only ten of its 943 occurrences in the Old Testament does it have the sense of carnal knowledge.[9]

Hardly convincing. For as theologian John Jefferson Davis retorts:

Mere word counting is no criterion of meaning; the use of a word in its specific context is the decisive consideration. In the book of Genesis, the word *yada* is used twelve times, and in ten of those instances it denotes sexual intercourse. Even more to the point, in the immediate context in 19:8, *yada* is used in a way that unmistakably refers to sexual intercourse. Lot said to the men of Sodom, in a desperate attempt to protect his guests, "Behold, I have two daughters who have not known man; let me bring them out to you, and do to them as you please; only do nothing to these men, for they have come under the shelter of my roof." Whatever one might conclude about Lot's judgment in this case, it is clear that he was offering his virgin daughters as a substitute to the men of Sodom who were demanding homosexual intercourse with his guests.[10]

Undeterred, Boswell persists. Building pretense upon pretense, he asserts that "Jesus himself apparently believed that Sodom was destroyed for the sin of inhospitality."[11] Then he cites the Gospel account:

And whoever will not receive you nor hear your words, when you depart from that house or city, shake off the dust from your feet. Assuredly, I say to you, it will be more tolerable for the land of Sodom and Gomorrah in the day of judgment than for that city. (Matthew 10:14–15)

Boswell's argument is obviously distorted—confusing a blatant rejection of the Gospel with a lack of hospitality.

But he is not finished yet. He asserts that the rest of the Old Testament does not view the destruction of Sodom as involving punishment for homosexuality: "Sodom is used as a symbol of evil in dozens of places, but not in a single instance is the sin of the Sodomites specified as homosexuality."[12] Citing Ezekiel 16:48–49, Boswell claims that "the sins of Sodom are not only listed categorically but contrasted with the sexual sins of Jerusalem as less serious."[13] However, in order to make his point, Boswell somehow fails to take into account the conclusion of the passage. In context, that final verse makes plain that the case law abomination of homosexuality was clearly in view:

"As I live," says the Lord God, "neither your sister Sodom nor her daughters have done as you and your daughters have done. Look, this was the iniquity of your sister Sodom: She and her daughter had pride, fullness of food, and abundance of idleness; neither did she strengthen the hand of the poor and needy. And they were haughty and *committed abominations* before me; therefore I took them away as I saw fit." (Ezekiel 16:48–50)

The word "abominations" here is the same word used in Leviticus 18:22 to describe explicit homosexual behavior. Additionally, those "abominations" are listed at the very end of the long catalog of Sodom's sins. Homosexuality was the culmination of their evil.

Boswell's refusal to take seriously Scripture's own definitions and categories is by no means unique. In their book *Is The Homosexual My Neighbor? Another Christian View* Letha Scanzoni and Virginia Mollenkott argue:

The Bible does not have a great deal to say about homosexuality, and in the original languages the term itself is never used. Whenever homosexual acts are mentioned, the acts are always committed in a very negative context, such as adultery, promiscuity, violence, or idolatrous worship. The fact that this negative context is often ignored may explain why Christians have traditionally shown harsh, unloving, often cruel attitudes toward homosexual persons.[14]

Whereas the defenders of homosexuality claim that they will tell us what the Bible *really* says about homosexuality, they inevitably reveal what they think about the Bible.

The fact is, most of these apologists just don't like what the Bible says. They are embarrassed by it. And so they attempt to explain it away—perhaps in a vain attempt to "defend" the honor and integrity of God.

Other apologists—with at least an increment of intellectual honesty—see through this ruse and simply confess that the Bible is wrongheaded on this issue. It is in error, they say, and thus we *ought* to be embarrassed by it. No need go through exegetical gymnastics to prove otherwise.

Bishop John Shelby Spong's omnisexual manifesto, *Living in Sin? A Bishop Rethinks Human Sexuality,* opts for this course.

So, for instance, Spong's portrayal of the destruction of Sodom and Gomorrah is deliberately mocking. Noting that "fundamentalists" use the story as evidence of Scripture's condemnation of homosexuality, he remarks:

> What a strange text to use for such a purpose. The biblical narrative approves Lot's offer of his virgin daughters to satisfy the sexual demands of the angry mob. It suggests that incest is a legitimate way of impregnating women when there is no man around save the father of those women. What society today would be willing to incorporate either of these practices into its moral code? Who among us is willing to accept the definition of women implicit in this account? If we reject the denigration of women as property or the practice of incest, both being based upon an inadequate view of morality, are we not also free to reject the society's faulty understanding of homosexuality as being also based upon inadequate moral grounds?[15]

The text, of course, gives no hint that heterosexual gang rape or incest are morally acceptable practices. There is no sign of approval of Lot's offer of his two daughters to the mob. Given the fact that Lot was originally attracted to Sodom (Genesis 13:10–13) and ended up living out his days as a homeless vagabond (Genesis 19:30) seems to indicate that he was far from God's blessing. Though he was "oppressed" and "tormented" by the behavior of the Sodomites (2 Peter 2:7–8), his own moral character evidently suffered as well. The fact that Lot had to be intoxicated and tricked into impregnating his daughters (Genesis 19:31–36) strongly indicates that incest was viewed as immoral by him. Furthermore, though the descendants of those incestuous unions were initially accorded a degree of respect due to their relationship with Abraham's descendants (Deuteronomy 2:9, 19), they were considered Israel's enemy because of their immoral deeds (Deuteronomy 23:3–6).

Of course none of this matters to Spong. He has already presuppositionally denuded the authority of Scripture. From that all else follows.

Recently, Christian journalist Bob Allen was preparing for an interview of Spong. He was asked by a coworker if he knew of any other evangelicals who had either interviewed or debated the Bishop.

A pained expression overshadowed Allen's face. "Oh yes," he replied, "but they were unable to really refute him because they shared his basic presuppositions—and he knew it. Spong is brilliant in using our inconsistencies against us."

The sad fact is that many of us are no less embarrassed by parts of the Bible than Spong. We stumble over its "hard sayings" and fumble over its "offensive words" (John 6:60–66).

Ultimately we will not be able to defend the Biblical condemnation of homosexuality if we are ashamed of Scripture elsewhere:

> For whoever shall keep the whole law and yet stumble in one point, he is guilty of all. For He who said, "Do not commit adultery," also said, "Do not murder." Now if you do not commit adultery, but you do murder, you have become a transgressor of the law. (James 2:10–11)

Whereas there is a clear covenantal discontinuity between the Old and New Testaments, *all* of the Bible is a reflection of God's holy character. We cannot defend parts of the Bible while allowing other parts to be neglected or scorned. To do so places us under Jesus' condemnation of the scribes and Pharisees who obeyed some of the Law but disobeyed the rest of it (Matthew 23:23).

Yet we do so nonetheless.

Courage to Believe

H. L. Mencken lived and died as a convinced atheist and opponent of the church. Yet when Mencken wrote an obituary for the committed

Christian scholar and well-known opponent of theological liberalism Gresham Machen, he called him "a man of great learning, and, what is more, of sharp intelligence."[16]

Why would an atheist, known for his creative and vociferous Christian bashing, pay such high compliments to a champion of conservative Christianity?

Mencken explains:

> My interest in Dr. Machen while he lived, though it was large, was not personal, for I have never had the honor of meeting him. Moreover, the doctrine that he preached seemed to me, and still seems to me, to be excessively dubious. . . . But Dr. Machen had the same clear right to believe in it that I have to disbelieve in it, and though I could not yield to his reasoning I could at least admire, and did greatly admire, his remarkable clarity and cogency as an apologist, allowing him his primary assumptions.[17]

A large part of Mencken's respect for Machen came as a result of Machen's fight with the liberals in the Presbyterian church who "presumed to repeal and reenact with amendments the body of doctrine" of Christian orthodoxy:

> Upon this contumacy Dr. Machen fell with loud shouts of alarm. He denied absolutely that anyone had a right to revise and sophisticate Holy Writ. Either it was the Word of God or it was not the Word of God, and if it was, then it was equally authoritative in all its details, and had to be accepted or rejected as a whole. Anyone was free to reject it, but no one was free to mutilate it or read things into it that were not there. Thus the issue with the Modernists was clearly joined, and Dr. Machen argued them quite out of court, and sent them scurrying back to their literary and sociological *Kaffeeklatsche.*[18]

Though Mencken was not convinced by his arguments that the Bible was infallible, he did think that Machen had "at least disposed of those who proposed to read it as they might read a newspaper, believing what they chose and rejecting what they chose."[19]

People might not like us if we proclaim the "whole counsel of God," but perhaps it is better to be respected and heard than liked and ignored.

Conclusion

The whole testimony of Scripture, from the beginning of the Old Testament record, through the Gospels, and on to the end of the New Testament is absolutely clear: homosexuality is sin whether committed in thought, word, or deed. Furthermore, God holds homosexuals responsible for their sin—just as He does any other practicing sinner. Despite the dogmatic instance of those who believe that human beings are fated by either biological or behavioral determinism, Biblical faith insists that we have control over our so-called sexual orientation and are thus responsible for our lives.

As Christian counselor Jay Adams has stated:

One is not a homosexual constitutionally any more than one is an adulterer constitutionally. Homosexuality is not considered to be a condition, but an act. It is viewed as a sinful practice which can become a way of life. The homosexual act, like the act of adultery, is the reason for calling one a homosexual (of course one may commit homosexual sins of the heart, just as one may commit adultery in his heart. He may lust after a man in his heart as another may lust after a woman).[20]

Of course homosexuality for some may not be a conscious and remembered choice any more than heterosexuality is for most. There may not have been any conscious process of deliberation, weighing the pros and cons and then finally coming to a decision. But that does not make sexual preference any less chosen. That does not make it any less voluntary or willful. The defense "I can't help it" is as indefensible as it is infantile.

The Gospel's message of the sinfulness of homosexuality has been reviled by some as an awful bigotry. It has even been equated with the evils of racism—which are categorically condemned in Scripture. But the reality is that treating homosexuality as a sin is the very opposite of bigotry. For instead of simply stereotyping homosexuals as predetermined products of either their biology or environment, the Gospel treats them the same as every other sinner who needs to repent and believe.

Calling homosexuality a sin may well seem to be a cruel, insensitive attitude—perhaps even a "homophobic" response of condemnation rather than of concern. But the truth is that it is the beginning of true freedom and joy for the homosexual. For if sexual preference were either a genetically encoded human condition—such as height or skin color—there would be no real hope. The homosexual would be shackled to his lusts forever, with no possibility of release. But once we can freely admit that homosexuality is just a sin, we can also see the way of deliverance and redemption.

This is the message of the Gospel: Christ died for sinners—to set them free from sin.

The apostle Paul knew this well. After listing homosexuality among other sinful practices that exclude people from the kingdom of God, he wrote to the church in Corinth:

> And such were some of you. But you were washed, but you were sanctified, but you were justified in the name of the Lord Jesus and by the Spirit of our God. (1 Corinthians 6:11)

The New Testament church, apparently, was filled with repentant ex-homosexuals who had found new life in Christ.

May it be so once again.

10

UNTO AGES OF AGES: TRADITION

We live in time so little time
And we learn all so painfully,
That we may spare this hour's term
To practice for eternity.[1]

ROBERT PENN WARREN

Winston Churchill once said that "the greatest advances in human civilization have come when we recovered what we had lost: when we learned the lessons of history."[2]

Sadly, that is a lesson lost on many—if not most—of our contemporaries. We are perhaps more inclined to agree with Henry Ford's quip, "History is bunk."[3]

One mark of the modern mind is an abrasive arrogance, that assumes the past is useless in dealing with the pressing problems of the present. Worse, some Christians, caught like their unregenerate neighbors in a malignant contemporaneity, actually think that their disdain for the historic Christian traditions is pleasing to God. Indeed, many think that the purpose of the Protestant Reformation was to overthrow the Christian traditions.

It is, of course, true that we must obey God rather than men. We must not be like the Pharisees, "teaching as doctrines the commandments of men" (Mark 7:7; Isaiah 29:13). Indeed, one of the cries of the Reformation was *Sola Scriptura*—Scripture alone.

199

But this by no means nullifies the value of the traditions of the church for the modern Christian. As theologian James Jordan has written:

> The Bible teaches that tradition is important, because it is the heritage of the Spirit. The Spirit has raised up apostles, prophets, evangelists, pastors and teachers, as well as other gifted persons. These persons are indeed gifts of the Spirit. We despise the Spirit if we do not pay attention to these gifts He has given in the past—forming the traditions of the church.[4]

Against Ecclesiastical Amnesia

History is not just the concern of historians and social scientists. It is not the lonely domain of political prognosticators and ivory tower academics. It is the very stuff of life. And, it is the very stuff of faith. In fact, the Bible puts a *heavy* emphasis on historical awareness—not at all surprising considering the fact that the vast proportion of its own contents record the dealings of God with men and nations throughout the ages.

Again and again in the Scriptures, God calls upon His people to *remember*. He calls on us to remember the bondage, oppression, and deliverance from Egypt (Exodus 13:3; Deuteronomy 6:20–23). He calls on us to remember the splendor, strength, and devotion of the Davidic kingdom (1 Chronicles 16:8–36). He calls on us to remember the valor, forthrightness, and holiness of the prophets (James 5:7–11). He calls on us to remember the glories of creation (Psalm 104:1–30), the devastation of the Flood (2 Peter 2:4–11), the judgment of the great apostasies (Jude 5–11), the miraculous events of the Exodus (Deuteronomy 5:15), the anguish of the desert wanderings (Deuteronomy 8:1–6), the grief of the Babylonian exile (Psalm 137:1–6), the responsibility of the restoration (Ezra 9:5–15), the sanctity of the Lord's Day (Exodus 20:8), the graciousness of the commandments (Numbers 15:39–40), and the ultimate victory of the cross (1 Corinthians 11:23–26). He calls on us to remember the lives and witness of all those who have gone before us in faith—forefathers, fathers, patriarchs, prophets, apostles, preachers, evangelists, martyrs, confessors, ascetics, and every righteous spirit made pure in Christ (1 Corinthians 10:1–11; Hebrews 11:3–40).

He calls on us to *remember*. As the psalmist has said:

> We must remember the deeds of the Lord in our midst. Surely, we must remember His wonders of old. I will meditate on all Your work, and muse

on Your deeds. Your way is holy; what god is like unto our God? You are
the God who works wonders; You have made known Your strength among
the peoples. You have by power redeemed Your people, the sons of Jacob
and Joseph. (Psalm 77:11–15)

And again:

Oh give thanks to the Lord, call upon His name. Make known His deeds
among the peoples. Sing to Him, sing praises to Him; speak of all His
wonders on the earth. Glory in His name; let the heart of those who seek
the Lord be glad. Seek the Lord and His strength; seek His face continually. Remember His wonders which He has done in our midst, His marvels
and the judgments uttered by His mouth. (Psalm 105:1–5)

When Moses stood before the Israelites at the end of his long life,
he did not exhort them with polemics or moralisms. He reminded them
of the works of God in history. He reminded them of their duty to *remember* (Deuteronomy 32:1–43).

When David stood before his family and friends following a great deliverance from his enemies, he did not stir them with sentiment or nostal-
gia. He reminded them of the works of God in history in a psalm of praise.
He reminded them of their duty to *remember* (2 Samuel 22:1–51).

When Solomon stood before his subjects at the dedication of the newly
constructed temple, he did not challenge them with logic or rhetoric. He
simply reminded them of the works of God in history in a hymn of wisdom. He reminded them of their duty to *remember* (1 Kings 8:15–61).

When Nehemiah stood before the families of Jerusalem at the con-
secration of the rebuilt city walls, he did not bombard them with theology or theatrics. He simply reminded them of the works of God in history in a song of the covenant. He reminded them of their duty to
remember (Nehemiah 9:9–38).

When Stephen stood before an accusing and enraged Sanhedrin, he
did not confront them with apology or condemnation. He simply reminded them of the works of God in history in a litany of faith. He
reminded them of their duty to *remember* (Acts 7:2–53).

Remembrance and forgetfulness are the measuring rods of faithfulness throughout the entire canon of Scripture. A family that passes its
legacy on to its children will bear great fruit (Deuteronomy 8:2–10). A
family that fails to take its heritage seriously will remain barren (Deuteronomy 8:11–14). A people that remembers the great and mighty

deeds of the Lord will be blessed (Deuteronomy 8:18). A people that forgets is doomed to frustration and failure (Deuteronomy 8:19–20). In fact, the whole direction of a culture depends on the gracious appointments of memory: "Wonders cannot be known in the midst of darkness. Righteousness cannot be done in a land of forgetfulness" (Psalm 88:12).

That is why the Bible makes it plain that there are only two kinds of people in the world: effectual doers and forgetful hearers (James 1:25). And that is why the ministry of the Holy Spirit in the lives of believers is primarily to bring to our *remembrance* the Word of Truth (John 14:26).

Philip Schaff, the prolific church historian during the previous generation, argued stridently that we must be eternally vigilant in the task of handing on our great legacy—to remember and then to inculcate that remembrance in the hearts and minds of our children:

> How shall we labor with any effect to build up the church, if we have no thorough knowledge of its history, or fail to apprehend it from the proper point of observation? History is, and must ever continue to be, next to God's Word, the richest foundation of wisdom, and the surest guide to all successful practical activity.[5]

Indeed, in this ongoing epic culture war—in this tortured clash between historic Christianity and ancient paganism—we dare not neglect our rich legacy. And we dare not keep it to ourselves:

> Listen, Oh my people, to my instruction; incline your ears to the words of my mouth. I will open my mouth in a parable; I will utter dark sayings of old, which we have heard and known, and our fathers have told us. We will not conceal them from our children, but tell to the generation to come the praises of the Lord, and His strength and His wondrous works that He has done. For He established a testimony in our midst and appointed a new law in the land, which He commanded to our fathers, that they should teach them to their children that the generation to come might know, even the children yet to be born that they may in turn arise and tell them to their children, that they should put their confidence in God, and not forget the works of God, but keep His commandments. (Psalm 78:1–7)

Seeing that the Spirit has been at work since the time of Christ, we would do well to look back at what He has done. After all, despite our almost adolescent propensity for asserting that the people of all previous centuries could not possibly know how to deal with the dilemmas of modernity, the church has *successfully* dealt with many of the issues we face today. The fact is that all too often modern Christians are prevented from fully understanding their situation because of their ignorance of their historical context.

Lord Acton, the great Christian historian from the last century, wrote:

> History must be our deliverer not only from the undue influence of other times, but from the undue influence of our own, from the tyranny of the environment and the pressures of the air we breathe.[6]

The English author and lecturer John H. Y. Briggs argues that an historical awareness is essential for the health and well-being of any society; it enables us to know who we are, why we are here, and what we should do. He says:

> Just as a loss of memory in an individual is a psychiatric defect calling for medical treatment, so too any community which has no social memory is suffering from an illness.[7]

The church is a society instituted by Jesus Christ. It is important that members of this society remember the legacy that God has graciously given them.

None of this is to imply that any tradition can speak with the same authority as Scripture does, of course. But tradition does speak with enough authority that we should pay careful heed. Jordan explains:

> Not all the prayers, music, and theology of the traditions are equally good. Not everything said in the past is of equal value. It is the Bible that judges the traditions. Nevertheless, the traditions play an important part in the life of the Christian. It is simply not possible for every individual Christian theologian to rethink every doctrinal and ethical matter out of the Bible. We rely on customs and traditions, on historic creeds and confessions, to do a lot of the work for us. Only when we face a serious crisis do we go back to the Bible and question our traditions.[8]

So, what view has the Christian church traditionally held through the centuries? What did the pioneers of our faith have to say about the issue of homosexuality?

When in Rome

As it spread throughout the Roman Empire, Christianity obviously confronted a pagan culture with a sexual ethic just as obviously alien to that of Scripture. "In their sexual code," writes Robin Lane Fox, the university lecturer in ancient history at New College Oxford, "Christians were conscious of standing apart from the pagan world."[9] They were well aware that they were aliens in a foreign land.

As one anonymous apologist wrote:

> Christians are not distinguishable from the rest of mankind in land or speech or customs . . . yet they live in their own countries as sojourners only; they take part in everything as citizens and submit to everything as strangers. Every strange land is native to them, and every native land is strange. They marry and have children like everyone else—but they do not expose their children. They have meals in common, but not wives. They are in the flesh, but they do not live after the flesh. They continue on earth, but their citizenship is in heaven. They obey the laws ordained, and by their private lives they overcome the laws. . . . In a word, what the soul is in the body, that is what Christians are in the world.[10]

This difference was especially evident in the area of homosexuality. As Fox observes, what few reservations existed with regard to same-sex relationships had nothing to do with it being inherently immoral:

> Pagans' sanctions against homosexuality concerned male prostitution and political ideas of a good citizen. . . . Among Romans, the most acceptable homosexuality was an act conducted by citizens on slaves or foreigners. In early Rome, an obscurely attested law does seem to have punished all homosexuality between citizens themselves. Christian authors still alluded to it, but it is clear that the law had long been defunct in normal political life. In Rome, as in Athens, there was special objection to those who were passive partners in a homosexual act. . . . By mid-third century A.D., Roman laws asserted strong penalties against male prostitutes but also proposed the confiscation of half the goods of a citizen who willingly submitted to another man. No cases are known to have been brought under it.[11]

Frances and Joseph Gies concur that perversion was commonplace and accepted in Rome. In their work, *Marriage and the Family in the Middle Ages,* they write:

The practice of homosexuality, especially male, was evidently widespread, at least among the Roman upper classes. Slave boys and slave girls were made to serve their master's pleasure.[12]

The early church's view of homosexuality, in contrast, was unhesitating and unanimous. Referring to the writings of the early church from the first century forward, the Anglican bishop of Crediton, England, Peter Coleman asserts:

Although the evidence is sparse, documents surviving from that period usually express undeviating hostility, and show that the leaders of the Church were aware of homosexual practices and firmly opposed to what they considered an immoral aspect of the pagan society in which they lived.[13]

Richard Hays of Yale Divinity School concurs:

Every pertinent Christian text from the pre-Constantinian period . . . adopts an unremittingly negative judgment on homosexual practice, and this tradition is emphatically carried forward by all the major Christian writers of the fourth and fifth centuries.[14]

To recent revisionists who would attempt to deny that the ancient church was unreservedly opposed to homosexual perversion, Robin Lane Fox bluntly replies:

As for homosexuality, Paul and the other apostles agreed with the accepted Jewish view that it was a deadly sin which provoked God's wrath. It led to earthquakes and natural disasters, which were evident in the fate of Sodom. The absence of Gospel teaching on the topic did not amount to tacit approval. All orthodox Christians knew that homosexuals went to Hell, until a modern minority tried to make them forget it.[15]

Perhaps the earliest extrabiblical Christian document that condemns homosexuality is the *Didache: The Teaching of the Twelve Apostles*. It was possibly written as early as A.D. 60, though it probably dates from between A.D. 100 and 150. Taking its cue from Deuteronomy 30:15, this manual of church instruction begins, "There are two paths to follow: one is life and the other is death. There is a profound difference between the two."[16] Continuing, the document makes it clear that prohibiting homosexuality was a standard part of the Christian distinction between those two paths:

> The second commandment of the Lord's instruction is this: Do not kill; do not commit adultery; do not corrupt boys; do not practice immorality; do not steal; do not practice witchcraft; do not use sorcery; do not kill an unborn child by abortion, nor kill a newborn child; do not covet your neighbor's possessions.[17]

Another authoritative pastoral document from the patristic church was the *Epistle of Barnabas,* which also was composed late in the first century or early in the second. Though its authorship is doubtful, it was well-respected by the church and accurately reflects its teaching. The author devotes the tenth chapter of his work to commenting on the meaning of the dietary laws that Moses gave:

> "You shall not eat the hare." Why? So that, he said, you may not become a child molester or be made like these. For the hare grows a new anal opening each year, so that however many years he has lived, he has that many anuses. Nor should you eat the hyena, he said, so that you may not become an adulterer or a seducer, or like them. Why? Because the animal changes its gender annually and is one year a male and the next a female. And he also rightly despised the weasel. You shall not, he said, become as these, who we hear commit uncleanness with their mouths, nor shall you be joined to those women who have committed illicit acts orally with the unclean. For this animal conceives through its mouth.[18]

While this may seem like a strange exposition, it is based on the common hermeneutical principle that different animals in Scripture represent different types of people (Deuteronomy 25:4 and 1 Corinthians 9:9–10; Deuteronomy 22:10 and 2 Corinthians 6:14; and Acts 10). Using the zoological knowledge of the day and his understanding of Biblical morality, the author condemns all sorts of gender-crossing perversion as well as pedophilia.[19]

The *Epistle of Barnabas* had wide-ranging influence. Its content was adopted by Clement of Alexandria in his manual of instruction for Christian parents, the *Paedagogus,* an exceedingly popular work. Clement's commentary on the dietary laws was even more concerned specifically with homosexuality. There he referred to Paul's condemnation of the practice in Romans, saying:

Such degradation is a defilement of the basest sort, and not to the offender only, but to all. Take it not lightly or in jest.[20]

One of the earliest apologists for Christianity, Aristides of Athens, wrote that Christians "have learned God's commandments, and they live by them in the hope of the world to come. For this reason they do not commit adultery or engage in sexual immorality."[21] Aristides makes it clear that homosexuality is included in his definition of "sexual immorality," saying, "The Greeks . . . follow shameful practices in having sexual activities with males."[22]

Indeed, another Christian apologist, Athenagoras, wrote to the emperors Marcus Aurelius and Lucius Aurelius Commodus midway through the second century explaining to them that accusations by the pagans that Christians were sexually immoral were not only false but hypocritical:

The harlot reproves the chaste. Our accusers have set up a market for fornication, have established infamous houses of every sort of shameful pleasure for the young, and do not even spare the males—males committing shocking acts with males. In all sorts of ways they outrage those with the more graceful and handsome bodies. They dishonor God's splendid creation, for beauty on earth is not self-made, but has been created by the hand and mind of God. It is these people who revile us with the very things they are conscious of in themselves and which they attribute to their gods. They boast of them, indeed, as noble acts and worthy of the gods. Adulterers and corrupters of boys, they insult eunuchs and those once married.[23]

After the conversion of Emperor Constantine, the Christianizing of the Roman Empire and its attendant culture—which had been proceeding apace since the coming of the Holy Spirit on Pentecost—was officially sanctioned. The Christian sexual ethic, therefore, was gradually established as the normative standard for all behavior.

Evangelizing the empire was by no means an easy task to accomplish. Not only did the church have to meet new responsibilities outside the sanctuary as the recognized religious leader of society, but its increasing popularity gave rise to an increasing problem with sin inside the sanctuary. This problem was dealt with partly by the teaching and preaching ministry of the church. John Chrysostom, for example, was courageous in reproving perversity and calling the church in Byzantium to repent despite much government opposition. He did not hesitate to accuse, saying:

> Those very people who have been nourished by godly doctrine, who instruct others in what they ought and ought not to do, who have heard the Scriptures brought down from heaven, these do not consort with prostitutes as fearlessly as they do with young men. The fathers of the young men take this in silence; they do not try to sequester their sons, nor do they seek any remedy for this evil.[24]

Nevertheless, the church continued to grow and meet the challenges of dealing with a changing society.

Interestingly though, this challenge was not primarily facilitated by the civil government. Both the behavior and the attitudes of the citizenry were changed by the nurture and the discipline of the local congregations.[25] The canon law of the early church established restorative penances for homosexual activity, for instance:

> They who have committed sodomy with men or brutes, murderers, wizards, adulterers, and idolaters, have been thought worthy with these which you do to others. We ought not make any doubt of receiving those who have repented thirty years for the uncleanness which they committed through ignorance; for their ignorance pleads their pardon, and their willingness in confessing it; therefore command them to be forthwith received, especially if they have tears to prevail upon your tenderness, and have since their lapse lived such a life as to deserve your compassion.[26]

Although this may seem severe to modern ears, and may attract accusations of "legalism," the church was, in fact, simply attempting to take sin seriously and to deal with it pastorally. In a society where, for ages, fathers were thought to have a legal right to kill their newborn sons and—more often—daughters if they did not want them, where the state gave slaveholders life-and-death powers over their slaves, where murder in the gladiator pits was a popularly accepted spectator sport, and the political rulers held absolute authority over the lives of their subjects, somehow the church had to inculcate into the populace a Christian world-and-life view—a Biblical ethic.

Thus, these acts of penance were instituted *not* as works of atonement, but as practical acts of sanctification. They served a double purpose: first, they demonstrated the sincerity of repentance and second, they constituted a form of restitution.

These rules of penance, or "penitentials," were first established in religious communities and nascent monasteries.[27] It is notable that the church leaders were realistic about the temptations that cloistered believers would face and advised them accordingly. Augustine of Hippo, for instance, wrote letters to cloistered celibate women warning them that their love for each other should be spiritual and not involve "shameless playing with each other."[28] Likewise, Basil of Caesarea, who was one of the founders of the monastic life, gave advice on avoiding homosexual temptation:

> It is frequently the case with young men that even when rigorous self-restraint is exercised, the glowing complexion of youth still blossoms forth and becomes a source of desire to those around them. If, therefore, anyone is youthful and physically beautiful, let him keep his attractiveness hidden until his appearance reaches a suitable state.[29]

While the penitentials began as rules for religious communities, they eventually became the rules of church discipline for all Christians—thus transforming the way people lived.

Though the primary responsibility to spread the Christian sexual ethic belonged to the institutional church, the civil government also had a role to play. Taking the Bible seriously, Christians knew that God punished whole societies with plagues, economic depressions, and wars when they refused to be salt and light in the society at large.[30]

In 588 A.D., the Emperor Justinian decreed:

> Because of such crime—blasphemy and sodomy—there are famines, earthquakes, and pestilences; wherefore we admonish men to abstain from the aforesaid unlawful acts, that they may not lose their souls. . . . We order the most illustrious prefect of the capital to arrest those who persist in the aforesaid lawless and impious acts after they have been warned by us, and to inflict on them the extreme punishments, so that the city and the State may not come to harm by reason of such wicked deeds.[31]

Even before Justinian, as early as 390 A.D., Emperor Theodosius declared sodomy a capital crime and various Christian realms continued to enforce that standard for almost two millennia.[32]

The Age of Faith

The Age of Faith has commonly been called the Dark Ages—as if the light of civilization had been unceremoniously snuffed out. It has similarly been dubbed the Middle Ages—as if it were a gaping parenthesis in mankind's long upward march to modernity.

It was, in fact, anything but dark or middling. Perhaps our greatest fault is that we have limited ourselves by a parochialism in time. It is difficult for us to attribute anything but backwardness to those epochs and cultures that do not share our goals or aspirations.

The medieval period was actually quite remarkable for its many advances—perhaps unparalleled in all of history. It was a true *nascence,* while the epoch that followed was but a *re-naissance.* It was a new and living thing that gave flower to a culture marked by energy and creativity. From the monolithic security of Byzantium in the East, to the reckless diversity of feuding fiefs in the West, it was a glorious crazy quilt of human fabrics, textures, and hues.

Now to be sure, the medieval world was racked with abject poverty, ravaging plagues, and petty wars—much like our own day. It was haunted by superstition, prejudice, and corruption—as is the modern era. And it was beset by consuming ambition, perverse sin, and damnable folly—again, so like today. Still, it was free from the kind of crippling sophistication, insular ethnocentricity, and cosmopolitan provincialism that now shackles us—and so it was able to advance astonishingly.

The titanic innovations medievalism brought forth were legion: it gave birth to all the great universities of the world from Oxford and Cambridge to Leipzig to Mainz; it oversaw the establishment of all the great hospitals of the world from St. Bartholomew's and Bedlam in London to St. Bernard's and Voixanne in Switzerland; it brought forth the world's most celebrated artists from Michelangelo Buonarotti and Albrecht Durer to Leonardo da Vinci and Jan van Eyck; it gave us the splendor of Gothic architecture—unmatched and unmatchable to this day—from Notre Dame and Chartres to Winchester and Cologne; it thrust out into howling wilderness and storm-tossed seas the most accomplished explorers from Amerigo Vespucci and Marco Polo to Vasco da Gama and Christopher Columbus; it produced some of the greatest minds and most fascinating lives mankind has yet known—were the list not so sterling it might begin to be tedious—Copernicus, Dante, Giotto,

Becket, Gutenberg, Chaucer, Charlemagne, Wyclif, Magellan, Botticelli, Donatello, Petrarch, and Aquinas.

But of all the great innovations that medievalism wrought, the greatest of all was spiritual. Medieval culture—both East and West—was first and foremost Christian culture. Its life was shaped almost entirely by Christian concerns. Virtually all of its achievements were submitted to the cause of the Gospel. From great cathedrals and gracious chivalry, to long crusades and beautiful cloisters, every manifestation of its presence was somehow tied to its utter and complete obeisance to Christ's kingdom.

Of course, the medieval church had its share of dangerous and scandalous behavior. It had gross libertines and rank heretics. It had false professors and bold opportunists. It had brutal ascetics and imbalanced tyrants. But then, there was no more of that sort of heterodoxy than we have today in evangelical, Catholic, or Orthodox circles—and perhaps, considering recent headlines, a good deal less.

At any rate, spiritual concerns played a larger role in the lives of medieval man and women than at almost any other time before or since. And, as might be expected, that all-pervading interest was evidenced in a prominent concern for chaste morality.[33] Thus, as the Christian faith permeated the societies of the West, the prohibition on sodomy was also propagated.

When Charlemagne first became emperor at the beginning of the medieval epoch, he worked to reform the monasteries which he felt had grown lax about homosexuality. Believing he was responsible for the creation of a Christian Europe, Charlemagne took it upon himself to exhort the monks "to strive to preserve themselves from such evils," saying that such perversity should not be committed "in any part of the realm, much less among those who should be especially chaste and devout."[34]

Other reformers also rebuked the monasteries for homosexuality. Around 1051, Peter Damien authored a blistering attack on the underground perversion. In *The Book of Gomorrah,* he wrote:

Absolutely no other vice can be reasonably compared with this one, which surpasses all others in uncleanness. For this vice is in fact the death of the body, the destruction of the soul; it pollutes flesh, extinguishes the light of the mind, casts out the Holy Spirit from the temple of the human breast, and replaces it with the devil, the rouser of lust; it removes truth utterly from the mind; it deceives and directs it toward falsehood; it sets snares in man's path and, when he falls into the pit, blocks it up so there is no escape; it opens the doors to hell and closes the gates of heaven; it makes the citizen of the heavenly Jerusalem the heir of infernal Babylon.[35]

For his exposé, Damien received a response from Pope Leo IX, who promised to attempt to end this perversity.

Less than two centuries later Pope Honorius III sent a pastoral letter to the Archbishop of Lund:

> We have received a petition from you requesting that we deign to provide mercifully for the fact that numerous subjects of yours, clerics and laymen, frequently engage in prohibited sexual relations, not only with persons related to them, but also by having sinful intercourse with dumb animals and by that sin which should neither be named nor committed, on account of which the Lord condemned to destruction Sodom and Gomorrah; and that some of these on account of the lengths and dangers of the journey, others on account of shame, would rather die in their sins than appear before us on such charges. Therefore, since divine mercy is greater than human perverseness and since it is better to count on the generosity of God than to despair because of the magnitude of a particular sin, we order you herewith to reprimand, exhort, and threaten such sinners and then to assign them, with patience and good judgment, a salutary penance, using moderation in its devising, so that neither does undue leniency prompt audacity to sin, nor does unreasonable severity inspire despair.[36]

One of the most widespread forms of teaching on homosexuality during that era was a book about animals called the *Physiologus*. According to one historian, E.P. Evans:

> Perhaps no book except the Bible has ever been so widely diffused among so many people for so many centuries.[37]

The *Physiologus* contained anecdotes about certain animals and used them as "character sketches" to illustrate various Christian truths. Following the tradition of the *Letter of Barnabas* and Clement's *Paedogogus,* the book used the mythical perversions of the weasel, the hyena, and the hare to point out that homosexuality is a perversion. According to historian John Boswell:

Its influence was incalculable, particularly during the High Middle Ages. Available in every Romance language as "the bestiary," it served as a manual of piety, a primer of zoology, and a form of entertainment.[38]

As in the early days of the Empire, civil magistrates also mitigated against homosexual influence in the society. Often though, since the state was viewed as an agency of God's wrath, and not His mercy, civil governments were much more severe. In the thirteenth century, Alfonso the Wise drafted a law code that was put in effect during the next century. In it he wrote:

Sodomy is the sin which men commit by having intercourse with each other, against nature and natural custom. And because from this sin arise many evils in the land where it is perpetuated, and it sorely offends God and gives a bad name not only to those who indulge in it but also to the nation in which it occurs. . . . For such crimes our Lord sent upon the land guilty of them famine, plague, catastrophe, and countless other calamities. Anyone can accuse a man of having committed a crime against nature before the judge of the district in which the crime was committed. If it is proved, both of those involved should be put to death. However, if one was forced or is under the age of fourteen he should not suffer this penalty, because those who are forced are not guilty, and minors do not understand how serious a crime they have committed. This same penalty shall apply to a man or woman who has intercourse with an animal. And the animal also shall be killed to obliterate the memory of the deed.[39]

Clearly, the medieval church continued in the honored tradition of the ancient church in its forthright condemnation of homosexuality.

The Reformation Tradition

The Protestant Reformation was an attempt to reform the one, true church and counteract corruptions that had developed within it. Under the slogan *Sola Scriptura,* the reformers attempted to bring the church in line with the Word of God, from which they believed it had departed. Their call for reformation touched on every area of life and godliness, including the area of sexual ethics.

Not surprisingly, the reformers, in maintaining faithfulness to Scripture, never varied from the Biblical standard of heterosexual monogamy.

Consequently, they did not hesitate to condemn homosexuality as sin. For example, Luther, in his commentary on Genesis, asserted:

> The heinous conduct of the people of Sodom is extraordinary, inasmuch as they departed from the natural passion and longing of the male for the female, which was implanted into nature by God, and desired what is altogether contrary to nature. Whence comes this perversity? Undoubtedly from Satan, who, after people have once turned away from the fear of God, so powerfully suppresses nature that he blots out the natural desire that is contrary to nature.[40]

John Calvin also condemned homosexuality. Commenting on a passage in Deuteronomy, he said:

> This passage treats all the infamous sorts of lechery, even the most loathsome kinds of them, whether incest or sodomy, or other such corruptions. And it is with good reason that God chooses out these particular kinds, for it is to the end that we should be touched with the more fear and terror when we go about any kind of lechery.[41]

One of the questions from the *Westminster Larger Catechism* asks: "What are the sins forbidden in the Seventh Commandment?" Sodomy is listed among the correct answers.[42]

Since the Reformation did not limit itself to the church, but affected all of life and culture, it necessarily influenced the thinking and policies of civil magistrates. Once again, the heirs of the Reformation continued in the long and honored traditions of the past. Even in the New World, this steadfast adherence was not abandoned. In Puritan New England, for example, the statutes were clear:

> Unnatural filthiness to be punished with death, whether sodomy, which is a carnal fellowship of man with man, or woman with woman, or buggery, which is a carnal fellowship of man or woman with beasts or fowls.[43]

Despite the encroaching moral darkness of the Enlightenment, the stigma of homosexuality was retained by the culture for quite some time. As late as 1750, two workers were publicly executed in Paris for homosexuality.[44]

Thus, the Reformation tradition as well, conformed to the Biblical condemnation of homosexuality as sin.

The Modern Church

Sadly, the twentieth century saw this remarkable two-thousand-year-old commitment suddenly dissipate. In an astonishingly short period of time the church lost its authoritative influence within the culture due to both internal compromise and institutional retreat—capitulating to the juggernaut of inhuman humanism.

Although there were many ways in which the church made itself vulnerable to the onslaught of humanism, perhaps the most significant was its practically idolatrous worship of "science." Even the most conservative Christians yielded to the seductive siren's call of scientism.

Evangelical historian George Marsden, in his compelling essay "The Collapse of American Evangelical Academia," writes:

> Among American Protestants there was no crisis of science versus religion associated with the first, or Newtonian, scientific revolution. The American Puritans and their heirs, by and large, embraced the new science with enthusiasm.[45]

The fact is, many nineteenth-century evangelicals largely based their faith on the supposed evidence of modern science. In effect, evangelicals asserted that Christianity was true *because* it met the standards of modern science.

Much of modern science was built on the assumptions of Enlightenment ideas, which denied the fallen nature of man and asserted that truth could be discovered irrespective of one's theological or ethical commitments. Thus, like a child playing Monopoly, modern science changes the rules as it goes along.[46] Darwin, Freud, Marx, and others introduced scientific theories and innovations that were much more blatantly anti-Christian than Newtonianism. As a result, the Christian faith was undercut. Since the church had already established Christianity on the basis of modern science, it now had to either alter Christianity or give up intellectual prestige.[47]

The church is still feeling the effect of this compromise of the authority of Scripture with the authority of theoretical science. The fact is that even science is filtered through our fallible predispositions, presuppositions, and prejudices. Modern science is built on the claim that experience is the only source of knowledge. In contrast, the Bible tells us that God's Word is the only reliable source of knowledge. Thus, our experience really can only test truth insofar as our experience is subject to God's Word.

Sadly, that is a difficult notion for us moderns to grasp.

The Diseasing of Christendom

Even the evangelical church has fallen prey to compromise in this area. This is especially true in the realm of psychology—a discipline that has direct bearing on understanding homosexuality, since it actually *created* the disease model for human behavior.

Dr. Patrick Carnes, for example, in his book *Out of the Shadows: Understanding Sexual Addiction,* treats all perpetrators of compulsive sexual behavior as victims of "sickness." He quotes the homosexual poet Walt Whitman, "I am larger, better than I thought. I did not know I held so much goodness."[48] And then he concludes that such "addicts" are not responsible for their sexual behavior:

> While our society is shifting to a more open attitude toward sexual expression, we still view the amount and kind of activity as a matter of personal choice. For the addict, however, there is no choice. No choice. The addiction is in charge. That addicts have no control over their sexual behavior is a very hard concept to accept when the addicts' trails have left broken marriages and parentless children, or worse, victims of sexual crimes.[49]

Not only does Carnes portray those guilty of sex crimes as addicts or "victims," he also labels those close relationships with addicts as "co-addicts." To explain what co-addiction is, he cites a newspaper story:

> Ruth Coe, the mother of convicted rapist Frederick Coe, was charged Friday with hiring a man she did not know was an undercover police officer to kill the prosecutor who tried her son and the judge who sentenced him to life in prison.[50]

Carnes comments:

> The plight of Ruth Coe is a tragic example of the *family illness* which affects those who care for the sexually compulsive.[51]

Lauded in *The Journal of the American Medical Association* as "interesting, readable, and original . . . of value to begin to understand these age-old sexual behaviors," the book has become a standard text in the field.[52]

In one respect, the adoption of this responsibility-evading perspective is not entirely unexpected. Carnes makes clear that he is merely attempting to adapt the popular "twelve-step program" of Alcoholics Anonymous for the treatment of sexaholism:

> A sex addict cannot, in our day and time, proudly announce his or her recovery—as alcoholics now can. Sexual addicts need to remember the decades of struggle that alcoholics had to go through in order to earn public acceptance of their illness. Even now large parts of the population still see alcoholism as a matter of moral degeneracy. We are perhaps decades away from a public understanding of the problem of sexual addiction.[53]

What makes this evasion/problematic for many evangelicals is that the disease model for alcoholism has long been accepted within conservative churches. Those who still believe that repeated heavy drinking is a sinful lifestyle, not an illness, are even rebuked by evangelical authors. "Treatment expert" Alexander DeJong, for example, writes:

> Many active alcoholics who are Christians remain hopelessly caught in the snare of their illness because they (and the Christian community which surrounds them) feel that their sickness is sin.[54]

As an Al-Anon publication stated:

> After centuries of treating alcoholism as a moral weakness, most present-day medical opinion considers alcoholism a disease which, like diabetes, can be arrested, but not cured. Many of the clergy, too, now accept alcoholism as sickness, and not sin.[55]

But if what the Bible condemns as the sin of drunkenness is, in fact, a disease, then doesn't that mean Christianity is either archaically misinformed at best, or a false religion at worst?

Dr. William Playfair, in *The Useful Lie,* a critique of the recovery industry, points out:

> The apostle Paul, who consumed alcohol in moderate quantities, said, "I will not be brought under the power of anything" (1 Corinthians 6:12). Speaking to others who consumed alcohol, he said, "Be not drunk." He

could have said, "Some of you cannot control your drinking. You are a special class of the 'one-drink, one-drunk' kind." But he didn't because there is no such thing. Interestingly, this same line of reasoning has been used by some Christians to justify the homosexual lifestyle. They create a special person of which Paul knows nothing. This special person then falls outside of Paul's condemnation of homosexuality, which is seen to be addressed only to heterosexuals who practice homosexuality, not to the "constitutionally homosexual person."[56]

Playfair is not imagining the relationship between alcoholism and homosexuality. The apostle Paul mentions both "drunkards" and "homosexuals" in a list that includes "thieves" and "adulterers." Furthermore, he characterizes such people as "unrighteous," and twice warns them that they will not "inherit the Kingdom of God" (1 Corinthians 6:9–10). If drunkenness is a disease, not a sin, then we have already lost half the battle when confronted with homosexuality.

Even worse, the disease model pioneered by AA in the case of heavy drinking is now being used by some evangelicals to explain every conceivable compulsive behavior, real or imagined. In fact, Carnes' idea of "co-addiction" has developed into the codependency industry—an industry with both a secular and a religious wing.

The self-professed secular humanist Wendy Kaminer, in her valuable book *I'm Dysfunctional, You're Dysfunctional: The Recovery Movement and Other Self-Help Fashions,* has noticed:

> Whether psychology has caught up to religion, infiltrated it, or been adopted by it, the most popular versions of both psychology and religion are becoming less and less distinguishable.[57]

The problem with this is that modern psychology and its view of addiction presupposes that people are inherently sinless.

Kaminer explains:

> Addiction "masks" true feelings and the true childlike self. Codependents are considered "adult children." If some are more like Scrooge than Peter Pan, all have a Tiny Tim within. Inner children are always good—innocent and pure—like the most sentimentalized Dickens characters, which means that people are essentially good. . . . Even Ted Bundy had a child within. Evil is merely a mask—a dysfunction. The therapeutic view of evil as sick-

ness, not sin, is strong in codependency theory—*it's not a fire and brim-stone theology.*[58]

Although the disease model still allows Christians to consider homosexual practice abnormal and undesirable, it greatly hampers the possibility of true repentance. The secular psychologist and author Stan Katz criticizes the disease model of human behavior, saying:

> We've all used the phrase "I can't help it" at one time or another. My children frequently say this to me when I catch them at something they know they shouldn't be doing, such as eating too much candy or falling behind in their homework. They know perfectly well they do have a choice, but they think that if I think they don't, I'll let them off the hook. Claiming powerlessness is easier than owning up to responsibility. I hear the same refrain among my patients, many of whom are depressed because they use drugs, mistreat their children or spouses, or keep getting involved in unsatisfying relationships. Unlike my children, most of them genuinely believe they are powerless to change their patterns. . . . Yet the essential reason for saying "I can't help it" is the same for these adults as it is for my children: It is easier to abdicate than to accept responsibility for one's actions.[59]

As a result of the disease model, evangelicals are becoming less and less inclined to deal with sin in a serious manner. One evangelical leader, for example, was asked how he would counsel two spouses who were committing adultery with each other. "I would make it very clear that I believe their adultery is a distortion of God's creation and that adulterous behavior is sin," he answered. "I would also try to help them take steps toward Jesus and to understand, as they grow closer to Him, they'll have to deal with the issue."

Actually, that's not quite the way it went.

Stephen Hayner, the president of InterVarsity Christian Fellowship, was asked how he would counsel a homosexual couple. He replied:

> I would make it very clear that I believe their homosexuality is a distortion of God's creation and that homosexuality is a sin. I would also try to help them take steps toward Jesus and to understand, as they grow closer to him, they'll have to deal with the issue.[60]

Lest anyone think Hayner's comments are somehow "taken out of context"—as has been asserted in the past—bear in mind that this statement was taken from an interview he gave in order to clarify his already quite confused position.[61]

Our point in replacing the "homosexuality" in Hayner's statement with "adultery" is to demonstrate that increasingly certain sins are not really being treated as sins at all—but rather as *bad habits*. Everyone knows—we hope—that the Gospel demands that all adulterous couples immediately cease their sinful behavior. Adulterers cannot possibly "take steps toward Jesus" while they continue to commit adultery. By practicing such sin they are running *away* from Jesus. As the apostle Paul states, such people will not inherit the Kingdom of God.

Why, then, should not the same standard apply to homosexuals? Perhaps because he believes that "most homosexuals . . . have no idea how they got this way and really don't want to be this way."[62] But Patrick Carnes says the same thing about pedophiles and rapists. Would Hayner tell a child molester that pederasty is a distortion of God's creation and that, as he grows closer to Jesus, he'll have to deal with the issue?

Repentance and Restoration

Thankfully, there are Christians who have resisted the modern trend and thus bear strong witness to what the Gospel teaches about homosexuality.

Regeneration, a Christian group in Baltimore directed by Alan Medinger, has facilitated the repentance and restoration of many homosexuals—some of whom are now married with children. Medinger is attempting to start more groups up and down the East Coast but, tragically, his own denomination, the Episcopal Church, is mostly either uncooperative or hostile, whereas most evangelicals are sympathetic but unwilling to get actively involved.[63]

White Stone Ministries has an office at Ruggles Baptist Church in Boston where Mike Mitchel and Linda Frank both counsel homosexuals who wish to alter their sinful sexual habits. Both know that repentance and restoration is possible because both were once homosexual themselves.[64]

Desert Stream Ministries is located in Santa Monica, California, where it brings a message of repentance and restoration to homosexuals. Its director, Andrew Comiskey, also an ex-homosexual, serves as president of Exodus International, an umbrella organization for over seventy-five similar ministries worldwide that carry the good news of repentance and restoration to homosexuals.[65]

Ron and Joanne Highley of New York City run L.I.F.E., a Bible-centered ministry to homosexuals. They publish testimonials of the fruits of repentance and restoration, including heterosexual marriage announcements and reports on the birth of subsequent children.[66]

Jesus People USA is a local Christian community in Chicago that ministers to many groups of people often overlooked by more traditional congregations, including homosexuals. They do not let modern science prevent them from presenting a message of repentance and restoration to homosexuals. They write:

> The environmental and psychological factors that constitute homosexual behavior are indeed various and complex. Liability is very much a part of this matter. We make choices on how we respond to stimuli. Compulsive behavior is not immune to the scrutiny of eternal judgement either.[67]

Conclusion

The great author from the first half of this century G. K. Chesterton once said:

> An imbecile habit has arisen in modern controversy of saying that such and such a creed can be held in one age but cannot be held in another. Some dogma, we are told, was credible in the twelfth century, but is not credible in the twentieth. You might as well say that a certain philosophy can be believed on Mondays, but cannot be believed on Tuesdays. You might as well say of a view of the cosmos that it was suitable to half-past three, but not suitable for half-past four. What a man can believe depends upon his philosophy, not upon the clock or the century.[68]

The proclamation of the Biblical message on homosexuality has been consistent and clear throughout the centuries. Only in the modern age has the visible church substantially departed from it. Nevertheless, there is still a remnant being used of God to bring repentance and restoration to homosexuals. Perhaps their example will bring repentance and restoration to the church of Jesus Christ.

In the present struggle to uphold our two-thousand-year-old heritage, it would stand us in good stead to pay heed to this pattern—this legacy—and to reclaim it.

After all, there is no need to reinvent the wheel. As historian David R. Carlin has said:

> The best way to develop an attitude of responsibility toward the future is to cultivate a sense of responsibility toward the past. We are born into a world that we didn't make, and it is only fair that we should be grateful to those who did make it. Such gratitude carries with it the imperative that we preserve and at least slightly improve the world that has been given us before passing it on to subsequent generations. We stand in the midst of many generations. If we are indifferent to those who went before us and actually existed, how can we expect to be concerned for the well-being of those who come after us and only potentially exist.[69]

PART IV

A CALL TO ARMS

And the possession?
The violence will be over
And an old passion,
Before I leave these ancient hills,
Descend abruptly into the modern city, crying:
Love![1]

LAURA RIDING

11

JUST SAY YES: HOPE

Speak that we may hear;
Listen while we confess
That we conceal our fear;
Regard us, while the eye
Discerns by sight or guess.[2]

ALLEN TATE

O ver three hundred years ago, the great Puritan writer John Bunyan
began his classic masterpiece, *Pilgrim's Progress,* with a desperate and woeful cry for direction:

> As I walked through the wilderness of this world, I lighted on a certain
> place where was a den, and I laid me down in that place to sleep, and as I
> slept I dreamed a dream. I dreamed, and behold I saw a man clothed in
> rags, standing in a certain place, with his face from his own house, a book
> in his hand, and a great burden on his back. I looked and saw him open the
> book, and read therein; and as he read he wept and trembled, and not being
> able to longer to contain, he brake out with a lamentable cry, saying: *What
> shall I do?*[3]

Over three hundred years later, the cry still arises. The burden still
exists. Concerned pilgrims still look out over the "wilderness of this
world," seeing the calamities of destruction, irresponsibility, depravity,
licentiousness, desperation, privation, debauchery, and blasphemy. They

witness a tattered, ragged, and bedraggled humanistic culture gone awry: perversity, poverty, ignorance, tyranny, exploitation, abuse, neglect, and violence. And, not surprisingly, they cry out, as if with one voice: *What shall I do? And, how do I do it?*

People want to know how they can make a difference. They want to know how they can help change the minds, hearts, and lives of those around them. They want to know how to integrate a Christian world-view and the nitty gritty details of life in this poor fallen world. They want to find out how they can actually do something more significant than writing a letter, giving a donation, or casting a vote. They want to stand for the truth, oppose debauchery, protect the innocent, comfort the distressed, and build for the future. They want to utilize their gifts, abilities, and skills.

But all too often, they just don't know how. Or, the task looks too ominous and they don't know where to start.

And so they cry out: *What shall I do?*

The answer is simple to assert yet difficult to fulfill—it is merely to uphold our responsibilities in every area: in the church, at home, and in the community.

Our Responsibility in the Church

The church is ultimately the most important institution on earth. All other institutions will pass away, but the church will remain through eternity. The church is the Bride of Christ (Revelation 21:9–10), loved by Him and united with Him as His own body. It possesses the keys of the kingdom (Matthew 16:18–19). It is a nation of priests (1 Peter 2:9), the holy city of New Jerusalem (Hebrews 22–24), and the discipler of the nations (Matthew 28:19). In both bringing *individual* sinners to repentance and restoration, or in calling for *national* repentance and restoration, the institutional church is of central importance to the implementation of God's good providence in our midst.

In order to meet the challenge of the humanist and homosexual assaults on our culture, the church must recover its proper place, perspective, and purpose—including the true preaching of the Word, the correct administration of the sacraments, and the proper practice of discipline. These marks of genuine spirituality are indispensable.

The true preaching of the Word necessarily involves faithful exposition of Scripture as it applies to all of life—including the whole realm of sexual ethics. The Bible clearly condemns lascivious living. But the Bible also clearly promises forgiveness, eternal life, and the Holy Spirit to those who will "repent, and be baptized in the name of Jesus Christ for the remission of sins" (Acts 2:38). The Bible bears a message of *both* judgment *and* mercy.

These truths must be expounded without compromise. If the church is to be faithful to Christ, it must proclaim the whole counsel of God—Law and Gospel, Wrath and Grace, Holiness and Love.

The church must preach *repentance*. People need to know that coming to Christ involves turning from sin. A Gospel without repentance is no Gospel at all. On this, Jesus was abundantly clear. He told the parable, for instance, about a king who issued an open invitation to His wedding feast:

> But when the king came in to see the guests, he saw a man there who did not have on a wedding garment. So he said to him, "Friend, how did you come in here without a wedding garment?" And he was speechless. Then the king said to the servants, "Bind him hand and foot, take him away and cast him into outer darkness; there will be weeping and gnashing of teeth." For many are called, but few are chosen. (Matthew 22:11–14)

Though we are saved by grace, true faith never stands alone in a vacuum but is always accompanied by a life of repentance from sin and obedience to Christ. We are saved *by* grace—but, we are saved *for* good works (Ephesians 2:10). As pastor and author John MacArthur declares:

> God's grace is not a static attribute whereby He passively accepts hardened, unrepentant sinners. Grace does not change a person's standing before God yet leave his character untouched. . . . True grace, according to Scripture, teaches us "to deny ungodliness and worldly desires and to live sensibly, righteously and godly in the present age" (Titus 2:12). Grace is the power of God to fulfill our New Covenant duties (1 Corinthians 7:19), however inconsistently we obey at times. . . . Faith, like grace, is not static. Saving faith is more than just understanding the facts and mentally acquiescing. It is inseparable from repentance, surrender, and a supernatural eagerness to obey.[4]

We desperately need to recover the Gospel message if we are to address the sins that beset our families, our communities, and our culture.

Even so, Christians must take care not to reduce the church's ministry to a *mere* message, as important as that message might be. The church as an institution is meant for more than simple proclamation. It is to be a means of incorporation as well. It is the church, as the *Westminster Confession* states, "through which all men are saved and union with which is essential to their best growth and service."[5]

The sacraments are an important element of this incorporation—vividly demonstrating the union of believers with the church and of the union of the church with Christ. Baptism and the Lord's Supper "put a visible difference between those that belong unto the church and the rest of the world," according to the *Confession*.[6]

It is through baptism that we "wash away our sins, calling on the name of the Lord" (Acts 27:16) and are made visible members of the church. It is through the Lord's Supper, as the reformer John Calvin declared, "that Christ's flesh, separated from us by such a great distance, penetrates to us, so that it becomes our food" and "by which Christ pours His life into us, as if it penetrated into our bones and marrow."[7]

As Jesus stated:

> Most assuredly, I say to you, unless you eat the flesh of the Son of Man and drink His blood, you have no life in you. Whoever eats My flesh and drinks My blood has eternal life, and I will raise him up at the last day. For My flesh is food indeed, and My blood is drink, indeed. He who eats My flesh and drinks My blood abides in me and I in him. As the living Father has sent Me, and I live because of the Father, so he who feeds on Me will live because of Me. This is the bread which came down from heaven—not as your fathers ate the manna and are dead. He who eats this bread will live forever. (John 6:53–58)

Any Christian outreach to homosexuals must make the church and the sacraments central to their ministry. This is especially important to those who have been heavily involved in habitual sin that has corrupted the core of their character. People who struggle with their identity need a new context in which to understand their new position in Christ. Christians can best provide this through incorporation in the institutional church—by emphasizing the whole life of the church including the sacraments. Baptism manifests the purifying work of the Spirit in washing away our old selves and the putting on of the new. The Lord's Supper manifests our union with Christ by virtue of His sacrifice on our behalf. Author Rick Ritchie argues:

We can be saved by merely trusting that the blood of Christ has paid for our sins, but how much more our faith is strengthened when God offers us the chance to partake of the ransom payment! We do not await a future judgment desperately hoping that some past experience of Christ in our hearts will be remembered. God has declared His favor toward us. If our mental experience of Christ is too ethereal for us to hang onto, our mouths are made of more solid stuff, and we can receive Christ orally.[8]

It is extremely important, however, that the sacramental blessings of Christ's grace not be given promiscuously. Baptism must not be administered to those who unrepentantly practice sin, for baptism in the Bible is never separated from repentance—from turning away from sin. Likewise, those who, after becoming members of the church, begin living in sin, must be confronted. The Bible says:

> Moreover if your brother sins against you, go and tell him his fault between you and him alone. If he hears you, you have gained your brother. But if he will not hear you, take with you one or two more, that "by the mouth of two or three witnesses every word may be established." And if he refuses to hear them, tell it to the Church. But if he refuses even to hear the Church, let him be to you like a heathen and a tax collector. Assuredly, I say to you, whatever you bind on earth will be bound in heaven, and whatever you loose on earth will be loosed in heaven. (Matthew 18:15–18)

Furthermore, the apostle Paul, writing to the church of Corinth about a member who was living in sin, exhorted them:

> In the name of our Lord Jesus Christ, when you are gathered together, along with my spirit, with the power of the Lord Jesus Christ, deliver such a one to Satan for the destruction of the flesh, that his spirit may be saved in the day of the Lord Jesus. (1 Corinthians 5:4–5)

Those baptized into the church who fall into sin and refuse to repent must be disciplined. They must be disbarred from the Lord's Supper— for their own sake as well as for the church's (1 Corinthians 11:28–31).

As uncomfortable as it may be, church discipline is simply not optional. As Paul warned the Thessalonian church:

> But we command you, brethren, in the name of our Lord Jesus Christ, that you withdraw from every brother who walks disorderly and not according to the tradition he received from us." (2 Thessalonians 3:6)

Sadly, there are many evangelical leaders who, in the guise of "compassion" openly disagree with Scripture on this point. According to *Christianity Today,* for instance, Stephen Hayner, the president of Inter-Varsity Christian Fellowship, said: "It is up to individual churches to determine whether to break fellowship with people over homosexuality."[9] Even worse, in Richard Foster's best-selling book *Money, Sex, and Power: The Challenge of a Disciplined Life* he writes:

> The Christian fellowship cannot give permission to practice homosexuality to those who feel unable to change their orientation or to embrace celibacy. But if such a tragic moral choice is made, the most moral context possible should be maintained. . . . Just because an ideal has been violated does not mean anything goes. A person continues to have moral responsibilities even when driven to engage in an activity that is less than the best. If we cannot condone the choice of homosexual practice, neither can we cut off the person who has made the choice. No, we stand with the person always ready to help, always ready to pick up the pieces if things fall apart, always ready to bring God's acceptance and forgiveness.[10]

Yes, a person "does have moral responsibilities even when driven to engage in an activity that is less than the best." He has a moral responsibility to repent. And, if he does not repent, the church has a moral responsibility to "cut off" or excommunicate that person.

To do otherwise, not only allows people to die in their sins, but endangers the church as well. Genuine compassion never sees fit to hedge its bets over and against God's perfect standards of justice and mercy.

Sin in the Camp

Flushed with confidence following their spectacular victory at Jericho, the people of Israel advanced to the much smaller, much weaker city of Ai. So certain were they of another victory that they sent up only a very small contingent to take the city (Joshua 7:2–3).

Much to their surprise, however, the men of Ai routed their vastly superior forces (Joshua 7:4–5).

Joshua and the leaders of the nation fell on their faces in fear and trembling before God. Trying to make rhyme or reason out of the lopsided battle, they begged for an explanation (Joshua 7:6–9). And what was God's reply?

The Lord said to Joshua: "Get up! Why do you lie thus on your face? Israel has sinned, and they have also transgressed My covenant which I commanded them. For they have even taken some of the accursed things, and have both stolen and deceived; and they have also put it among their own stuff." (Joshua 7:10–11)

One man, Achan, had violated God's specific commands, hiding sin in his tent, and thus had brought judgment and condemnation upon the entire nation. Ai was lost, and lives were lost. All because Achan was in the camp. All because sin was in the tent.

A church that does not graciously and mercifully discipline the unrepentant—but instead promiscuously tolerates them—is in grave danger. Jesus threatened the church of Pergamos saying:

You have there those who hold to the doctrine of Balaam, who taught Balak to put a stumbling block before the children of Israel, to eat things sacrificed to idols, and to commit sexual immorality. (Revelation 2:14)

He told them: "Repent, or else I will come to you quickly and will fight them with the sword of my mouth" (Revelation 2:16).

Now, of course the church must not only practice discipline, but restoration as well. In fact, the whole purpose of discipline is righteous restoration. Of those who have been excommunicated but then repent, the apostle Paul wrote:

This punishment which was inflicted by the majority is sufficient for such a man, so that, on the contrary, you ought rather forgive and comfort him, lest perhaps such a one be swallowed up with too much sorrow. Therefore, I urge you to reaffirm your love to him. (2 Corinthians 2:6–9)

According to the apostle, there are at least three steps to full restoration.

First, the sinner must be truly forgiven. That means that the sin will never be held against him. It must not be repeated to him or to others. It must not be stored away as the basis for a grudge. The case is closed. Period.

Secondly, the church must "comfort him." The Greek word used here is *parakaleo,* which actually means to help, assist, counsel, and persuade, as well as comfort. Christian counselor Jay Adams asserts that this Biblical "comfort" may involve intensive pastoral care and nurture:

Counseling about the problems and the sins that led to their ouster in the first place. Help in becoming reassimilated into the body. Help in making new social contacts and reinstating old ones. Help in reconciling themselves to others to whom they spoke hard words or toward whom they did despicable things. They will need guidance in finding their place in the body so that they can once again begin to use their gifts—none of this business about making them wait six months to rejoin the choir. They may need medical assistance; Satan can be rough, and if they have been in his hands any length of time, they will probably bear the marks that show it. They may need financial help.[11]

Finally, the repentant person must be formally reinstated to fellowship in the church. He should be given back all rights and privileges of church membership and, most important, be permitted to partake in Holy Communion. Again, according to Adams:

This does not mean, of course, that he can simply leap back into the saddle of leadership: office-bearing is not an automatic right of membership. But it must be made clear, to both the congregation and the repentant person, that he is being joyfully received back into full fellowship within the covenant family, once again in complete communion with Christ and His people.[12]

Remember, the church—though it must truthfully represent Christ's wrath—is primarily an institution of grace. Church discipline is designed by God to effect repentance, reconciliation, and restoration.

Obviously, there are a number of obstacles that inhibit the exercise of church discipline today. And chief among those obstacles is the very structure of church organization: denominationalism. Theologian John Frame comments that "those churches that seek to implement Biblical discipline are frequently frustrated by denominationalism."[13] Why? Because it is all too easy—and all too common—for a person to leave a church in which he has come under discipline and simply go down the street to another. Few churches actually ask prospective members for a letter of good standing from their last church. Thus, denominational barriers make this already difficult intercongregational communication even worse. It may eventually "foster an ungodly competitiveness, rather than cooperativeness,"[14] which makes discipline even more ineffectual.

There are, however, some ways of dealing with the problems brought about by these kinds of divisions. Churches need to recognize the discipline of other churches—even those of different denominations whenever possible and wherever legitimate. If a person says he was forced to leave a previous church because of his theological confession, the church to which he is applying for membership should investigate his story before accepting him. The present assault on the integrity of the Gospel and the church can only be thwarted by a united church.

Additionally, the church has a clear mandate to minister to those who suffer as a consequence of their sin and to those who are victims of the sins of others. That is why, for instance, AIDS should be seen as a glorious opportunity for ministry—not a threat to it.

Historically, it has been the institutional church that has founded hospitals as a natural outgrowth of the Gospel. The church needs to fully recover its legacy. As theologian Michael Tolliver has asserted:

> The task of evangelism doesn't end with a proclamation of the Gospel. As important as that is, the Bible makes it as clear as day that if we want to win the hearts of men and women for Christ we are going to have to match our words with deeds. We are going to have to authenticate the claims of the Gospel with *holy activity*.[15]

Our Responsibility at Home

Like the church, the family is a divine institution which is immensely important to the temporal welfare of a culture and the fulfillment of the Cultural Mandate. That early mandate was addressed first and foremost to the family:

> Be fruitful and multiply; fill the earth and subdue it; have dominion over the fish of the sea, over the birds of the air, and over every living thing that moves across the earth. (Genesis 1:26–28, 2:24)

The Biblical family consists of a faithful relationship between one man and one woman and the children God gives them. Obviously, this definition is under attack today, as author Gary DeMar notes:

> There are, what Alvin Toffler calls, a bewildering array of family forms: homosexual marriages, communes, groups of elderly people banding together to share expenses and sometimes sex, tribal groupings among certain ethnic minorities, and many other forms coexist as never before. These counterfeit families attempt to restructure the family around an evolving order rather than a Biblical model.[16]

The most important resource the Christian family has that the homosexual movement can never counter or subvert is *children*:

> Behold, children are a heritage from the LORD, the fruit of the womb is his
> reward. Like arrows in the hand of a warrior, so are the children of one's
> youth. Happy is the man who has his quiver full of them; they shall not be
> ashamed, but shall speak with their enemies in the gate. (Psalm 127:3–5)

It is essential, therefore, for families to take whatever means necessary to protect their best witnesses for the Biblical sexual ethic—their
own progeny.

According to Scripture, the education of children is the responsibility of the parents. Children are exhorted not to keep company with sinners but to listen instead to their parents. Parents ought not, therefore,
give their children over to ethical subverters in either the public or the
private sector, in either education or entertainment.

Jesus stressed the immensity of our responsibility to children when
He said:

> Whoever causes one of these little ones who believe in Me to sin, it would
> be better for him if a millstone were hung around his neck, and he were
> drowned in the depth of the sea. (Matthew 18:6)

The fact is, the family is the primary agent of stability in a society.
It is the family that is charged with the responsibility of infusing children with the principles of God's Law (Deuteronomy 6:6–7). It is the
family that is charged with the responsibility of upbraiding, restraining,
and rebuking unrighteous behavior (Proverbs 23:13–14). It is the family
that is charged with the responsibility of balancing liberty with justice,
freedom with responsibility, and license with restriction (Deuteronomy
11:18–21). It is the family that is charged with the responsibility of being culture's basic building block (Genesis 9:1–7).

The family is central to virtually every societal endeavor under
God: from education (Proverbs 22:6) to charity (1 Timothy 5:8), from
economics (Deuteronomy 21:17) to spirituality (Ephesians 6:1–4), from
the care of the aged (1 Timothy 5:3–13) to the subduing of the earth
(Genesis 1:26–28).

And to all these responsibilities is added another. The family is central to the ministry of cultural cohesion. Thus, when the family fails, disaster looms large.

When the Family Fails

This truth was tragically illustrated in the life of Samuel. It seems that the failure of his family life actually brought the entire nation of Israel to the brink of disaster:

> Now it came to pass when Samuel was old that he made his sons judges over Israel. The name of his firstborn was Joel, and the name of his second, Abijah; they were judges in Beersheba. But his sons did not walk in his ways; they turned aside after dishonest gain, took bribes, and perverted justice. (1 Samuel 8:1–3)

Samuel was a very busy man. As the judge over Israel, he was forced to make the long and arduous "circuit from Bethel to Gilgal to Mizpah" (1 Samuel 7:16). His duties left little time for the diligent oversight of his home life in Ramah, and though he sincerely attempted to rule his family well from afar, the result was nothing short of disastrous.

Samuel's neglect of family affairs was exposed in his sons after he had appointed them to be judges succeeding him. They failed to walk in a manner befitting righteousness, turning aside after dishonest gain, accepting bribes, perverting justice. From their judicial seat in Beersheba, they exasperated the people and defiled judgment (1 Samuel 8:3).

This personal tragedy, as awful as it was for Samuel, was just the beginning of his woes. The citizens of Israel, seeing the wickedness of Samuel's family and the senescence of Samuel himself, began to panic. They began to fear for the future and cry out for a king who would restore the stability of their cultural and political order:

> Then all the elders of Israel gathered together and came to Samuel at Ramah, and said to him, "Look, you are old, and your sons do not walk in your ways. Now make for us a king to judge us like all the nations." (1 Samuel 8:4–5)

The elders of the nation came together in Samuel's home to confront the aged leader with their fears and to present him with their demands. Samuel's family failure had undermined national security. Thus, they wanted him to take immediate political action in order to preserve life and liberty in the land. They wanted a king. Like all the other nations around them, they wanted a king.

Samuel was grieved. His entire life's work had been committed to preserving the standard of Biblical Law and justice in Israel. Now it seemed that his undersighted neglect at home was nullifying his every accomplishment:

> But the thing displeased Samuel when they said, "Give us a king to judge us." So Samuel prayed to the Lord. And the Lord said to Samuel, "Heed the voice of the people in all that they say to you; for they have not rejected you, but they have rejected Me, that I should not reign over them. According to all the works which they have done since the day that I brought them up out of Egypt, even to this day—with which they have forsaken Me and served other gods—so they are doing to you also. Now therefore, heed their voice. However, you shall solemnly forewarn them, and show them the behavior of the king who will reign over them." So Samuel told all the words of the Lord to the people who asked him for a king. And he said, "This will be the behavior of the king who will reign over you: He will take your sons and appoint them for his own chariots and to be his horsemen, and some will run before his chariots. He will appoint captains over his thousands and captains over his fifties, will set some to plow his ground and reap his harvest, and some to make his weapons of war and equipment for his chariots. He will take your daughters to be perfumers, cooks, and bakers. And he will take a tenth of your grain and your vintage, and give it to his officers and servants. And he will take your menservants and your maidservants and your finest young men and your donkeys, and put them to his work. He will take a tenth of your sheep. And you will be his servants. And you will cry out in that day because of your king whom you have chosen for yourselves, and the Lord will not hear you in that day." (1 Samuel 8:6–18)

In desperation, Samuel attempted to warn the people of the inherent dangers of their scheme. There would be taxation. There would be conscription. There would be coercion. There would be tyranny. It was inevitable.

But the people could not be swayed:

> Nevertheless the people refused to obey the voice of Samuel; and they said, "No, but we will have a king over us, that we also may be like all the

nations, and that our king may judge us and go out before us and fight our battles." (1 Samuel 8:19–20)

The prospect of tyranny looked much better to the people than an eroding social and political order under Samuel's debauched family. A king and his tyranny, then, it would be:

> And Samuel heard all the words of the people, and he repeated them in the hearing of the Lord. So the Lord said to Samuel, "Heed their voice, and make them a king." And Samuel said to the men of Israel, "Every man go to his city." (1 Samuel 8:21–22)

Throughout his life, Samuel worked hard, traversing the countryside, weaving a social and political fabric impervious to the rending attacks of lawlessness, godlessness, and truthlessness. He poured himself into this work—virtually to the exclusion of all else—only to discover late in life that his sorely neglected family was unraveling every stitch.

When the family fails, the entire social and political system suffers. When the family fails, the church suffers. When the family fails, the whole culture suffers.

But just as Samuel's family failure had a dramatic and negative impact on the health of the entire nation, so Issachar's family's success had a dramatic and positive impact on the health of the entire nation.

When the Family Succeeds

Issachar was the ninth son of Jacob, the fifth of Leah (Genesis 30:68, 35:23). The family descended from him consisted of four great tribal clans: the Tolaites, the Punites, the Joshubites, and the Shimranites (Numbers 26:23–24). At Sinai they numbered 54,000 (Numbers 1:29), but by the end of the desert wandering, when the people were counted at Kadesh Barnea, their population had swollen to 64,300 (Numbers 26:25).

Issachar's family was not merely huge. Rather, it was a Godly family: "The sons of Issachar were men. They had understanding of the times, and knew what Israel ought to do" (1 Chronicles 12:32).

The sons of Issachar included such heroes of the faith as Tola, the deliverer and judge (Judges 10:1–2), and Barak, the commander of Deborah's army (Judges 4:6–10; 5:1). They were among those named who rose up courageously against Sisera and Jabin (Judges 5:15), and who fought bravely beside David during the Ziklag exile (1 Chronicles 12:19–40).

So great was their valor, that the name of the sons of Issachar shall forever be enshrined above one of the gates in the New Jerusalem (Ezekiel 48:33).

Such a wealth of godliness and faithfulness does not materialize in a family by chance. Family purity does not occur in a vacuum.

The sons of Issachar very obviously were nurtured in the admonition of the Lord (Ephesians 6:4). The sons of Issachar very obviously were raised up by godly parents who set the commandments of God upon their hearts, who talked about them when they sat at home, when they walked along the way, when they lay down, and when they rose up (Deuteronomy 6:6–7). The sons of Issachar very obviously were taught, while still quite young, the way they should go—so, when they were old, they did not depart from it (Proverbs 22:6).

Notice the familiar refrain in the family lives of Moses (Exodus 2:1–10), Samson (Judges 13:2–25), David (Ruth 4:13–22), John the Baptist (Luke 1:5–25), Paul (Philippians 3:4–8), and Timothy (2 Timothy 3:14–15). Like these other godly men of valor, the sons of Issachar knew the joys of righteous homes. And the nation was enhanced immeasurably by it.

The sons of Issachar "understood the times." They "knew what Israel should do." And they did it. As a family.

Our Responsibility in the Community

There was a long period in the early to mid-twentieth century when evangelicals eschewed involvement in politics altogether. More recently, however, Christians have begun to awaken to their responsibility to "make disciples of all the nations" (Matthew 28:19).

Sadly, this new surge in Christian involvement has been forced into a primarily negative posture—that is, it has been forced into a defensive mode. We have had to oppose attempts by federal, state, and local governments to force us to accept homosexuality as a legitimate lifestyle. We have had to oppose housing codes that penalize Christian landlords who refuse to rent facilities to people who have adopted sinful practice as their way of life. We have had to oppose the use of tax monies to fund homosexual pornographic propaganda. We have had to oppose attempts by the government to punish those who attempt, in their home or workplace, to maintain a healthy and wholesome atmosphere. We have had to oppose hate-crime legislation that attempts to penalize people for their opinions of homosexuality. We have had to oppose school curriculums that portray the homosexual lifestyle as a legitimate option. In essence, we have had to oppose the use of the government coercion by the homosexual lobby to force us to conform to their agenda.

As necessary as this defensive posture has been, it cannot be anything but a short-term strategy. As Christians, our long-term goals for the civil government must include a positive upholding of goodness, justice, and mercy—as it is defined in Scripture. After all, Jesus Christ is not just the Head of the church, but He is also the King of kings and Lord of lords (Revelation 19:16):

> Now therefore, be wise, O kings; be instructed, you judges of the earth. Serve the LORD with fear, and rejoice with trembling. Kiss the Son, lest He be angry, and you perish in the way, when His wrath is kindled but a little. Blessed are all those who put their trust in Him. (Psalm 2:10–12)

As the present cultural crisis amply demonstrates, when a culture departs from Christ's standards, frightful consequences are meted out to the wicked and the innocent alike. It is essential to the health and welfare of our civilization that we be governed by God's wisdom, not man's wisdom. We must therefore attempt to elect representatives who take the Bible seriously and we must put forward a positive program of civil justice and corporate mercy.[17]

Sadly, some evangelicals will consider this call to action to be somehow sub-Christian. One anonymous evangelical leader in Colorado Springs recently told *Christianity Today* that "evangelicals . . . need to decide if we're about anti-gay legislation or proclaiming the Gospel, and the two are not necessarily the same thing."

On the contrary, though civic involvement may not directly involve the Gospel, we *cannot* proclaim the Gospel and be silent about the assaults on decency, morality, and family integrity all about us.

Chuck and Donna McIlhenny, when confronted with this question during their tumultuous ministry in San Francisco, recalled Martin Luther's bold assertion:

> If I profess with the loudest voice and clearest exposition every portion of the truth of God except precisely that little point which the world and the

Devil are at that moment attacking, I am not confessing Christ, however boldly I may be professing Christ. Where the battle rages, there the loyalty of the soldier is proved, and to be steady on as the battlefield besides, is mere flight and disgrace if he flinches at that point.[18]

We cannot preach the Gospel on the one hand and, at the same time, stand silently by while the culture at large spites God's commandments.

Compelling Interests

The common law tradition—international, national, state, and local—has always recognized the compelling interests of the religious community in shaping both the general moral tenor of the culture and the specific ethical parameters of public policy. Eliminating Christian influence in the public square not only debilitates the effectiveness of the church, it threatens the cohesiveness of the society.

The Supreme Court recently reaffirmed this crucial role in legislating morality when it upheld Georgia's sodomy statute in *Bowers v. Hardwick*. According to the majority opinion:

The law is constantly based on notions of morality, and if all laws representing essentially moral choices are to be invalidated under the due process clause, the courts will be very busy indeed.[19]

In a concurring opinion, the Chief Justice said:

In constitutional terms there is no such thing as a fundamental right to commit homosexual sodomy. . . . To hold that the act of homosexual sodomy is somehow protected as a fundamental right would be to cast aside millennia of moral teaching.[20]

The State does not merely recognize the religious community as a subjective force for moral good in the society, it also recognizes the objective authority that the religious community shares with the government in stipulating, protecting, and maintaining family integrity.

It is the church, for instance, that wields the authority to actually define and create families by solemnizing the legal and covenantal vows of marriage. The State has always conceded this jurisdiction to the church and its clergy. This is not simply a sacred tradition or symbolic ritual; it is an integral aspect of our legal system.

Thus, challenges to state sodomy laws are not only petitions for declaratory and injunctive relief against the State, they are an attack on the designated authority of the church. If the courts do bow to homosexual pressure tactics and decriminalize aberrant behavior on the basis of due process, it is the church that is constrained as well as the State. The church, then, either becomes a symbolic and servile adjunct of the State or its authority to define and create families is stripped away altogether.

Should that ever happen—and certainly that is the stated goal of the radical homosexual movement—the entire American tradition of family law code and decentralized jurisdictions would necessarily collapse under the weight of governmental absolutism. And just as surely, the freedom and integrity of the church would be compromised severely.

It is important, therefore, that these kinds of social concerns not escape the purview of the application of the Gospel. If Christ is Lord, He is Lord over the totality of life.

And that includes politics.

Thus, it is well within the compelling interests of both individual Christians and whole congregations to involve themselves in the civil sphere. The whole gamut of political activity—from non-partisan educational efforts to partisan campaigns—is a legitimate outworking of our call to be faithful in the midst of this poor fallen world.

Now more than perhaps ever before, Christians need to be contacting their legislators and magistrates, testifying at community hearings and town meetings, petitioning school boards and city councils, writing letters and disseminating literature, supporting Christian advocacy groups and educational ministries, identifying good candidates to support and weak candidates to defeat. In short, we must take seriously our responsibilities as citizens—for the sake of our nation, for the sake of our children, and even for the sake of the church itself.

Right and Wrong

It is the sad tendency of modern men to either do the right thing in the wrong way or to do the wrong thing in the right way. We either hold to the truth obnoxiously or we hold to a lie graciously. We are either a rude angel or a polite devil. Often what poses as a cruel orthodoxy is defeated by what poses as a kind heresy.

That is what makes the current debate over sexual ethics so terribly complex. Those who hold to the Biblical standard are often anything but the picture of Christian decorum, whereas those who play fast and free with the moral tenor of the faith are often generous to a fault.

Consequently, it is not enough to simply assert that Christians do what God wants them to do—in the church, in the state, and in the home. They must *be* what God wants them to be as well.

According to the *Westminster Confession of Faith,* the church has been entrusted with "the ministry, oracles, and ordinances of God, for the gathering and perfecting of the saints, in this life, to the end of the world."[21] In order to faithfully and wisely carry out this stewardship, the mission of the church must be organized around what Francis Schaeffer called "two contents, two realities."[22]

The first content is sound doctrine. The church must teach it, exhort it, nurture it, and highlight it in all that it does in both its evangelism and its discipleship, from its worship to its societal presence.

The second content is honest answers to honest questions. The Great Commission and the Cultural Mandate are the church's highest priorities in its mission to the world. They must be carried out and perpetrated in gentleness, openness, kindness, and helpfulness.

The first reality is true spirituality. Holiness, godliness, and spiritual discipline must be the distinctive marks of the true church. Prayer, fasting, almsgiving, and fixedness in the Word should be just as evident in the lives of the members as are fervent evangelism and glorious worship.

The second reality is the beauty of human relationships. Within the church there should be abundant evidence of true *koinonia.* At the same time, relations between the church and the community should show forth service, tenderness, understanding, empathy, and compassion.

Thus while an unswerving commitment to truth must be maintained in the church, it must be contextualized by an equally unswerving commitment to servanthood.

Without that, right appears to be wrong while wrong appears to be right.

The Good Samaritan

It was supposed to be a test. Straightforward. Simple. A test of orthodoxy. A test of theological skillfulness. Not a trap, really. Just a test:

And behold, a certain lawyer stood up and put Jesus to the test, saying, "Teacher, what shall I do to inherit eternal life?" And He answered him, "What is written in the law? How does it read to you?" And he answered and said, "You shall love the Lord your God with all your heart, and with all your soul, and with all your strength, and with all your mind; and your neighbor as yourself." And He said to him, "You have answered correctly; do this, and you will live." (Luke 10:25–28)

Christ's word-perfect-never-miss-a-beat response should have been music to the ears of any good Pharisee. He unhesitatingly upheld the Mosaic Law. He was careful "not to exceed what is written" (1 Corinthians 4:6). He was impeccably orthodox.

If that were the end of the story, it would be less a story than a dry recitation of doctrine: true, good, and necessary, but not particularly gripping. But of course, the story doesn't end there.

The lawyer just wouldn't let Jesus off the hook. He continued to cross-examine the Lord. He pressed the issue. Sinful men love to do this. They want God on the hot seat. They want God in the dock:

Wishing to justify himself, he said to Jesus, "And who is my neighbor?" Jesus replied and said, "A certain man was going down from Jerusalem to Jericho, and he fell among robbers, and they stripped him and beat him, and went off leaving him half dead. And by chance a certain priest was going down on that road, and when he saw him, he passed by on the other side. And likewise a Levite also, when he came to the place and saw him, passed by on the other side. But a certain Samaritan, who was on a journey, came upon him; and when he saw him, he felt compassion, and came to him, and bandaged up his wounds, pouring oil and wine on them, and he put him on his own beast, and brought him to an inn, and took care of him. And on the next day he took out two denarii and gave them to the innkeeper and said, 'Take care of him; and whatever more you spend, when I return, I will repay you.' Which of these three do you think proved to be a neighbor to the man who fell into the robbers' hands?" And he said, "The one who showed mercy toward him." And Jesus said to him, "Go and do the same." (Luke 10:29–37)

What started out to be a test—a theological confrontation over the Law—was suddenly transformed by the Lord Jesus into a moment of conviction. The Pharisee found himself in the valley of decision. And at the same time he was on the horns of a dilemma—because of a Samaritan of all things.

Seven hundred years earlier, Assyria had overrun and depopulated the northern kingdom of Israel, including Samaria. They had a cruel policy of population-transfer that scattered the inhabitants of the land to the four winds. Then, the empty countryside was repopulated with a ragtag collection of vagabonds and scalawags from the dregs of the Empire (2 Kings 17:24–41). Instead of regarding these Samaritan new-comers as prospects for Jewish evangelism, the people of Judah, who continued in independence for another full century, turned away in con-tempt, and the racial division between Samaritan and Jew began its bit-ter course.

The Samaritans were universally despised by good Jews. They were half-breeds who observed a half-breed religious cultus. Worse than the pagan Greeks, worse even than the barbarian Romans, the Samaritans were singled out by the Jews as a perfect example of despicable deprav-ity. They were close enough geographically and culturally to know of the truth, yet they resisted.

But now Jesus was elevating a Samaritan to a position of respect and honor, describing him as the good neighbor, the hero of the parable. It was as though Jesus had slapped the religious leaders of Israel in their collective faces.

After demanding an expansion of Christ's textbook answer, the Pharisee might have expected a parable that encouraged him to show love to all men, even to Samaritans. But never in a thousand years would he have guessed that Christ would show how such a despised one could be nearer to the kingdom than a pious but compassionless Jew.

The Pharisee had asked a passive question, expecting a passive an-swer: "Who is my neighbor?" (Luke 10:29). But Jesus responded with an active command: "Go and do the same." (Luke 10:37). Jesus did not supply the teacher with information about whom he should or shouldn't help, because failure to keep the commandment springs not from a lack of information, but a lack of obedience and love. It was not keener un-derstanding that the teacher needed, but a new heart. Like that of the Samaritan.

Both Law and Love

The Samaritan in the story is a paragon of virtue. He strictly observed the law, shaming the priest and Levite who "passed by on the other side" (Luke 10:31–32). He paid attention to the needs of others (Deuteronomy

22:4) and showed concern for the poor (Psalm 41:1). He showed pity toward the weak (Psalm 72:13) and rescued them from violence (Psalm 72:14). Knowing the case of the helpless (Proverbs 29:7), he gave of his wealth (Deuteronomy 26:12–13), and shared his food (Proverbs 22:9).

But perhaps even more significant than his strict adherence to the law was the compassion that the Samaritan demonstrated. He wasn't simply "going by the rules." His was not a dry, passionless obedience. He had "put on a heart of compassion, kindness, humility, gentleness, and patience" (Colossians 3:12). He "became a father to the needy, and took up the case of the stranger" (Job 29:16). He loved his neighbor as himself (Mark 12:31), thus fulfilling the law (Romans 13:10).

The Samaritan fulfilled the demands of both law *and* love. He demonstrated both obedience and mercy. He heeded the Spirit *and* the letter. He combined faithfulness *and* compassion. He had wed Word *and* deed.

At another time, Jesus was asked to summarize the law of God—the standard against which all spirituality is to be measured. He replied: "You shall love the Lord your God with all your heart, and soul, and mind. This is the great and foremost commandment. And the second is like it; you shall love your neighbor as yourself. On these two commandments depend the law and the prophets" (Matthew 22: 37–40).

Jesus reduced the whole of the law—and thus, the whole of the faith—to love. Love toward God, and then, love toward man. But at the same time, Jesus defined love in terms of law.

In one bold deft stroke, Jesus freed the Christian faith from both legalism and subjectivism. He linked law and love, thus unclouding our purblind vision of both. Love was held in check by responsible objectivity while law was held in check by passionate applicability.

That is the faith of the Good Samaritan—faithful but compassionate, unswerving but merciful, obedient but kind—because that is "the faith once and for all delivered to the saints" (Jude 3).

This is the kind of faith we should exhibit before a watching world, the kind of fidelity which must be our hallmark. If we ever hope to bear witness to the unadulterated Gospel, we must "speak the truth." But we must do it "in love" (Ephesians 4:15).

That is the only way that right can truly be right and wrong can truly be wrong.

The Brass Tacks

"Okay, okay," you say. "But now, where do we begin? The church I attend is very small. We're willing to do what we need to do to be faithful to God's call. But our resources are few. Realistically, how can we help? What can we do?"

Well, we simply start at the beginning. We begin with the Word of God.

Not only must we nurture our own people with the rich truths of practical Biblical instruction, instilling in them a vision for service and sacrifice; we must get the Good News to the sick and suffering. Jesus made it clear that the Gospel was not privileged information to be preciously protected within the confines of a covenantal cabal. No, the Word of Hope and Truth is to be broadcast high and low, from the rooftops and in the hedgerows, along the highways and in the market square. We must always speak the truth in love, with gentleness and discretion (Ephesians 4:15; Colossians 4:5, 6), but first and foremost, we must always speak it (Mark 16:15).

There are innumerable ways that we effectively do this. Ways that any church—large or small, rich or poor—can undertake immediately.

One Methodist church in Dallas recently began operating a twenty-four hour AIDS hotline. Volunteers from several Sunday school classes sign up for four-hour shifts and simply share the Gospel with frightened or despondent callers from the large gay community in town. "We realized that the only information people were getting," the pastor said, "was little more than propaganda. We felt obligated to provide *really* helpful medical information, *really* helpful spiritual and emotional counsel, and *really* helpful direction for the future."

The volunteers go through an extensive six-week training course where they learn not only how to share Christ and the Biblical hope, but also how to steer callers toward responsible medical, moral, and hygienic practices. "The response has been remarkable," said the pastor. "Not only has the church been able to help the distressed and extend its evangelistic reach into the darkest corners of our community, but we've grown as a congregation, spiritually, emotionally, and even numerically. Folks can see by our commitment to this that we *really* mean business."

A Bible church in Philadelphia has used a different approach to getting the Word out to AIDS patients. Every Friday and Saturday night four teams of volunteers go visiting, room to room, in four different hospitals, sharing the Gospel, lending a listening ear, and providing Bibles, Christian literature, and gifts.

"Some of the people we've been able to minister to," the organizer of the program says, "are folks we *never* would have reached otherwise. Not by television. Not by radio. Not by evangelistic crusades. Not by any of the traditional approaches that our church has used for years. It took us going to *them*. It took us reaching into *their* world." Volunteers in the program have been amazed at the response they've gotten.

"I met one young man," a volunteer related, "who had *never* before heard the Gospel. He was so completely overwhelmed by our willingness to visit him, to talk to him, to comfort him, and to just listen to him, that he broke down in tears, uncontrollably sobbing every time we came around. All his friends and loved ones had abandoned him. He was penniless and pathetic. He had given up all hope and was just waiting to die. One Saturday night he literally begged me to show him from the Bible how to become a Christian. He said that he *knew* that Christianity was real, that it was mankind's only hope, because he had *seen* it lived out. Well, you can just imagine what that did for *me*. I mean, suddenly *my* faith was being built up. I was seeing with my own eyes the power of service, the power of obedience, and the power of God for salvation! It has been an extraordinary experience for me. Now I know what Jesus meant when He said, 'It is more blessed to give than to receive.' Giving has been the greatest gift of all."

Another volunteer concurred. "I wouldn't trade this experience for anything in the world. My faith is stronger. My commitment is surer. And my life is happier. It's amazing how a simple thing like visiting the sick can change such dire circumstances as the AIDS plague into an open window for the kingdom."

A Nazarene church in San Diego has opened an AIDS crisis counseling center three days a week where AIDS sufferers and their families can receive Biblical instruction and nurture for difficult days ahead.

An Orthodox church in Detroit opens its doors once a month so that families facing the disruptive tragedy of AIDS can meet together to talk, to listen, to lend support to one another, and to learn God's perspective on sin, sickness, and sorrow.

A Baptist church in Denver recently established a day center for AIDS patients and their families near the downtown medical center. Bible studies and informal discussions are led by volunteers from the diaconate at least twice a day. Several ladies in the church provide refreshments and hospitality at mealtimes. And a quiet lounge with an adjacent library is made available throughout the rest of the day, as a kind of haven and refuge from the storms of affliction.

A college group from a large charismatic church in Seattle has established a reading and information center in the gay section of town where Bibles, Christian books, tracts, magazines, and responsible medical information are distributed free of charge.

In a similar vein, an interdenominational college group at the University of Nebraska, inspired by the nineteenth-century London colportage societies of Charles Haddon Spurgeon, have begun a door-to-door distribution of Christian literature in the gay community, both on campus and off.

Each of these varied activities and programs, and dozens of others springing up daily all over the country, are united by their commitment to communicate the Word of God to every man. They are united in their knowledge that the Truth offers healing (Proverbs 12;18; 16:24), life (Proverbs 15:4), and liberty (John 8:32). Jesus has commissioned us to go forth with the Word to heal and reconcile any and all who will hear and heed (Matthew 10:1, 6–8). Now is no time to retreat. Now is no time to seek first our security, hiding the Word under a bushel basket of fear and trembling.

But our task doesn't end with an evangelistic proclamation of the Gospel message. As important as that is, the Bible makes it plain that we have to match our words with deeds as well. Faith without corresponding works is altogether worthless. It is, in fact, dead (James 2:14–26).

It is important that as our ministry to AIDS sufferers develops that we do more than preach and pass out tracts. We must *live out* our faith, and *flesh out* our compassion with *deeds* of kindness and charity.

One small Brethren church in the Virginia suburbs of Washington, D.C., is attempting to wed Word and deed in their work among impoverished AIDS patients in the black community. "We recognized very quickly," one of the associate pastors said, "that the skyrocketing costs of AZT treatments and prolonged hospital stays were going to economically devastate the families of the patients. We began to develop a plan to try to help out as best we could."

Early in 1982, at a time when most people were just beginning to hear about AIDS, the church was already buying up a block of small frame homes in the inner city, renovating them, and renting them at rock-bottom prices to families struck by the AIDS tragedy. "We wanted to make certain that the families would be able to stay together," said the minister, "but not *just* stay together. We wanted them to be able to stay together in a home environment." The church maintains an active ministry to each of the fourteen families it currently houses. Eight of the families have not joined the church, and six of them have been unable to pay the rent for several months in a row now.

"Our intentions are not either proselytism or property management, so membership and rent checks are not big issues with us," said the minister. "Obeying Christ and meeting the needs of the helpless are what we care about."

Of course, the charity dispensed by the church program is not without standards. "We try to make certain that our love is Scriptural and not simply sentimental. We don't want to be promiscuous in our care, so we require each family to meet certain requirements and to carry out particular responsibilities. We want to make certain that we *really* help these families. The worst thing we could do is to create for them a whole new environment of dependency."

A Reformed church in Dallas has a charity outreach to AIDS sufferers that is no less ambitious. A group of volunteers keeps track of hospital admission and follows up through the chaplaincy offices to make certain that the patient's physical needs are met. They cover rent payments, buy groceries, pay utility bills, secure medical services, and provide job referrals. "Once the patients are diagnosed with full-blown AIDS," says the project coordinator, "they are all too typically abandoned by their friends, fired from their jobs, evicted from their apartments, and excluded from normal everyday life. Most of them have between two and three years to live, but already they are set out to die, cut off from virtually everything they've known and depended on. What are they supposed to do? Where are they supposed to go?"

The church has met with a good deal of resistance in their efforts to rehabilitate the patients and to meet their immediate needs, but they've also had a number of incredibly gratifying experiences. According to the coordinator, the purpose of the program is to "turn a terrible situation into a good one. Instead of turning the folks out into the howling wilderness we are attempting to drive them into the arms of the church and into the heart of the kingdom."

Two Baptist churches in Chicago have joined forces to provide part-time job referrals for AIDS-afflicted families so that they can provide free or nearly free medical care, counseling, day care, housing, and transportation.

An on-campus Presbyterian outreach has put together a foodbank for families of AIDS patients and sponsors a unique combination food drive and evangelistic thrust at the University of Alabama each year.

A large charismatic Episcopal church in Knoxville has opened a halfway house and hospice for impoverished AIDS patients who have nowhere else to go.

Each of these ministries has grown out of the peculiar circumstances and traditions of the sponsoring churches, but each of them shares a commitment to wedding Word and deed, faith and works. Each of them is committed to sharing the Gospel with uncompromising faithfulness, but in addition to that, they are each committed to fleshing out the Gospel in tangible acts of goodness and mercy. They know that it is only as the naked are clothed, the hungry fed, and the helpless cared for, that healing will cover our land (Isaiah 58:6–8).

Conclusion

The world is hungry for truth. And we are called to sound forth with its sonorous notes:

> For if the trumpet makes an uncertain sound, who will prepare himself for the day of trouble? (1 Corinthians 14:8)

But if we merely assert the truth, we have only done half our job. God has not called us to be mere citadels of fidelity. He has not called us to be mere bastions of veracity. We are to be winsome ambassadors as well. Thus, when we answer Bunyan's age-old cry, both Word and deed must therefore be evident—both faithfulness and compassion.

That—and that alone—is the authentic Christian faith. That—and that alone—is sufficient for the day.

CONCLUSION:
LANCE'S REPRISE

To walk where autumn heaps their promises
And, unregenerate by false faith, to tread
World-gazing prophecies as leaves to leaves;
To let sibylline fragments fly.[1]

DONALD DAVIDSON

"There is no peace for the wicked" (Isaiah 48:22; 57:21). With that booming phrase, the great evangelical prophet Isaiah punctuated his final series of sermons to his beloved people, the citizens of Judah. With a remarkable economy of words, Isaiah was able to capture the essence of his concerns. He was able to summarize his life's message. He was able to outline his theology. He was able to illustrate with absolute clarity the spiritual emphasis of his entire ministry.

All that, in one phrase.

Isaiah—as a true prophet—had dedicated himself to proclaiming to the people God's eternal purposes for them. He was a diligent bearer of the glad tidings of peace. God had established a "covenant of peace" with the people (Isaiah 54:10). And it was an irrevocable, everlasting covenant (Isaiah 61:8). Thus, they would be at peace with the nations (Isaiah 26:12) and at peace with God (Isaiah 27:5). They would experience "peace like a river" (Isaiah 66:12) and "like the waves of the sea" (Isaiah 48:18). There would be "peace to him who is far off and peace to him who is near" (Isaiah 57:19). It would be a "perfect peace" (Isaiah 26:3) wrought by the "Prince of Peace" (Isaiah 9:6).

251

But, Isaiah was quick to add, this great and glorious peace would only come upon God's faithful covenant people. "There is no peace for the wicked" (Isaiah 48:22). And sadly, as Isaiah uttered this phrase, the citizens of Judah appeared to be anything but God's faithful covenant people. They were treading the darksome path of wickedness.

Their worship had deteriorated into meaningless ritual (Isaiah 1:11–15). They had become proud and complacent (Isaiah 32:10). They tolerated perversion and wickedness in their midst (Isaiah 30:1–3). Even their own hearts were inclined "toward wickedness, to practice ungodliness and to speak error against the Lord, to keep the hungry person unsatisfied and to withhold drink from the thirsty" (Isaiah 32:6). They were flirting with disaster (Isaiah 5:13–17). For, "there is no peace for the wicked" (Isaiah 48:22).

Thus the God of peace commanded the prophet of peace to reiterate, once and for all, the program for peace, saying:

> Cry loudly, do not hold back; raise your voice like a trumpet, and declare to My people their transgression, and to the house of Jacob their sins. Is this not the fast I choose? To loosen the bonds of wickedness? To undo the bands of the yoke, to let the oppressed go free, and break every yoke? Is it not to divide your bread with the hungry and bring the homeless poor into the house? When you see the naked, to cover him, and not to hide yourself from your own flesh? Then your light will break out like the dawn, and your recovery will speedily spring forth. And your righteousness will go before you. The glory of the Lord will be your rear guard. Then you will call, and the Lord will answer. You will cry, and He will say, "Here I am." If you remove the yoke from your midst, the pointing of the finger, and speaking wickedness, and if you give yourself to the hungry, and satisfy the desire of the afflicted, then your light will rise in darkness, and your gloom will become like midday. And the Lord will continually guide you, and satisfy your desire in scorched places, and give strength to your bones. And you will be like a watered garden, like a spring of water whose waters do not fail. And those from among you will build the ancient ruins. You will raise up the age-old foundations. And you will be called the repairer of the breach, and the restorer of the streets in which to dwell. (Isaiah 58:1, 6–12)

Did the people want peace, perfect peace, the peace that surpasses all understanding? Did they want to restore their culture, raise the foundations, and reclaim their lost legacy? Then they would have to repent of their wickedness and do the works of righteousness. They would have to show forth the fruits of grace. They would have to uphold their covenant responsibility. They would have to do what God had called them to do. And they would have to be what God had called them to be.

Lance Ahlman understood that only too well.

But of course, that had not always been the case. The flowers of odious savors sweet had long bedeviled his sensibilities. His passions, as magic and mysterious as the fog of Puck, had led him hither and yon in search of peace. Judging experience by sentiment and sentiment by experience, he found himself running in vicious circles. He was riven by the ravages of immediacy. In the end, he simply realized that he might actually be wrong—about himself, about others, even, about the very nature of nature.

Even after he had given up the gay lifestyle in despondent desperation, he remained unsettled. "I just came to the place where I realized that being *nice* and *tolerant* and *accepting* were perhaps the cruelest things I could ever be," he told me.

"I came to the place where I realized that I was doing my old homosexual friends no favors at all by standing idly by while they not only crippled their own lives but wreaked havoc on the culture at large. I came to the place where I realized that the most compassionate thing I could do was to stand firm on the everlasting truth of Almighty God. I must take my place among His faithful covenant people. I don't really have any other choice. After all, there is no peace for the wicked—and wickedness in times like these has to be defined as standing in the wings, doing nothing while all the world struggles under the weight of falsehood and injustice."

From Here to There

At a time when disintegrating forces of deception and perversity are raging all across the cultural landscape, the urgency of peacemaking—of coming to the place of faithfulness and compassion—becomes all too evident. But, no matter what we do, no matter how hard we try, and no matter what we say, a turnaround won't happen overnight. Peace isn't won in a day.

Even at Jericho, when God miraculously delivered the city into the hands of His people, they had to march around the walls for days on end. They had to wait.

Cultural restoration is a multigenerational task. It takes time. It takes work.

Jonathan knew that. So he did not hesitate—not even for a moment. He went to work immediately. He understood the urgency of the situation, so he acted boldly. He knew that the restraints of time demanded decisiveness.

Israel was laboring under the terrible bondage of the Philistines. The army of Jonathan's father, King Saul, was defenseless and demoralized, owning no swords and no spears:

> So it came about on the day of battle that neither sword not spear was found in the hands of any of the people who were with Saul and Jonathan, but they were found with Saul and his son Jonathan. (1 Samuel 13:22)

Imagine that. An entire army with no weapons. Only the king and his son had any really efficient armaments. No power. No resources. No army. No decent weapons. No hope?

Perhaps the people should wait for another day to work for their deliverance. Perhaps they should wait for the day of advantage. Perhaps they should do nothing for now, waiting for a more opportune moment. After all, cultural restoration doesn't happen overnight. Peace isn't won in a day.

But, no. Not Jonathan.

He knew that God desires for his people to "walk by faith and not by sight" (2 Corinthians 5:7). "Perhaps," thought Jonathan, "the Lord will work for us, for the Lord is not restrained to save by many or by few" (1 Samuel 14:6).

So Jonathan and his armor bearer set out, alone, to attack the Philistine garrison and gain the promised "peace of the land." The story is exciting just in the retelling:

> Then Jonathan said, "Behold, we will cross over to the men and reveal ourselves to them. If they say to us, 'Wait until we come to you'; then we will stand in our place and not go up to them. But if they say, 'Come, up to us,' then we will go up, for the Lord has given them into our hands; and this shall be the sign to us." And when both of them revealed themselves to the garrison of the Philistines, the Philistines said, "Behold, Hebrews are coming out of the holes where they have hidden themselves." So the men of the garrison hailed Jonathan and his armor bearer and said, "Come up to us and we will tell you something." And Jonathan said to his armor bearer,

"Come up after me, for the Lord has given them into the hands of Israel." Then Jonathan climbed up on his hands and feet, with his armor bearer behind him; and they fell before Jonathan, and his armor bearer put some to death after him. And that first slaughter which Jonathan and his armor bearer made was about twenty men within about half a furrow in an acre of land. And there was a trembling in the camp, in the field, and among all the people. Even the garrison and the raiders trembled, and the earth quaked so that it became a great trembling. (1 Samuel 14:8–15)

The odds were against him. One man with his armor bearer, against the entire Philistine garrison. It was suicidal.

Maybe. It looked that way. But then, looks can be deceiving. Appearances are sometimes quite out of line with facts.

So, what were the facts?

Jonathan knew that the land belonged to God, not to the Philistines (Psalm 24:1). He knew that God had placed the land into the care of His chosen people, the Jews (Joshua 1:2). He knew that they had sure and secure promises that if they would obey God's word and do God's work, they would be prosperous and successful (Joshua 1:8), that every place which the sole of their feet trod would be granted to them (Joshua 1:3), and that no man would be able to stand before them all the days of their lives (Joshua 1:5). He knew that if the people would only "dwell in the shelter of the Most High," in the "shadow of the Almighty" (Psalm 91:1), He would deliver them "from the snare of the trapper and from the deadly pestilence" (Psalm 91:3). He would cover them "with his pinions" (Psalm 91:4), and protect them from "the terror by night" and "the arrow that flies by day" (Psalm 91:5). And though a thousand should fall at their left hand and ten thousand to the right, affliction would not approach them; they would only look and see "the recompense of the wicked" (Psalm 91:7–8). They would be protected from the teeth of the devourer, encompassed with supernatural power (Psalm 91:10).

Those were the facts.

Though it looked as if God's people were broken, scattered, defeated, and woebegotten, in truth they were more than conquerors (Romans 8:37). They were overcomers (1 John 5:4).

Philistine dominion was fiction. Israel cowering in fear was foolish fantasy. Pessimism about their ability to stand and not be shaken was novel nonsense (Hebrews 12:28).

Jonathan knew that.

So, he acted. He acted boldly. He acted decisively. He acted on the basis of the truth and reliability of God's Word, not on the seemingly impossible circumstances that faced him. He acted on faith and not on sight. He acted realistically, knowing that God's definition of things is the real reality, the only reality. He acted with passion and zeal for the things he knew to be God's will.

And God honored him, blessing Jonathan with enormous success. Jonathan stood against the tide. By all rights, he should have been crushed under its weight, but instead, the tide turned. He won the day and saved the nation.

Faith and Victory

"Now faith is the assurance of things hoped for, the conviction of things not seen" (Hebrews 11:1). "By it the men of old gained approval" (Hebrews 11:2). Against all odds, against all hope they obtained victory. They snatched glory out of the jaws of despair. They hurdled insurmountable obstacles to "lay hold" of the good things of the Lord (Hebrews 6:18). By faith, they believed God for the remarkable, for the impossible (Matthew 19:26; Hebrews 11:1–40). Abraham (Genesis 12:1–4), Sarah (Genesis 18:11–14), Isaac (Genesis 27:27–29), Jacob (Genesis 48:1–20), Joseph (Genesis 50:24–26), Moses (Exodus 14:22–29), Rahab (Joshua 6:23), Ruth (Ruth 1:16–17), Gideon (Judges 6–8), Barak (Judges 4–5), Samson (Judges 13–16), Jephthah (Judges 11–12), David (1 Samuel 16–17), Isaiah (Isaiah 1–6), Samuel, and all the prophets (1 Samuel 1; Hebrews 11:32) "conquered kingdoms, performed acts of righteousness, obtained promises, shut the mouths of lions, quenched the power of fire, escaped the edge of the sword, from weakness were made strong, became mighty in war, and put foreign armies to flight" (Hebrews 12:33–34). Though they were mocked and persecuted, imprisoned and tortured, impoverished and oppressed, they were unshaken and eventually obtained God's great reward (Hebrews 11:35–40):

> Therefore, since we have so great a cloud of witnesses surrounding us, let us also lay aside every encumbrance, and the sin which so easily entangles us, and let us run with endurance the race that is set before us, fixing our eyes on Jesus, the author and perfecter of faith, who for the joy set before Him endured the cross, despising the shame, and has sat down at the right hand of the throne of God. (Hebrews 12:1–2)

The future is ours.

But the days are urgent. Humanism's empire of perversity and idolatry, of greed and gluttony, is collapsing like a house of cards. Peace is nowhere to be found.

The battlefields of Europe, Southeast Asia, Central America, and the Middle East testify that humanism's hope for peace on earth is a false hope. The economic ruin of Nicaragua, Ethiopia, Afghanistan, Yugoslavia, and Russia testify that humanism's hope for utopia is a false hope. The ovens of Auschwitz, the abortuaries of L.A., the bathhouses of New York, and the nurseries of Bloomington testify that humanism's hope of medical and genetic perfectibility is a false hope. The ghettos of Detroit, the barrios of West San Antonio, the tent cities of Phoenix, and the slums of St. Louis testify that humanism's hope of winning the "war on poverty" is a false hope. The entire record of the twentieth century gives vivid testimony that humanism's hope of an enlightened and perfectable culture is a false hope.

But the Biblical hope has never yet been found wanting.

So—what are we waiting for?

It must be admitted that "there are giants in the land" (Numbers 13:32) and that "we appear to be grasshoppers in our own sight, and in theirs" (Numbers 13:32).

But God has given us His promises and established His priorities, laid out His strategies, and illumined His principles. And His program cannot fail.

Time to Go to Work

Jonathan faced the Philistines. He took God at His Word. He went to work, and emerged victorious.

Similarly, against all odds, Ehud faced the power of Moab (Judges 3:12–30); Shamgar faced the power of the Philistines (Judges 3:31); Deborah faced the power of Canaan (Judges 4–5); Gideon faced the power of Midian (Judges 6–8); the apostles faced the power of the Roman empire, (Acts 8–28); and each one emerged victorious.

Against all odds.

Isn't it about time for us to demonstrate to an unbelieving world that God can still beat the odds? Isn't it about time for us to prove to a fallen and depraved generation that God can raise up a weak and unesteemed people against all odds, and win? Isn't it about time we laid the foundation of peace? Isn't it?

> For though we walk in the flesh, we do not war according to the flesh, for the weapons of our warfare are not of the flesh, but divinely powerful for the destruction of fortresses. We are destroying speculations and every lofty thing raised up against the knowledge of God, and we are taking every thought captive to the obedience of Christ. (2 Corinthians 10:3–5)

In Christ, we are actually overwhelmingly powerful (Ephesians 6:10–18; Romans 8:37–39). Even the gates of hell cannot prevail against us (Matthew 16:8). If, that is, we would only yield to Him and do our job—standing faithfully with the covenant people of God through the ages. If we would only take the Gospel hope beyond, to "the uttermost parts of the earth" (Acts 1:8), if we would only "make disciples of all nations" (Matthew 28:19), if we would only "rebuild the ancient ruins, raise up the age old foundations, and repair the breach" (Isaiah 58:12).

It is time to go to work. It is time to lay the foundations of peace. We may have to work with few, or even no resources. Like Jonathan (1 Samuel 14:6). We may have to improvise, utilizing less than perfect conditions and less than qualified workers and less than adequate facilities. Like Nehemiah (Nehemiah 1:20). We may have to battle the powers that be, the rulers and the principalities. Like Peter, James, and John (Acts 4:20). We may have to go with what we've got, with no support, no notoriety, and no cooperation. Like Jeremiah (Jeremiah 1:4–10). We may have to start "in weakness and in fear and in much trembling" (1 Corinthians 2:3), without "persuasive words of wisdom" (1 Corinthians 2:4). Like the apostle Paul (1 Corinthians 2:1). Instead of allowing their limitations and liabilities to discourage and debilitate them, the heroes of the faith went to work—God's power being made manifest in their weakness (1 Corinthians 1:26–29).

It is time for us to go to work.

Cultural restoration doesn't happen overnight. Peace isn't won in a day. So the sooner we get started, the better off we'll be. The sooner we get started, the quicker the victory will come. In order to get from here to there, we need to set out upon the road. At the very least.

There will never be an ideal time to begin the work that God has set before us in maintaining the integrity of the church—on the issue of sexual morality or a thousand other fronts. Money is always short. Volunteers are always at a premium. Facilities are always either too small, or too inflexible, or in the wrong location, or too expensive. There is never enough time, never enough energy, and never enough resources.

So what?

Our commission is not dependent upon conditions and restrictions. Our commission is dependent only upon the unconditional promises of God's Word. God has called us to peace (1 Corinthians 7:15), to be peacemakers (Matthew 5:9), "so then let us pursue the things that make for peace" (Romans 14:9).

We should just go. Do what we ought to. We should make peace. Starting now.

"There is no peace for the wicked." But if we will do our job, and do it now, then the Lord's peace shall be reckoned unto us.

Jonathan knew the odds were against him, lopsidedly so, when he faced the Philistines single-handedly. But he also knew that God blessed obedience. He knew that God blessed valor. He knew that God's work done in God's way would never lack for God's provision and protection. So, he set out. And he won. He gained peace for the land.

"Really, that is what I am depending on," Lance told me recently. "Like Jonathan, I know that I've got an uphill battle—in the church as well as in the world. But I also know that I've got to walk by faith and not by sight. I've got to walk in the supernatural anointing of Almighty God, casting down strongholds, taking every thought, every word, every deed, every man, woman, and child captive for Christ. There is no other choice."

Lance is already an amazing emblem of God's grace. May he be an emblem of God's call upon the church as well. Amen and Amen.

NOTES

Acknowledgments

1. William Pratt, ed., *The Fugitive Poets: Modern Southern Poetry in Perspective* (Nashville, TN: J. S. Sanders, 1991), 14.

Introduction: Lance's Story

1. William Pratt, ed., *The Fugitive Poets: Modern Southern Poetry in Perspective* (Nashville, TN: J. S. Sanders, 1991), 84.
2. George Grant and Mark A. Horne, *Unnatural Affections: The Impuritan Ethic of Homosexuality in the Church* (Franklin, TN: Legacy Communications, 1991).
3. George Grant, ed., *Caveat: Homosexuality, the Military, and the Future* (Franklin, TN: Legacy Communications, 1993).
4. George Grant, ed., *Gays in the Military: The Moral and Strategic Crisis* (Franklin, TN: Legacy Communications, 1993).

Chapter 1—A Walk on the Wilde Side

1. William Pratt, ed., *The Fugitive Poets: Modern Southern Poetry in Perspective* (Nashville, TN: J. S. Sanders, 1991), 103.
2. Ibid., 130.

Chapter 2—De-Lighting America

1. William Pratt, ed., *The Fugitive Poets: Modern Southern Poetry in Perspective* (Nashville, TN: J.S. Sanders, 1991), 33.
2. Peter Leithart, "The Promiscuous Society" (unpublished manuscript), 14–15.

3. Ibid.
4. Leigh W. Rutledge, *Unnatural Quotations: A Compendium of Quotations By, For, or About Gay People* (Boston: Alyson Publishers, 1988), 175.
5. Ibid.
6. Paul Veyne, ed., *A History of Private Life: From Pagan Rome to Byzantium* (Cambridge, MA: Harvard University Press, 1987), 183–206.
7. Ibid.
8. Millicent Flannigan, *The Innovation of Family Stability in the Pagan Societies of the Ancient World* (Philadelphia: Presbyterian Missions Society, 1891), 101–167.
9. Ibid, 88–98.
10. Broward Jewish World, October 16, 1990.
11. Camille Paglia, *Sex, Art, and American Culture: Essays* (New York: Vintage, 1992), 22–23.
12. George Grant, *The Last Crusader: The Untold Story of Christopher Columbus* (Wheaton, IL: Crossway, 1992).
13. George Grant, *Third Time Around: The History of the Pro-Life Movement from the First Century to the Present* (Franklin, TN: Legacy Communications, 1991).
14. In comprehending the impact of the missions movement in the nineteenth century on heathen cultures, the work of Thomas Sowell in his book *Preferential Policies: An International Perspective* (New York: William Morrow, Publishers, 1990) is indispensable. The book surveys various times and places where particular races have received special treatment under law—either negatively or positively. In a chapter entitled, "Majority Preferences in Minority Economies," Sowell analyzes countries where minority groups have aroused the envy of the majority by achieving at a significantly higher rate. In Nigeria for example, the majority northern tribes were and are Muslim. During the period of British colonial rule, missionaries were legally confined to ministry among the minority in the south. According to Sowell, "The net result was that education and hospitals, among other features of Western culture, were concentrated among the peoples of the southern Nigeria." When the British left, the Ibos of the south completely dominated the positions of power and prestige in both the public and private sphere. The northern majority voted themselves "affirmative action" programs and provoked a civil war in an attempt to balance the obvious discrepancies (pp. 69–76). Again, in Sri Lanka, multicultural harmony was carefully preserved under British rule. The Buddhist Sinhalese majority, however, remained resistant to Christian missions—particularly

missionary schools. The Tamil minority learned English and pursued various avenues of upward mobility. In the end the Tamils occupied the vast majority of the higher positions in the post-colonial society (pp. 76–87). The point of all this? Sowell argues that Nigeria and Sri Lanka—as well as a number of other examples from Indonesia to Brazil—clearly illustrate the tremendous impact that Christian missions have made to the social, legal, and economic structure of pagan cultures around the world. And they illustrate the gracious benefit that the seamless ethic of pro-education, pro-health, pro-work, pro-development, pro-family, and pro-life values affects the everyday life of formerly oppressed and impoverished peoples.

15. George Grant, *Bringing in the Sheaves: Transforming Poverty into Productivity* (Franklin, TN: Legacy Communications, 1993).
16. Robin Lane Fox, *Christians and Pagans* (New York: Alfred A. Knopf, 1987).
17. Peter Jones, *The Gnostic Empire Strikes Back: An Old Heresy for the New Age* (Phillipsburg, NJ: Presbyterian and Reformed Publishing, 1992), ix.
18. Ibid., x.
19. Ibid.
20. Ibid., 124.
21. Rutledge, 156.
22. Leithart, 73.
23. Carl Becker, *The Heavenly City of Eighteenth-Century Philosophers* (New Haven: Yale Univ. Press, 1932), 21.
24. Francis A. Schaeffer, *How Should We Then Live?* (Wheaton, IL: Crossway, 1976).
25. Leithart, 65.
26. Jean-Jacques Rousseau, *A Discourse on the Origin of Inequality* (Chicago: Encyclopedia Britannica, 1952), 340.
27. Owen Chadwick, *The Secularization of the European Mind* (Cambridge, UK: Canto Books, 1975).
28. John Koster, *The Atheist Syndrome* (Brentwood, TN: Wolgemuth and Hyatt, 1988).
29. Thomas Paine, *Common Sense and Other Essays* (New York: Signet Classics, 1977), 19.
30. James H. Billington, *Fire in the Minds of Men: Origins of the Revolutionary Faith* (New York: Basic Books, 1980), 55.
31. Eugene H. Methvin, *The Rise of Radicalism* (New Rochelle, NY: Arlington House, 1973).
32. Ibid., 42.
33. Billington, 103.

34. Ibid., 52.
35. Richard Deacon, *The Cambridge Apostles: A History of Cambridge University's Elite Intellectual Secret Society* (New York: Farrar, Straus and Giroux, 1986), 202.
36. Ibid., 55.
37. Ibid., 59.
38. Ibid.
39. Ibid., 56.
40. Ibid., 64.
41. Ibid., 54.
42. Ibid.
43. *The Advocate,* December 15, 1992.
44. David Chilton, *Power in the Blood: A Christian Response to AIDS* (Brentwood, TN: Wolgemuth and Hyatt, 1987), 32.
45. Marshall Kirk and Hunter Madsen, *After the Ball: How America Will Conquer Its Fear and Hatred of Gays in the 90s* (New York: Doubleday, 1989), 45.
46. Frank du Mas, *Gay Is Not Good* (Nashville, TN: Thomas Nelson, 1979), 111.
47. New England Journal of Medicine 309, (1983), 576–582.
48. A. P. Bell and M. S. Weinberg, *Homosexualities: A Study of Diversity Among Men and Women* (New York: Simon and Schuster, 1978), 312.
49. Paglia, 24.
50. Tony Marco, *Gay Rights: A Public Health Disaster and Civil Wrong* (Ft. Lauderdale, FL: Coral Ridge Ministries, 1992), 26.
51. *National Review,* November 1, 1985.
52. du Mas, 109.
53. Enrique T. Rueda and Michael Schwartz, *Gays, AIDS, and You* (Old Greenwich, CT: Devon Adair, 1987), 54.
54. Randy Alcorn, *Christians in the Wake of the Sexual Revolution* (Portland, OR: Multnomah, 1985), 138–139.
55. *The Advocate,* January 12, 1993.
56. Ibid., 64.
57. Frank Browning, *The Culture of Desire: Paradox and Perversity in Gay Lives Today* (New York: Crown, 1993), 100.
58. K. Jay and A. Young, *The Gay Report* (New York: Summit, 1979), 500.
59. *The Conservative Chronicle,* February 17, 1993.
60. Kirk and Madsen, 308.
61. Ibid., 308–309.
62. Ibid., 309.
63. Ibid., 311.

64. Ibid., 33.
65. Ibid.
66. A study in the *New England Journal of Medicine* found that on average homosexuals ingest the fecal matter of 23 different men each year. Indeed, in a nation-wide survey, 17 percent of homosexuals said that they eat their partner's feces or smear it on themselves, and 12 percent say they give and receive enemas as a "part of sex." Meanwhile some 40 percent of all those surveyed admitted to "showering in their partners' urine" from time to time. *NEJM* 309, 1983, 576–82.
67. Pat Califia, *Sapphistry: A Book of Lesbian Sexuality* (Tallahassee, FL: Naiad Press, 1988), 52.
68. Ibid., 52–53.
69. *Atlanta Journal/Constitution,* September 27, 1991.
70. *The Congressional Record,* February 15–21, 1987.
71. Ibid.
72. *Bay Area Reporter,* Feb. 13, 1992.
73. Ibid.
74. Marco, 11–12.
75. William Dannemeyer, *Shadow in the Land: Homosexuality in America* (San Francisco: Ignatius Press, 1989), 120–121.
76. Ibid., 120.
77. K. Jay and A. Young, *The Gay Report* (New York: Summit, 1979), 275, 279, 281.
78. Ibid., 17.
79. Ibid., 88.
80. Enrique T. Rueda, *The Homosexual Network* (Old Greenwich, CT: Devin Adair, 1982), 214.
81. Marco, 12.
82. Ibid, 9.
83. Ibid.
84. *Psychological Reports,* 1986, #58, 327–337.
85. Reisman, 32.
86. *Journal of Interpersonal Violence,* 1991, 6, 323–336.
87. Kirk and Madsen, 311.
88. *Common Cause,* July 1991.
89. *Nebraska Medical Journal,* 70, 1985.
90. *Common Cause,* August 1991.
91. Ray, 35.
92. Florence King, *Reflections in a Jaundiced Eye* (New York: St. Martin's, 1989), 97.
93. She goes on to counsel her readers on the supposedly safe and alledgedly erotic uses for such things as candle wax, clamps. clips, ene-

mas, whips, paddles, and other items that do not bear description. Califia, 111.

94. Alcorn, 140.

95. *Deneuve,* February 1993.

96. Judith Reisman, *A Content Analysis of Two Decades of The Advocate and The Gayfellow Pages* (Washington, D.C.: The Institute for Media Education, 1992), 34.

97. Roger Magnuson, *Are Gay Rights Right?* (Portland, OR: Multnoman, 1990), 40–41.

98. Califia, 5–7.

99. Ibid.

100. Adam Parfrey, ed., *Apocalypse Culture* (Los Angeles: Feral House, 1990), 34–35.

101. Ibid., 29.

102. Ibid., 35.

103. Ibid.

104. Browning, 224–225.

105. Charles Morris, *The Marvelous Record of the Closing Century* (Philadelphia: American Book and Bible, 1899), 610.

106. Ibid.

107. James S. Dennis, *Christian Missions and Social Progress* (Old Tappan, NJ: Revell, 1909), 130.

108. Ibid., 347.

Chapter 3—Indecent Exposure: Culture

1. William Pratt, ed., *The Fugitive Poets: Modern Southern Poetry in Perspective,* (Nashville, TN: J. S. Sanders, 1991), 71–72.

2. Ibid., 101.

3. *The Village Voice,* April 27, 1993.

4. *The Tennessean,* April 26, 1993.

5. *New York Times,* April 26, 1993.

6. *Vanity Fair,* May 1993.

7. *DC Commentary,* May 1993.

8. *Florida Feminist Voices,* April 1993.

9. Ibid.

10. Ibid.

11. *Media Watch,* May 1993.

12. Ibid.

13. Ibid.

14. Ibid.

15. *Family Research Council Washington Watch,* May 11, 1993.
16. Camille Paglia, *Sexual Personae: Art and Decadence from Nefertiti to Emily Dickinson* (New York: Vintage, 1991), 25.
17. Paglia, 105.
18. Michael Medved, *Hollywood vs. America: Popular Culture and the War on Traditional Values* (New York: HarperCollins, 1992), 312–313.
19. *The Atlanta Journal/Constitution,* October 8, 1992.
20. *The Atlanta Journal/Constitution,* March 19, 1992.
21. Ibid., 167–168.
22. Ibid., 168.
23. *Movie Guide,* January 1993.
24. *The Advocate,* January 12, 1993.
25. Ibid.
26. Ibid.
27. Ibid.
28. Marshall Kirk and Hunter Madsen, *After the Ball: How America Will Conquer Its Fear and Hatred of Gays in the 90s* (New York: Doubleday, 1989), 179.
29. *The New York City Tribune,* December 1989.
30. *The Atlanta Journal/Constitution,* April 4, 1990.
31. *USA Today,* February 11, 1991.
32. Medved, 310.
33. *The Advocate,* December 15, 1992.
34. David Chilton, *Power in the Blood: A Christian Response to AIDS* (Brentwood, TN: Wolgemuth and Hyatt, 1987), 26–27.
35. Ibid., 27.
36. Ibid., 44–45.
37. Frank Browning, *The Culture of Desire: Paradox and Perversity in Gay Lives Today* (New York: Crown, 1993), 212–13.
38. Ibid., 214.
39. Ibid., 214–215.
40. *Empowerment,* March 1993.
41. *USA Today,* November 29, 1990.
42. *The Atlanta Journal/Constitution,* November 3, 1992.
43. *New York Native,* July 15, 1991.
44. *The New York Times,* July 6, 1992.
45. Margaret Cruikshank, *The Gay and Lesbian Movement* (New York: Routledge, 1992), 69.
46. *The New York Times,* July 6, 1992.
47. Kathy McCoy, *The Teenage Body Book: Guide to Sexuality* (New York: Simon and Schuster, 1983).

48. Ibid., 54–55.
49. Wardell Pomeroy, *Girls and Sex* (New York: Dell, 1981).
50. Wardell Pomeroy, *Boys and Sex* (New York: Dell, 1981).
51. *Genre,* December 1992.
52. Ibid.
53. Ibid.
54. *The New York Times,* July 6, 1992.
55. *The Atlanta Journal/Constitution,* December 1, 1991.
56. *The Atlanta Journal/Constitution,* September 24, 1992.
57. Dan Delbex, ed. *Damron Address Book* (San Francisco: The Damron Co., 1993).
58. Ibid.
59. *Marietta Daily Journal,* March 21, 1991.
60. Delbex, *Damron Address Book,* 256.
61. Ibid., 619.
62. Kirk and Madsen, 301–302.
63. *The New York Times,* September 23, 1992.
64. *The Atlanta Journal/Constitution,* December 1, 1991.
65. *The Atlanta Journal/Constitution,* September 24, 1992.
66. Ibid.
67. Ibid.
68. *The Tennessean,* February 14, 1993.
69. *The New York Times,* June 2, 1992.
70. Ibid.
71. Marlin Maddoux, *Free Speech or Propaganda? How the Media Distorts the Truth* (Nashville, TN: Thomas Nelson, 1990), 13.
72. *The New American,* February 22, 1993.
73. *Texas Education Review,* December 1992.
74. Ibid.
75. *Notable Quotables,* October 12, 1992.
76. *C-SPAN,* February 20, 1993.
77. *The Texas Education Review,* September 1992.

Chapter 4—Fatal Distraction: Education

1. William Pratt, ed., *The Fugitive Poets: Modern Southern Poetry in Perspective* (Nashville, TN: J. S. Sanders, 1991), 59.
2. William Dannemeyer, *Shadow in the Land: Homosexuality in America* (San Francisco: Ignatius, 1989), 159.
3. Thomas Sowell, *Inside American Education: The Decline, the Deception, the Dogmas* (New York: Free, 1993), ix.

4. George Grant and Mark Horne, *Unnatural Affections: The Impuritan Ethic of Homosexuality and the Modern Church* (Franklin, TN: Legacy, 1991), 27.

5. *U.S. Taxpayer's Bulletin,* August 1992.

6. *Ohio Bureau for Safe Sex Information,* July 1992.

7. Ibid.

8. Connie Marshner, *Decent Exposure: How to Teach Your Children About Sex* (Franklin, TN: Legacy, 1993), 31.

9. *Miami Herald,* 8 November 1992.

10. *Insight,* 27 September 1992.

11. Idem.

12. Ibid.

13. Prodigy interactive personal service, 19 March 1993.

14. George Grant, *Grand Illusions: The Legacy of Planned Parenthood* (Franklin, TN: Adroit, 1992).

15. "Celebrating Seventy Years of Service," 1986 Annual Report, Planned Parenthood Federation of America, 8–13.

16. Only 32 percent of teens who have had no sex education are sexually active, compared to 46 percent of those who have had "comprehensive" sex education courses. Louis Harris and Associates, *American Teens Speak: Sex, Myths, TV, and Birth Control* (New York: Planned Parenthood Federation of America, 1986), 6.

17. Harris, 7; *Family Planning Perspectives,* July/August 1986.

18. *Family Planning Perspectives,* July/August 1986.

19. Roberta Weiner, ed., *Teen Pregnancy: Impact on the Schools* (Alexandria, VA: Capitol, 1987), 17.

20. Ibid., 17, 24.

21. Wendy Baldwin, *Adolescent Pregnancy and Childbearing Rates, Trends, and Research Findings from the CPR-NICHD* (Bethesda, MD: Demographic and Behavioral Science, NICHD, 1985), 17.

22. Weiner, 10.

23. Harris, 8, 18, 60; Ruff, 48; and Marsiglio and Mott, 141.

24. Marshner, 190.

25. *Empowerment,* March 1993.

26. Ibid.

27. Ibid.

28. Ibid.

29. *Lambda Report,* February 1993.

30. *Alyson Wonderland Book Catalog,* 1992–93, 28.

31. L. Tsang, ed., *The Age Taboo* (Boston: Alyson, 1981), 144.

32. Ibid.

33. Ibid.

34. James T. Bennett and Thomas J. DiLorenzo, *Official Lies: How Washington Misleads Us* (Alexandria, VA: Groom, 1992), 212.

35. Ibid.

36. Ibid., 213.

37. Ibid., 212.

38. David Thibodauz, *Political Correctness: The Cloning of the American Mind* (Lafayette, LA: Huntington, 1992), 145–46.

39. *Break Point with Chuck Colson,* January 1993.

40. *The Advocate,* 15 December 1992.

41. Ibid.

42. Bennett and DiLorenzo, 193.

43. Ibid., 190.

44. S. Alexander Rippa, *Education in a Free Society* (New York: David McKay, 1967), 110.

45. Charles Leslie Glenn, Jr., *The Myth of the Common School* (Amherst, MA: Univ. of Massachusetts Press, 1988), 79.

46. Mary S. Calderone and Eric W. Johnson, *The Family Book About Sexuality* (New York: Bantam, 1981), 226.

47. Glenn, 80.

48. William Kailer Dunn, *What Happened to Religious Education? The Decline of Religious Teaching in Public Elementary School, 1776–1861* (Baltimore: Johns Hopkins Univ. Press, 1958), 137.

49. *The Advocate,* 15 December 1993.

50. Glenn, 143.

51. Ibid., 145.

52. Ibid., 132.

53. Ibid., 183.

54. Ibid.

55. *Blumenfeld Educational Letter,* January 1987.

56. Ibid., 26.

57. *Texas Education Review,* May 1992.

58. Robert L. Dabney, *Discussions* (Harrisonburg, VA: Sprinkle, 1879), 195.

59. Ibid.

60. *Fort Lauderdale Sun-Sentinel,* 6 September 1991.

Chapter 5—Statutory Hate: Politics

1. William Pratt, ed., *The Fugitive Poets: Modern Southern Poetry in Perspective* (Nashville, TN: J. S. Sanders, 1991), 31.

2. *Washington Newsletter,* March 1990.

3. *The Rothbard-Rockwell Report,* August 1991.
4. Camille Paglia, *Sex, Art, and American Culture: Essays* (New York: Vintage, 1992), 34–35.
5. Margaret Cruikshank, *The Gay and Lesbian Liberation Movement* (New York: Routledge, 1992), 2.
6. Marshall Kirk and Hunter Madsen, *After the Ball: How America Will Conquer Its Fear and Hatred of Gays in the 90s* (New York: Doubleday, 1989), 108.
7. *ContraMundum,* Winter 1993.
8. *Media Report on Liberty,* Winter 1992.
9. Ibid.
10. Ibid.
11. Ibid.
12. Kirk and Madsen, 176.
13. Cruikshank, 80.
14. *Lambda Report,* February 1993.
15. Maggie Gallagher, *Enemies of Eros: How the Sexual Revolution Is Killing Family, Marriage, and Sex and What We Can Do About It* (Chicago: Bonus, 1989), 192.
16. Chuck McIlhenny and Donna McIlhenny with Frank York, *When the Wicked Seize a City* (Lafayette, LA: Huntington, 1993), 152.
17. Ibid., 153.
18. *Out,* February/March 1993.
19. Ibid.
20. Ibid.
21. Ibid.
22. *Concerned Women,* July 1990.
23. Ibid.
24. *The Advocate,* 26 January 1993.
25. *The New American,* 8 February 1993.
26. *The Advocate,* 26 January 1993.
27. *The New American,* 8 February 1993.
28. Ibid.
29. *Washington Newsletter,* July 1991.
30. *American Journal of Psychology,* July, 1980, 806–10.
31. Ibid., 807.
32. Ibid., 809.
33. Ibid., 810.
34. *The Advocate,* 28 March 1989.
35. Ibid.
36. Ibid.
37. *U.S. News and World Report,* 6 April 1992.

38. Ibid.
39. Reproduced and distributed by the No Special Rights Committee.
40. *World,* 6 March 1993.
41. Ibid.
42. Ibid.
43. *Lambda Report,* February 1993.
44. Ibid.
45. Ibid.
46. *Washington Blade,* 12 March 1993.
47. *The Sicler Report,* April 1993.

Chapter 6—Dead Certainties: Medicine

1. William Pratt, ed., *The Fugitive Poets: Modern Southern Poetry in Perspectiv,* (Nashville, TN: J.S. Sanders, 1991), 60.
2. Martin Duberman, Martha Vicinus, and George Chauncey, eds., *Hidden from History: Reclaiming the Gay and Lesbian Past* (New York: Meridian, 1990), 296.
3. Ibid., 297.
4. Ibid., 298.
5. Ibid., 299.
6. Ibid.
7. Ibid., 305.
8. Ibid., 311–312.
9. Ibid., 312.
10. Camille Paglia, *Sexual Personae: Art and Decadence from Nefertiti to Emily Dickinson* (New York: Vintage, 1991), 233.
11. Ibid., 233–234.
12. Ibid., 234.
13. Maggie Gallagher, *Enemies of Eros: How the Sexual Revolution Is Killing Family, Marriage, and Sex and What We Can Do About It* (Chicago: Bonus, 1989), 256–257.
14. Walter Kaufman ed. and trans. *The Portable Nietzsche* (New York: Penguin, 1982), 499–500.
15. Mark Lynn Peters, *Freud's De-Materialistic Philosophy* (New York: Blannell-Harwig, 1975), 112.
16. William Dannemeyer, *Shadow in the Land: Homosexuality in America* (San Francisco: Ignatius, 1989), 25.
17. *World,* 24 April 1993.
18. Dr. Judith A. Reisman and Edward W. Eichel, *Kinsey, Sex, and Fraud: The Indoctrination of a People* (Lafayette, LA: Huntington, 1990).

19. Ibid., 221.
20. Ibid., 9.
21. Alfred C. Kinsey, Wardell B. Pomeroy, and Clyde E. Martin, *Sexual Behavior in the Human Male* (Philadelphia: Saunders, 1948), 177.
22. Ibid., 178.
23. W. H. Masters, V. E. Johnson, and R. C. Kolodny, eds., *Ethical Issues in Sex Therapy and Research,* (Boston: Little, Brown, 1977), 13.
24. Darrel Jones, *Hearken: Voices of Reason and Unreason,* (London: Palm Meadow, 1990), 341.
25. Ronald Bayer, *Homosexuality and American Psychiatry* (New York: Praeger's, 1981), 36.
26. Dannemeyer, 131.
27. Tony Marco, *Gay Rights: A Public Health Disaster and Civil Wrong* (Ft. Lauderdale, FL: Coral Ridge Ministries, 1992), 45.
28. Ibid., 273.
29. W.H. Masters, V.E. Johnson, and R.C. Kolodny, *Human Sexuality* (Boston: Little, Brown, 1984), 319.
30. *USA Today,* 17 December 1991.
31. *The New York Times,* 17 December 1991.
32. *The New York Times,* 7 January 1992.
33. Ibid.
34. *Newsweek,* 22 March 1993.
35. *Science,* August 1991.
36. *Bay Area Reporter,* 5 September 1991.
37. Marco, 49.
38. Charles Tittle, *Society of Subordinates,* (Bloomington, IN: Indiana Univ., 1972), 17.
39. Ibid., 71.
40. Camille Paglia, *Sex, Art, and American Culture: Essays* (New York: Vintage, 1992), 23.
41. *Time,* 17 August 1992.
42. Ibid.
43. Ibid.
44. Ibid.
45. Ibid.
46. Idem, p. 31.
47. *Family Research Newsletter,* April-June 1991.
48. Ibid.
49. *The American Spectator,* August 1984.
50. Franklin E. Payne, *What Every Christian Should Know About the AIDS Epidemic: The Medical and Biblical Facts,* (Augusta, GA: Covenant, 1991), pp. 71–72, 100.

51. Marco, p. 13.
52. Ibid., 14.
53. Ibid., 14.
54. Idem, p. 27.
55. Ibid., 254.
56. *Time,* 3 August 1992.
57. *American Journal of Public Health,* December 1985, p. 493–96.
58. Ibid., 1449–50.
59. *The Washington Post,* 24 June 1990.
60. Marco, 21.
61. Frank Browning, *The Culture of Desire: Paradox and Perversity in Gay Lives Today* (New York: Crown, 1993), 119.
62. Ibid., 120.
63. Randy Shilts, *And The Band Played On: Politics, People, and the AIDS Epidemic* (New York: St. Martin's, 1987), 200.
64. Ibid., 118.
65. Ibid., 26.
66. Ibid., 27.
67. Marshall Kirk and Hunter Madsen, *After the Ball: How America Will Conquer Its Fear and Hatred of Gays in the 90s* (New York: Doubleday, 1989), 355.
68. Browning, 84.
69. Ibid., 85–86.
70. Ibid., 86.
71. Franklin E. Payne, M.D., *What Every Christian Should Know About the AIDS Epidemic: The Medical and Biblical Facts About AIDS,* (Augusta, GA: Covenant, 1991), 36–50.
72. Ibid., 36, 39–45.
73. James T. Bennett and Thomas J. DiLorenzo, *Official Lies: How Washington Misleads Us* (Alexandria, VA: Groom Books, 1992), p. 251.
74. Dr. Robert Root-Bernstein, *Rethinking AIDS: The Tragic Cost of Premature Consensus* (New York: Free, 1993), 47.
75. Ibid.
76. *The American Spectator,* February 1992.
77. Ibid.
78. Ibid.
79. Root-Bernstein, 319.
80. *The American Spectator,* February 1992.
81. Ibid.
82. Root-Bernstein, 319.
83. *American Spectator,* February 1992.
84. Ibid.

85. Shilts, 170.
86. Root-Bernstein, 352.
87. Ibid.
88. Ibid., 353.
89. *Washington Newsletter,* May 1990.
90. *American Spectator,* May 1992.
91. *Time,* 3 August 1992.
92. *AIDS: Issues and Answers,* October 1992.
93. Root-Bernstein, 39–42.
94. Ibid., 2.
95. *The Sunday Tribune,* January 31, 1988.
96. Ibid.
97. *The American Spectator,* May 1992.
98. *Bio-Medical Ethics Report,* July 1990.
99. Root-Bernstein, 24.
100. *The American Spectator,* May 1992.
101. Ibid.
102. Ibid.
103. *Policy Review,* Summer 1990.
104. Ibid.
105. Root-Bernstein, p. 115.
106. Ibid, p. 372.
107. H.L. Mencken, *A Carnival of Buncombe* (Chicago: Univ. of Chicago, 1980), 69.

Chapter 7—Troop Immorale: Military

1. William Pratt, ed., *The Fugitive Poets: Modern Southern Poetry in Perspective,* (Nashville, TN: J. S. Sanders, 1991), 64.
2. *The Wall Street Journal,* 2 December 1992.
3. Ibid.
4. Ibid.
5. Ibid.
6. Ibid.
7. Ibid.
8. Ibid.
9. *American Journal of Psychiatry,* April 1984.
10. Ibid.
11. Ibid.
12. Ibid.
13. Ibid.

14. Ibid.
15. Ibid.
16. Ibid.
17. Ibid.
18. Clyde Hammersmith and Judith Tarr, eds., *The Changing Shape of American Culture* (New York: Bredesen, 1990), 66.
19. George Grant, ed., *Gays in the Military: The Moral and Strategic Crisis* (Franklin, TN: Legacy, 1993), 1–9.
20. Ibid., 23.
21. Ibid., 64.
22. Ibid., 10–11.
23. Ibid., 12.
24. Ibid., 13.
25. Ibid., viii.
26. Ibid., 24.
27. Ibid.
28. *Lambda Report,* March 1993.
29. *The Advocate,* 15 December 1992.
30. Grant, 25.
31. *The Village Voice,* 27 April 1993.
32. Grant, 25.
33. Ibid.
34. Ibid.
35. *Conservative Chronicle,* 17 February 1993.
36. Grant, 46.
37. Ibid., 47.
38. Ibid., 52–53.
39. Ibid., 57.
40. Ibid., 25.
41. Ibid.
42. Ibid., 49.
43. Ibid.
44. Ibid., 49–50.
45. *Lambda Report,* March 1993.
46. *Policy Network Newsletter,* April 1993.
47. Ibid.
48. Ronald D. Ray, *Military Necessity and Homosexuality* (Louisville, KY: First Principles, 1993), 16–22.
49. Ibid.
50. Ibid.
51. Harold Fellows, *Political Curmudgeons* (London: Jencks and Lloyd, 1966), 45.

52. Grant, 28.
53. Ibid.
54. *Washington Post*, 5 July 1990.
55. Jon Winokur, *The Portable Curmudgeon* (New York: Penguin, 1987), 220.
56. E. J. Dionne, *Why Americans Hate Politics* (New York: Simon and Schuster, 1991), 9.
57. Ibid., 18.
58. *Remnant Review*. 6 November 1992.
59. A. James Reichley, *The Life of the Parties: A History of American Political Parties* (New York: Free, 1992).
60. Michael Drummond, *Participatory Democracy: A New Federalism in the Making* (New York: L. T. Carnell, 1923), 19.
61. Ibid., p. 22.
62. Ralph Ketcham, *The Anti-Federalist Papers* (New York: Mentor, 1986).
63. Drummond, 17.
64. Ross Lence, *Union and Liberty: The Political Philosophy of John C. Calhoon* (Indianapolis, IN: Liberty, 1992).
65. Ray, 91–104.
66. Grant, viii.
67. *Vanity Fair*, May 1993.
68. *Fort Lauderdale News-Sentenal*, 14 May 1989.
69. Ibid.
70. Norman Dorsen, ed., *Our Endangered Rights: The ACLU Report on Civil Liberties Today*, (New York: Pantheon Books, 1984), x.
71. Ibid., xi.
72. Ibid.
73. *The Boston Globe*, 26 August 1977.
74. *The Christian News-Observer*, Spring 1988.
75. Gary Amos, *Defending the Declaration: How the Bible and Christianity Influenced the Writing of the Declaration of Independence* (Brentwood, TN: Wolgemuth and Hyatt, 1989).
76. Charles S. Hyneman and Donald Lutz, eds., *American Political Writing During the Founding Era, 1760–1805* (Indianapolis, IN: Liberty, 1983).
77. Herbert W. Titus and Gerald R. Thompson, *America's Heritage: Constitutional Liberty*, unpublished class syllabus, CBN University School of Law, 1988.
78. Tim LaHaye, *Faith of Our Founding Fathers* (Brentwood, TN: Wolgemuth and Hyatt, 1987).

79. John W. Whitehead, *The Separation Illusion* (Milford, MI: Mott Media, 1977).
80. Gardiner Spring, *The Obligations of the World to the Bible: A Series of Lectures to Young Men* (New York: Taylor and Dodd, 1839), 95–98.
81. Robert Goguet, *The Origin of Laws* (New York: John S. Taylor, 1821), 302.
82. Ibid., 99.
83. Cotton Mather, *Essays to Do Good* (Boston: Massachusetts Sabbath School Society, 1845), iv.
84. Harold K. Lane, *Liberty! Cry Liberty!* (Boston: Lamb and Lamb Tractarian Society, 1939), 32–33.
85. Alexis de Tocqueville, *Democracy in America* (New York: Brandt Textbook, 1966), xvi.
86. Spring, 101–2.
87. Aleksandr Solzhenitsyn, *A Warning to the West* (New York: Harper and Row, 1978), 64.
88. *ACLU Annual Report 1986–1987*, 10.
89. Spring, 98.

Chapter 8—An Impuritan Ethic: Church

1. William Pratt, ed., *The Fugitive Poets: Modern Southern Poetry in Perspective* (Nashville, TN: J. S. Sanders, 1991), 89.
2. Michael Scott Horton, *Made in America: The Shaping of Modern American Evangelicalism* (Grand Rapids, MI: Baker, 1991).
3. *World,* 5 January 1991.
4. Charles Colson, *The God of Stones and Spiders: Letters to a Church in Exile* (Wheaton, IL: Crossway, 1991).
5. *Houston Post,* 16 August 1991.
6. Ibid.
7. Ibid.
8. Francis Schaeffer, *The Great Evangelical Disaster* (Wheaton, IL: Crossway, 1984).
9. James W. Skillen, *The Scattered Voice: Christians at Odds in the Public Square* (Grand Rapids, MI: Zondervan, 1991).
10. *New York Times,* 28 August 1991.
11. *National and International Religion Report,* 12 August 1991.
12. *World,* 23 February 1991.
13. *World,* 27 July 1991.
14. *Christianity Today,* 19 August 1991.
15. *National and International Religion Report,* 22 July 1991.

16. Ibid.
17. Ibid.
18. Ibid.
19. *World,* 10 August 1991.
20. *World,* 29 June 1991.
21. Ibid.
22. Ibid.
23. *Christianity Today,* 22 July 1991.
24. Ibid.
25. *World,* 23 February 1991.
26. Ibid.
27. Camille Paglia, *Sex, Art, and American Culture* (New York: Vintage, 1992), 27.
28. Ibid.
29. Ibid., 30.
30. Ibid., 36.
31. *National and International Religion Report,* 12 August 1991.
32. *National and International Religion Report,* 29 July 1991.
33. *World,* 13 July 1991.
34. *Genre,* December 1992.
35. John Shelby Spong, *Rescuing the Bible from Fundamentalism: A Bishop Rethinks the Meaning of Scripture* (San Francisco: Harper, 1991).
36. John Shelby Spong, *Living in Sin: A Bishop Rethinks Human Sexuality* (San Francisco: Harper and Row, 1988).
37. *World,* 29 September 1990.
38. *World,* 10 August 1991.
39. *Newsweek,* 81.
40. Letha Scanzoni and Virginia Ramey Mollenkott, *Is the Homosexual My Neighbor? Another Christian View* (San Francisco: Harper, 1978).
41. Ibid., 71.
42. David A. Fraser, ed., *The Evangelical Round Table: The Sanctity of Life* (Princeton, NJ: Princeton Univ. Press, 1988), 159.
43. Ibid.

Chapter 9—Revealing Notions: Truth

1. William Pratt, ed., *The Fugitive Poets: Modern Southern Poetry in Perspective* (Nashville, TN: J.S. Sanders, 1991), 54.
2. Ibid., 70.

3. Cornelius van Til, *The Defense of the Faith* (Phillipsburg, NJ: Presb. Ref., 1955), 8.
4. James Bricknell Houston, *Genesis: Sermons and Commentary* (Philadelphia: Presbyterian Book Distributors, 1878), 28.
5. William Brandt, *The Standard Home* (Philadelphia: Carlyle, 1909), 253.
6. *Genre,* December 1992.
7. Margaret Cruikshank, *The Gay and Lesbian Liberation Movement* (New York: Routledge, 1992), 92.
8. John Boswell, *Christianity, Social Tolerance, and Homosexuality: Gay People in Western Europe from the Beginning to the Christian Era to the Fourteenth Century* (Chicago: Univ. of Chicago Press, 1980), 93.
9. Ibid., 94.
10. John Jefferson Davis, *Evangelical Ethics: Issues Facing the Church Today* (Phillipsburg, NJ: Presb. and Ref., 1985), 115.
11. Boswell, p. 94.
12. Ibid., 94.
13. Ibid.
14. Letha Scanzoni and Virginia Ramey Mollenkott *Is the Homosexual My Neighbor?* (San Francisco: Harper and Row, 1978), 54.
15. John Spong, *Living in Sin?* (San Francisco: Harper and Row, 1988), 141.
16. *Baltimore Evening Sun,* 18 January 1937.
17. Ibid.
18. Ibid.
19. Ibid.
20. Jay Adams, *Competent to Counsel* (Phillipsburg, NJ: Pres. and Ref., 1970), 139.

Chapter 10—Unto Ages of Ages: Tradition

1. William Pratt, ed., *The Fugitive Poets: Modern Southern Poetry in Perspective* (Nashville, TN: J.S. Sanders, 1991), 130.
2. Martin Forbes, *History Lessons: The Importance of Cultural Memory,* (New York: Palamir, 1981), 61.
3. Herbert Collier, *Historical Uncertainty,* (Radford, UK: The Univ. of Radford Press, 1949), 76.
4. *Rite Reasons: Studies in Worship,* December 1990.
5. *Church History,* February 1990.
6. Tim Dowley, ed. *Eerdmans' Handbook to the History of Christianity* (Grand Rapids, MI: Eerdman's, 1977), 2.

7. Ibid.

8. *Rite Reasons,* December 1990.

9. Robin Lane Fox, *Pagans and Christians* (New York: Alfred A. Knopf, 1989), 341.

10. T. R. Glover, *The Conflict of Religions in the Early Roman Empire* (Washington, DC: Canon, 1974, 1909), 159–60.

11. Fox, 342.

12. Frances and Joseph Gies, *Marriage and the Family in the Middle Ages* (New York: Harper and Row, 1987), 29.

13. Kendall S. Harmon, *Should Practicing Homosexual Persons be Ordained in the Episcopal Church Today?* (Shaker Heights, OH: Episcopalians United, 1991), 26.

14. *Journal of Religious Ethics,* 14/1, 1986.

15. Fox, p. 352.

16. Jan L. Womer, ed. and trans., *Morality and Ethics in Early Christianity* (Philadelphia, Fortress, 1987), 30.

17. Ibid, p. 31.

18. John Boswell, *Christianity, Social Tolerance, and Homosexuality: Gay People in Western Europe from the Beginning of the Christian Era to the Fourteenth Century* (Chicago: Univ. of Chicago Press, 1980), 137–138. Boswell argues in this work that Christianity, from the time of the New Testament until the later Middle Ages, was tolerant, if not accepting, of homosexual practice. The scholar Robin Lane Fox considers Boswell's thesis "quite unconvincing" (*Pagans and Christians,* 738), and we must concur. Even a laymen can see the flaws in his handling of the Biblical text, and there is no reason to believe that he handles other source documents with any more accuracy. Furthermore, much of Boswell's case for the ancient and medieval church relies on his conclusion that "the source of anti-gay feelings among Christians must be sought elsewhere" than Scripture (117). This highly inaccurate statement on the Bible's teaching allows Boswell to portray all "anti-gay feeling" in the church as an aberration, and all tolerance as representative. Since his understanding of Scripture is flawed, his interpretation of church history is also distorted. It is tolerance that is an aberration, not "anti-gay feelings."

19. Alan Ballard, *The Dietary Laws: A Reformed Perspective,* (Glasgow, UK: Clarion, 1972), 190.

20. Ibid.

21. Womer, p. 36.

22. Ibid, p. 38.

23. Cyril C. Richardson, ed., *Early Christian Fathers* (New York: Collier, 1970), 337–38.

24. Boswell, p. 131.
25. Peter Leithart, "The Promiscuous Society" (unpublished manuscript), 52.
26. Lawrence L. Pouvre, *Canons and Councils* (London: Holy Trinity Evangelical Book Trust, 1967), 49.
27. Harold J. Berman, *Law and Revolution: The Formation of the Western Legal Tradition* (Cambridge, MA: Harvard, 1983), 69.
28. Boswell, 158.
29. Ibid, p. 159.
30. See especially Deuteronomy 28–29.
31. Reay Tannahill, *Sex in History* (New York: Stein and Day, 1980), 56.
32. Ibid.
33. Again, the brilliant academic apologist for homosexuality and abortion from Yale University, John Boswell, has written a stunning refutation of this centuries' old contention in his book *The Kindness of Strangers: The Abandonment of Children in Western Europe from Late Antiquity to the Renaissance* (New York: Pantheon, 1988). Though his research into primary source documents is comprehensive and his mastery of the material is obvious, Boswell succumbs to the tempting impulse of forcing the facts to fit his own libertine presuppositions. The result is an impressive display of creative historical revisionism: the reason that the medieval church took such great pains to care for the abandoned and even institutionalized oblation, according to Boswell, was simply to keep a steady stream of recruits and cheap labor flowing into the monastery system. That is *prima facie* absurd. Thus, despite the fact that he has done the academic community a great service by tracking down innumerable obscure documents—many of which I have actually used in this study—the ultimate value of Boswell's work is diminished greatly by the twisted propaganda techniques that he used to draw his conclusions.
34. Boswell, 177
35. Ibid, p. 211.
36. Ibid, p. 380.
37. E. P. Evans, *The Bestiary: A Book of Beasts* (New York: 1954), 232.
38. Boswell, 141.
39. Ibid., 289. Notice the similarity between this law and Leviticus 20:13, 15–16.
40. Jaroslav Pelikan, ed., *Luther's Works* (St. Louis: Concordia, 1961), 3:255.
41. James Jordan, ed. *The Covenant Enforced: Sermons on Deuteronomy 27 and 28* (Tyler, TX: ICE, 1990), 51–52.

42. *The Confession of Faith of the Presbyterian Church in the United States Together with the Larger Catechism and the Shorter Catechism* (Atlanta: John Knox, 1965), 232.
43. John Cotton, *Abstract of the Laws of New England* (London: 1641), 342.
44. Peter Gay, *The Enlightenment: An Interpretation* (New York: Alfred A. Knopf, 1969), 431.
45. Alvin Plantinga and Nicholas Wolterstorff, ed., *Faith and Rationality: Reason and Belief in God* (Notre Dame: Univ. of Notre Dame, 1983), 222–23.
46. See Thomas Kuhn, *The Structure of Scientific Revolutions* (Chicago: Univ. of Chicago, 1962).
47. There is however another way to defend the faith that is both rational and faithful. See Richard Pratt, *Every Thought Captive* (Phillipsburg, NJ: Presb. and Ref., 1979); John Frame, *The Doctrine of the Knowledge of God* (Phillipsburg, NJ: Presbyterian and Reformed, 1987); and Cornelius Van Til, *The Defense of the Faith* (Phillipsburg, NJ: Presb. and Ref., 1955).
48. Patrick Carnes, *Out of the Shadows: Understanding Sexual Addiction* (Minneapolis, MN: CompCare, 1983), 164.
49. Ibid., ix.
50. *Spokane Review,* 21 November 1981.
51. Carnes, 87.
52. Ibid.
53. Ibid., 161–62.
54. Alexander C. DeJong, *Help and Hope for the Alcoholic* (Carol Stream: Tyndale, 1982), 22.
55. *Al-Anon Family Groups* (New York: Al-Anon Family Group, 1986), 8.
56. William L. Playfair with George Bryson, *The Useful Lie* (Wheaton, IL: Crossway, 1991), 102.
57. Wendy Kaminer, *I'm Dysfunctional, Your Dysfunctional: The Recovery Movement and Other Self-Help Fashions* (New York: Addison-Wesley, 1992), 125.
58. Ibid., 18.
59. Dr. Stan J. Katz and Aimee E. Liu, *The Codependency Conspiracy: How to Break the Recovery Habit and Take Charge of Your Life* (New York: Warner, 1991), 128.
60. *Christianity Today,* 15 January 1990.
61. See George Grant and Mark Horne, *Unnatural Affections: The Impuritan Ethic of Homosexuality and the Modern Church* (Franklin, TN: Legacy, 1991), 16. We quoted Hayner from an article in *World* magazine. Hayner claims the article, which was based on a *Religious News*

Service report, misquoted him. Though we have the highest regard for
the integrity and objectivity of *World*'s staff, we decided to defer to
Hayner since to our knowledge there is no recording of the original
speech in which he allegedly made even more controversial remarks
than in the *Christianity Today* news report.

62. *Christianity Today,* 15 January 1990.
63. William Dannemeyer, *Shadow in the Land: Homosexuality in America*
(San Francisco: Ignatius, 1989), 113–114.
64. Ibid., 114.
65. Ibid., 114, 116–17.
66. Ibid., 115.
67. *Cornerstone,* Issue 94.
68. G. K. Chesterton, *Orthodoxy,* (New York: Dodd, Mead, 1908), 74–75.
69. *Church History,* February 1990.

Chapter 11—Just Say Yes: Hope

1. William Pratt, ed., *The Fugitive Poets: Modern Southern Poetry in
Perspective* (Nashville, TN: J.S. Sanders, 1991), 94.
2. Ibid., 79.
3. John Bunyan, *Pilgrim's Progress,* (New York: Penguin, 1965), 51.
4. John MacArthur, *The Gospel According to Jesus: What Does Jesus
Mean When He Says "Follow Me"?* (Grand Rapids, MI: Zondervan,
1988), 31.
5. *The Confession of Faith of the Presbyterian Church in the United
States Together with the Larger Catechism and the Shorter Catechism*
(Atlanta: John Knox, 1965), 121–122.
6. Ibid., 126.
7. John Calvin, *Institutes of the Christian Religion,* (Philadelphia: Westminster, 1960), 1370.
8. *Modern Reformation,* July/August 1991.
9. *Christianity Today,* 15 January 1990.
10. Richard Foster, *Money, Sex, and Power: The Challenge of a Disciplined Life* (San Francisco, Harper and Row, 1985), 112.
11. Jay Adams, *Handbook of Church Discipline* (Grand Rapids: Zondervan, 1986), 95.
12. Ibid.
13. John Frame, *Evangelical Reunion: Denominations and the Body of
Christ* (Grand Rapids, MI: Baker, 1991), 47.
14. Ibid.

15. Michael Tolliver, *The Grace of God,* (Philadelphia: Presbyterian Board of Publication, 1891), 43.

16. Gary DeMar, *Ruler of the Nations: Biblical Principles for Government* (Ft. Worth, TX: Dominion, 1987), 185.

17. To prevent any misunderstanding, we should state plainly that just because the Bible does not recognize the civil right to practice homosexual copulation does not mean that homosexuals do not have any civil rights at all. They have the same civil rights as anyone else—such as the right to a fair trial. The Bible prohibits the development of a police state by commanding rulers not to violate the laws of Christ.

18. Chuck McIlhenney and Donna McIlhenney with Frank York, *When the Wicked Seize a City* (Lafayette, LA: Huntington, 1993), 85.

19. *Bowers v. Hardwick,* 2846.

20. Ibid., 2847.

21. *The Confession of Faith,* 232.

22. Francis A. Schaeffer, *Two Contents, Two Realities,* (Downers Grove, IL: InterVarsity), 1972.

Conclusion

1. William Pratt, ed., *The Fugitive Poets: Modern Southern Poetry in Perspective* (Nashville, TN: J.S. Sanders, 1991), 45.

INDEX

A

Able, Richard 148
Acer, David 132
Achan 232–235
ACLU 16
ACT-UP 16, 41, 104–105
Acton, Lord 205
Adams, Jay 199, 234–235
Advocate 33, 36, 56, 85, 102
AIDS 12–13, 19, 91–92, 123–140
    248–252
Alcorn 35, 44
Alexander 88
Alfonso the Wise 215
Allen, Bob 197
Amebiasis 124
American 2000 88
American Psychiatric Association
    114, 117–118
Ames, Fisher 162–163
Aspin, Les 1250–154
Athenagoras 209
Augustine 211

B

Bateman, Newton 84
Bacchus 1–2, 141
Bailey, J. Michael 119–120
Balak 176–177
Barnabas 208–209, 215

Basil 211
Bauer, Gary 94
Bayer, Ronald 117
Becker, Carl 28
Bennett, James 81–82, 84,
    131–132
Bergalis, Kimberly 132
Billington, James 30
bisexuality 121–123
Blumenfeld, Samuel 88
Boswell, John 194–195
Bowers v. Hardwick 153–154
    242–243
Brandt, William 188
Briggs, John H.Y. 18
Brokaw, Tom 69
Browning, Frank 36, 59–60, 127,
    129–130
Bunyan, John 227
Bush, George 100

C

Califia, Pat 38, 41–42, 44, 80
Calvin, John 216
Cambridge Apostles 31
Cameron, Paul 120–121, 123–124
Campola, Tony 176
Carey, George 166
Carey, Gregory 119
Carlin, David 224

Carnes, Patrick 218–219
Carroll, Gerry 148
Carson, William 155
CDC 134–140
Centers for Disease Control
    134–140
Chesterton, G.K. 155–156
    223–224
child molestation 42–43
Children's Defense Fund 16
Chilton, David 33,35
Chrysostom, John 210
civil liberties 91–107
Clausewitz, Carl Von 158
Clement 209, 215
Clinton, Bill xi, 51–54, 105–107,
    147–151
Coates, Dan 149
Colson, Chuck 83, 166
comics 63–64
courts 154–155
Crane, Hart 51
Cruikshank, Margaret 93, 96

D

Damien, Peter 213
Dannemeyer, William 40, 73, 118
Davidson, Donald 91
Deacon, Richard 31
Dejong, Alexander 219
DeMar, Gary 236
DeWitt, John 157
Di Lorenzo, John 81–82, 84,
    131–132
Dionne, E.J. 156–157
discrimination 91–107
disease 123–140
Dobson, James 107
Doell, Dan 105
Donaldson, Sam 68–69
Duesberg, Peter 137–140

Dugas, Gaetan 127

E

East Village 11–19
Eddleman, Henry 145–147
Eidsmoe, John 151–152, 153–154
Enlightenment 28–34, 112–114
Episcopal Church 169–170
Evans, E.P. 214

F

family values 98–99
Farah, Joseph 57
Fernandez, Joseph 79
fisting 43–44
forgiveness 5
Foster, Richard 232
Fox, Robin Lane 206–207
Freeman, John 105
Fumento, Michael 132–134

G

Gallagher, Maggie 97–98, 113
Gallo, Robert 137–138
Gay Related Immuno-Deficiency
    131–134
Gay Pride Parade 1–4, 41, 51–54
Gay Bowel Syndrome 124
Gebhard, Paul 116–117
giardiasis 124
Gilmore, James 147
Glenn, Charles 86–87
gnosticism 27–29
Goguet, Robert 159–160
Goyer, Henry 145–147
Great Commission 25–27
Greenlee, Karen 44–45
Greenpeace 16
Greg, James B.H. 187–188

GRID 131–134
Gries, Joseph and Frances 207

H

Hart, Jeffrey 151
hate crimes 91–107, 149
Hayner, Stephen 222
Hays, Richard 207
healing 5
Heckler, Margaret 136
Heidinger, James 168
Henry, Patrick 157
hepatitis 124
heterosexual risks 131–134
HIV 134–140
Hodge, Charles 87
Hollywood 54–56
homophobia 80–81, 91–92
Honorius III 214
Hooker, Thomas 160
Horton, Michael Scott 166

J

Jay, John 160
Jefferson, Mark 156
Jipping, Tom 155
Johnson, Magic 132
Jones, Peter 27–28
Jordan, James 202, 205–206
Justinian 211

K

Kaminer, Wendy 220–221
Kantor, Bill 68
Katz, Stan 221
Kennedy, D. James 158, 166–167
Keynes, John Maynard 30–32
King, Florence 44
Kinsey, Alfred 114–117

Kirk, Marshall 33–34, 37, 43, 56, 66, 93–94, 96,

L

LaBarbara, Peter 79–80
legislating morality 158–161
Leithart, Peter 24, 28
Leo, John 76–77, 103–104
LeVay, Simon 120–121
liberty 91–107
Lorian, Victor 133
Luther, Martin 216
Lytle, Andrew Nelson 9

M

Machen, J. Gresham 198
Maddoux, Marlin 67–68
Madison, James 160
Madsen, Hunter 33–34, 37, 43, 56, 66, 93–94, 96
Magnuson, Roger 41
Mann, Horace 84–87
Mapplethorpe 43–44
Marco, Tony 35, 40, 42, 125
Maris, Jason Del 102–103
Marsden, George 217
Marshner, Connie 75, 78
Mas, Frank du 34
Masters and Johnson 118–119
Mawyer, Martin 95, 150
McIlhenny, Chuck and Donna 242
media 51–54, 56–61, 67–69
medicine 109–141
Medved, Michael 54–56
Mencken, H.L. 140–141, 198
mercy ministry 248–252
Methodist Church 167–169
military 109–112, 143–163
Mixner, David 51–52, 106, 158

Mollenkott, Virginia 174–176, 195–196
Montagnier, Luc 125–126
Moore, Merrill 1
Morris, Gouvenor 157
Morrison, Robert 150–151, 153

N

NAMBLA 16, 40, 180
necrophilia 44–45
Newport 109–112
Nietzsche, Friedrich 113–114

P

Paglia, Camille 25, 34, 54, 59, 92–93, 112–113
Paine, Thomas 29–30
Payne, Franklin 131, 136–137
pedophilia 40, 116
Pilgrim's Progress 227
Pillard, Richard 119–120
Plato 24
Playfair, William 220
Pomeroy, Wardell 118–119
Powell, Colin 149
Prager, Dennis 24
Presbyterian Church 170–173
promiscuity 34–37
publishing 61–65

Q

Queer Nation 16, 41, 104

R

Rainie, Harrison 68
Ransom, John Crowe xi
Ray, Ronald 155
Reisman, Judith 40, 44, 115–117

Renaissance 28–29
reverse discrimination 91–107
Riding, Laura 225
Ritchie, Rick 231
Robespierre 29
Root-Bernstein, Robert 132–133, 135–140
Rousseau, Jean 112–114

S

San Francisco 22–23
Scanzoni, Letha 174–176, 195–196
Schaeffer, Francis 167
Schaff, Phillip 204
Schumpter, Joseph 117
sex education 63–64, 71–89
sexually transmitted diseases (STD's) 123–140
shigellosis 124
Shilts, Randy 127–129, 135
Sierra Club 16
Solzhenitsyn, Aleksandr 162
Sowell, Thomas 37, 73
Spong, John Shelby 173–174, 196, 197
Spring, Gardiner 161–162
Sproul, R.C. 166
Staley, Scott 100
Stevenson, Alec Brock 181
Strachey, Lytton 31–32
straight bashing 99–105
Studds, Gerry 149

T

Tate, Allen 49, 143, 183, 227
television 56–59
Terzian, Philip 68
Theodosius 212
Thibodaux, David 82
thought crimes 99–101

Tittle, Charles 121
Tolliver, Michael 235
Toqueville, Alexis de 161
traditional morality 23–29
travel guides 64–67

V

Van Til, Cornelius 185

W

Wallace, Joyce 133
Warren, Robert Penn 11, 201
Wedin, William 122
Westminster Standards 216, 230, 244
Will, George 156
Wills, Jesse 165
Women's Action Coalition 16